December 1, 2005

To my colleague and friends,
Harry Allison and Barbara Henke—

    you play an important role
in the history of the College.
I am pleased to present this
book to you with my best
wishes.

                John Hicks

Funding for this project made possible by :

THE UNIVERSITY OF TULSA

ROBERT W. LAWLESS, PRESIDENT (1996-2004)

THE COLLEGE OF LAW, MARTIN H. BEKSKY, DEAN (1995-2004)

THE CHAPMAN TRUSTS, SHARON J. BELL, TRUSTEE

OKLAHOMA HORIZONS SERIES

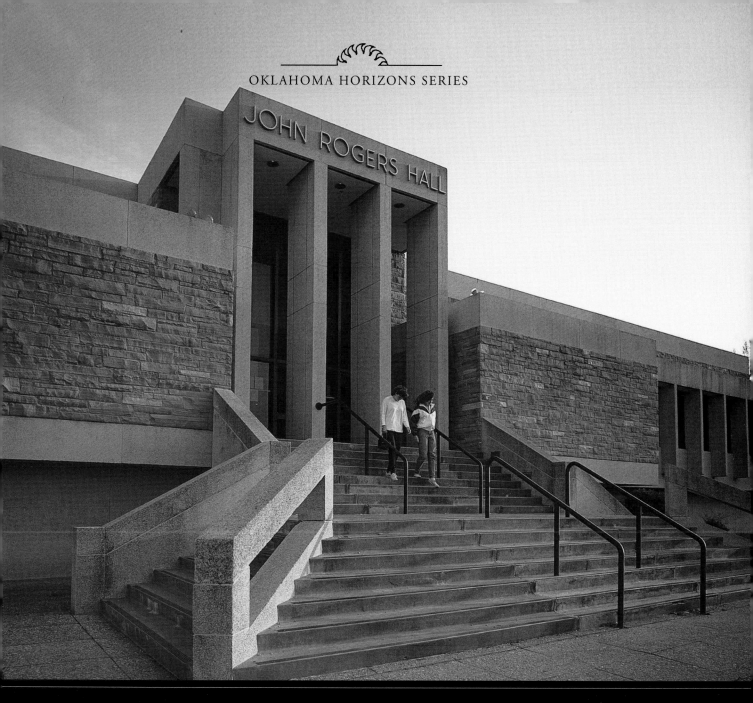

A History of

THE UNIVERSITY OF TULSA COLLEGE OF LAW

by John Forrester Hicks

series editor: **GINI MOORE CAMPBELL**
associate editor: **BOB BLACKBURN**

RIGHT: The law library located in the first Tulsa County Courthouse from 1927 to 1949. Paul Stithem Studio. *Courtesy The University of Tulsa College of Law archives.*

CONTENTS

UNIVERSITY OF TULSA

COLLEGE OF LAW

O ur human nature makes us curious about the past. On an individual level, we humans desire to know our family history. Genealogy is of interest to most people sometime in their lives and a passion for many. On a larger level, people are often interested in the history of their clan or culture, or, from a political perspective, are interested in the history of their town, state or country. Indeed, this human curiosity often extends to other families, clans, cultures, towns, states and countries.

This impulse is often directed toward educational institutions. Because of strong feelings of attachment, alumni and others want to know about the origins of their alma mater. Because the institution usually lasts far beyond the memory of any person or generation, its past must be recorded in some fashion if it is to be preserved.

The University of Tulsa College of Law has moved into its ninth decade and its origins and development have become increasingly clouded by the mists of time. As a young professor, my focus on the present and the future made me oblivious to this reality. Over the years, however, as my own personal attachment to the school grew along with an interest in its origins, I came to realize that, if the past was to be preserved, someone had to act. Thus, I began to search out and collect documents, newspaper clippings and, ultimately, recollections of alumni, faculty, staff, attorneys and others who could shed light on the school's history during different eras.

It has truly been a labor of love for me to be able to find and preserve this history of the College of Law. The school has come to mean much more than a place of employment to me. The institution and its people—students, faculty, staff, alumni and many others—have become my family and my way of life. By the same token, each person whose life has intersected with the College also has his or her own story of the impact the school has had on their lives.

So, what follows is a glimpse into the past of this institution. It does not, cannot tell the whole story. No history can. But, my hope is that it provides some understanding of the origin and development of this institution so many care for—The University of Tulsa College of Law.

LEFT: This tapestry, entitled "The Balance of Justice," hangs in the atrium of the student lounge in John Rogers Hall. *Courtesy of The University of Tulsa College of Law archives.*

ACKNOWLEDGMENTS

The Mabee Legal Information Center, one of two major expansions, is located immediately to the left of John Roders Hall. *Courtesy The University of Tulsa College of Law archives.*

Developing the idea to preserve the history of the College of Law was a solitary endeavor. But, to research, write and publish a book chronicling that history required the collaboration of many people. I am indebted to a great number of faculty, staff, administrators, students, alumni and friends of the law school for their varied contributions.

A lack of extensive documentation relating to the early-day school and its founders required me to turn to the personal knowledge of a wide variety of people both within and outside the University in order to provide a more complete account of that period. Each recent contributor is individually acknowledged in the endnotes. Dean Martin Belsky was most supportive as we approached the transition from manuscript to publication. Each recent University President, in turn—Ben Henneke, J. Paschal Twyman, Robert Donaldson and Robert Lawless—provided valuable insight into the relationship between the law school and the University during the period of his presidency. In particular, Rick Ducey, Director of the Mabee Legal Information Center, and Lou Lindsey, Associate Director, were extremely helpful and cooperative, providing photographs and documents relating to the law library and other subjects. I am indebted to all these individuals for their assistance.

In creating the manuscript, no one labored longer or harder than Cyndee Jones, my faculty asststant in the College of Law Secretariat. From first word to final proofing, she was my colleague in this endeavor. Dean Martin Belsky and Professors Tom Holland ('71) and Catherine Cullem ('80) made valuable contributions to early drafts, as did Rick Ducey and Lou Lindsey. Jennifer Struble ('03), first, as a student, and, later, as a graduate, provided valuable technical assistance with the endnotes and text. Alumnae Sharon Bell ('85) and Jan Slater Anderson ('91) provided both encouragement and assistance on the manuscript. Roger Blais, University of Tulsa provost, and Barbara Geffen, general counsel to the University, provided helpful insight from the University perspective.

Finally, no acknowledgment by me would be complete without the recognition of two special people in my life. My mother, Hazel Overton Hicks, had such belief in this project at the beginning and encouraged me to undertake it. My wife, Sandy Altman Hicks, has been my chief supporter in every way at the end of it. Thank you.

Thanks to all the many people already referenced, as well as those not mentioned, for, without you, I could not have completed this book. I, alone, accept responsibility for whatever deficiencies exist. Any praise for its accomplishments however, must be shared with a great many. I trust they also share with me satisfaction in preserving the history of the first eighty years of The University of Tulsa College of Law.

Kendall Hall, built in 1908, served for years as the main academic building on the Henry Kendall College campus. It was in this building that law was first taught in Tulsa. The original building was replaced in 1975 by the current Kendall Hall. *Courtesy The University of Tulsa archives.*

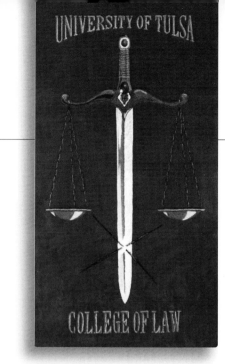

Chapter I

THE TULSA LAW SCHOOL YEARS *(1923 - 1943)*

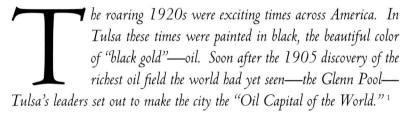

The Background (1920s)

The roaring 1920s were exciting times across America. In Tulsa these times were painted in black, the beautiful color of "black gold"—oil. Soon after the 1905 discovery of the richest oil field the world had yet seen—the Glenn Pool—Tulsa's leaders set out to make the city the "Oil Capital of the World." [1]

By this time the ambitious plan was succeeding. Behind such high profile and rich oil magnates as Josh Cosden and W. G. Skelly stood an army of business, professional and civic leaders, and workers who developed the myriad business, banking, residential, and cultural enterprises such a capital needed.

Optimism was in the air. Tulsa was going somewhere. Banks were being formed to handle the financial needs of the industry; skyscrapers were being built to house the white-collar workers in the industry; numerous support businesses for the industry were being created; homes, from mansions on the bluff of the Arkansas River, to modest dwellings, were being built; and beautiful churches were rising skyward downtown. And tomorrow would be even better.

Tulsa had long valued education. At the very beginning of the oil boom, city leaders believed that good educational facilities were needed to attract leaders in the oil industry to Tulsa. In 1907 city leaders lured Henry Kendall College, then a Muskogee institution, to Tulsa with the offer of twenty acres and $100,000.[2] Henry Kendall College became the University of Tulsa in 1920 and has been an educational leader in the city since that time.

The oil industry started the city throbbing with activity. This activity—commercial, industrial, residential, cultural—in turn generated the need for lawyers to handle the legal work this activity created. By 1923 there were several hundred lawyers in Tulsa.[3]

Where were lawyers to be educated? By the turn of the century the historic method of training lawyers—apprenticeship with a practitioner—was rapidly being replaced by formal education. Universities were forming law departments to educate aspiring attorneys-to-be. The University of Oklahoma had organized a law school in 1909.[4] This law school offered only a full-time program and was more than 120 miles away from Tulsa. What was an enterprising young man or woman to do who lived in Tulsa, needed to work full time, and, yet, wanted to advance in life with the help of a legal education?

Washington E. "Wash" Hudson was the law school's first dean and served from 1923 to 1943. *Courtesy The University of Tulsa College of Law archives.*

Very early during its existence in Tulsa, Henry Kendall College integrated legal education into its curriculum. During 1910-1911, President Seth Reed Gordon instituted preparatory courses in law.[5] His successor, Reverend Frederick W. Hawley, continued this start by organizing a law curriculum during the 1911-1912 school year. Tulsa attorneys taught in twenty-seven areas of legal study, such as torts, criminal law, evidence, and corporation law.[6] Thus began a partnership between The University of Tulsa, as Henry Kendall College was to later become, and Tulsa attorneys in the teaching of law which continued in various forms over the years.

This foray into legal education at Henry Kendall College was not permanent. The curriculum of the college was fluid because the institution kept trying a variety of approaches in an effort to attract students. After a few years, non-law areas were deemed more appropriate for the college to pursue and, by the early 1920s, there was once again a lack of opportunity for legal education in the Tulsa area. A second foray into legal education began which would be much more fruitful and permanent.

A group of five Tulsa attorneys—Washington E. "Wash" Hudson, Emory E. Hanson, Robert D. Hudson, M.C. Rodolf, and I.J. Underwood—obtained a charter from the state on May 17, 1923, incorporating the Tulsa Law School. This was a free-standing institution, not connected with any other educational institution. For the next twenty years this school would provide legal education for the Tulsa community. The first phase in the life of the law school

had begun, albeit apart from the university.

Of these five men, all respected members of the Tulsa Bar, Wash Hudson and Emory E. Hanson were by far the most important to the fledgling school. Hudson was named the dean of the new school and would remain so until the

school merged into The University of Tulsa in 1943. Hanson was the executive secretary and would prove to be the driving force behind the school, not only during its first twenty years as an independent institution, but also during its first few years as a part of The University of Tulsa.

Wash Hudson was the right man at the right time to head the law school in Tulsa. Born in Tennessee shortly after the Civil War, he received an A.B. degree from South Kentucky College and an LL.B.

Washingtion E. "Wash" Hudson in later years, standing by a marker commemorating his contributions to water resources development in Oklahoma. *Courtesy The University of Tulsa College of Law archives.*

degree from Vanderbilt University. He moved to Oklahoma Territory in 1902 for his health and located at Lawton at the opening of the Kiowa/Comanche/Apache country. He was reputed to have been a friend of Geronimo. Years of drought in southern Oklahoma caused him to look to other areas of the state.

"I represented the banks and the railroads and I had passes on the railroads so I began traveling over the state.

"Finally I got here [northeastern Oklahoma] and looked this area over. I said 'Someday in this area a great city will be built.'"[7]

He moved to Tulsa in 1909. He continued his law practice and became involved in politics. He was elected to the State House of Representatives in 1914. As chair of the House Oil and Gas Committee, he helped write the state's first conservation laws. He served one term from 1915 to 1917.

Six years later he was elected to the State Senate and served from 1923 to 1927. His political astuteness is evidenced by the fact that he was chosen majority floor leader during his first year in the Senate. Ever after, he was known as "Senator Hudson."

A small man with a high, squeaky voice, he was flamboyant both as a lawyer and as a person. About 1914 he joined the Ku Klux Klan. His stated reason? Tulsa was a booming oil town and law and order had broken down. "The businessmen and the bankers were all members. We cleaned things up."[8] He said he joined only after being assured there was nothing against religion. He is reported to have quit the Klan in 1922, the night a speaker from the

East denounced Catholics, Negroes, and Jews.[9] Klan membership rolls discovered in 1993 indicate that Hudson may have, in fact, either remained a member or rejoined the organization. His name appears on 1928 to 1931 membership rolls.[10]

Wash Hudson's most enduring interest and possibly his greatest contribution to Oklahoma was water resources development. As he rode over northeastern Oklahoma in horse and buggy, he became impressed with the possibilities for harnessing the power of the Grand River. In the 1920s he tried to interest private investors in building a dam on the river. Although this idea was never accomplished, he did interest investors in buying land for a dam and lake. He and the investors created a corporation whose purpose was to build a dam to produce electric power for lead and zinc mining.

In 1935 the state took an interest in the project, which was transferred to the Grand River Dam Authority and ultimately completed. Hudson served as a member of the authority for a number of years. In honor of his efforts a monument commemorating his work was dedicated at the Grand River Dam near Langley. Lake Hudson, located in Mayes County, is named in his honor. In the rotunda of the State Capitol building is a life-size portrait of Senator Robert S. Kerr, who, like Senator Hudson, was also a proponent in the development of Oklahoma's water resources. In the background of the portrait appears a map of northeastern Oklahoma which includes Lake Hudson, an enduring monument to the founding dean of the law school.

Senator Hudson was the ideal person for the task at hand. A well-

known, "old time" lawyer who could spin tales in and out of court, an influential politician who could help a law school secure the necessary approvals from the state legislature and the state supreme court, Senator Hudson was ready-made to help create a law school, get it started and serve as its public head.

However, he was not an academician and apparently was not interested in the day-to-day detail work of running an educational institution. To complement Hudson as "Mr. Outside," this new enterprise needed a "Mr. Inside." The right person was Emory E. Hanson.

Unlike the flamboyant Wash Hudson, E.E. Hanson was a shy, retiring man. Although extremely important in the creation and early days of the law school, he became a dim figure with the passage of time. In this sense he mirrors the early law school he helped found and nurture. He was known, but not well known. He left no "paper trail," only vague oral impressions by the people who knew him. He was born in 1889 and attended college at Illinois Wesleyan University. Whether he attended law school or simply "read law" under the tutelage of a lawyer is uncertain. He was not listed in Martindale-Hubbell as having attended law school.[11] However, the 1925-26 Tulsa Law School bulletin listed him as having an LL.B.[12] He was admitted to the practice of law in 1919.[13] Thus, in the early 1920s he was a young lawyer at a time when Wash Hudson was already established and well known as a lawyer and politician.

Who was the "founder" of the Tulsa Law School? Was it the brain child of only one person, perhaps Wash Hudson or E.E. Hanson, or was it the joint effort of these two men alone or along with others?[14] There are no definitive answers. The role each man played in the founding and early life of the school is certain—Hudson, as dean, was the public representative of the school who loaned his name, reputation, and political know how to the institution; while Hanson, as secretary/treasurer and registrar, was the day-to-day operator of the school who dealt with students, secured faculty, and obtained a location for classes to be held. He would later be considered and referred to as "Dean Hanson" by students.[15]

The other three incorporators played a lesser, although important, role in the founding of the law school. They were all prominent Tulsa attorneys and formed the nucleus of the first faculty. Robert D. "Bob" Hudson was, perhaps, the most important. He was the son of Wash Hudson. Bob Hudson was generally considered to be one of the best trial lawyers ever to practice law in Tulsa, a true "lawyer's lawyer." Like his father, he attended Vanderbilt Law School. He was appointed a court of common pleas judge when that court was first created in 1924. He was only 24 years old and the youngest judge in Oklahoma at the time. He was later appointed a district court judge in 1927 and served for a number of years, after which he practiced law with his father, with Norma Wheaton, an early Tulsa Law School graduate and pioneer woman attorney, and with Tom Brett, later United States District Court judge. The Robert D. Hudson Chapter of the American Inns of Court was named for him. He, like his father, was caught up in controversy over membership in the Ku Klux Klan. His name

appears on a Klan membership roll discovered in 1993.[16] In 1995, following an investigation and debate over Hudson's membership in the Klan and its meaning, members narrowly voted to change the name of the chapter.[17] The chapter was later named the Council Oak Inn. A number of members left this inn and started the Hudson-Wheaton-Hall Inn.[18] This inn was named after Bob Hudson, Norma

Wheaton, and Amos T. Hall, a pioneer African American attorney in Tulsa.

Everything was in place in the early 1920s. The City of Tulsa needed and wanted an institution that could provide legal education to its citizens. Men and women in the city were eager to be teachers and students of the law. All the necessary elements were present for a law school to be founded.

Emory E. "E.E." Hanson served as executive secretary of the Tulsa Law School from 1923 to 1943 and assistant dean of The University of Tulsa School of Law from 1943 to 1946. *Courtesy The University of Tulsa College of Law archives.*

The First Beginning
(1923-25)

The soft mellow rays of a dying September sun [shine] in the windows of a small office room. A small group of young men and women are seated around the room and in their midst an earnest-faced instructor is talking; every eye is upon him as he stands there, explaining and expounding his subject.... Now, darkness has clothed the earth, the piercing brightness of street lights falls upon the little building. The door opens and the little group emerges, talking and laughing. Tulsa's first Law School has just finished its first class. The year was 1923.[19]

How much of this early-day description of the beginning of legal education in Tulsa, located in the University of Tulsa *Kendallabrum* for 1925-1926, is fanciful and how much is fact? What of the place, the people, and the date of the first law school class?

In the beginning, the Tulsa Law School had no home of its own. Were classes initially held in a "small office room" somewhere in downtown Tulsa, as the yearbook description states? Depending on exactly when classes were first held, that is a possibility. Even if that were the case, however, classes were soon moved. Beginning in the fall of 1923, classes were regularly held in the basement of the then-new Central High School in downtown Tulsa, and, also, in the Administration Building of the school system. Each fall and spring, E.E. Hanson or Wash Hudson would appear before the Tulsa School Board and request the use of space in these facilities.[20] Classes would begin at 6:00 p.m. and run until 8:00 p.m.

Eighteen students are reported to have begun the study of law.[21] A fact worth noting about the student body is that it was composed of both men and women, as the quotation above suggests. From the very beginning, women were involved in legal education at the Tulsa Law School. In fact, one of the first graduates of the school was a woman, Mrs. Clem A. Harwood. In contrast, the story of racial minorities at the school is quite different, as is discussed in later chapters.

BELOW: Central High School, on Cincinnati Avenue in downtown Tulsa, was the first home of the law school and served as the main site for law classes from 1923 to 1949. The building later served as the headquarters for AEP-Public Service Company of Oklahoma. Photo by Miller Photography. *Courtesy The University of Tulsa College of Law archives.*

The enrollment of the new law school was reported to have grown rapidly. A newspaper article written in the fall of 1925 talks of 40 on-going students and says that 50 new students are "expected."[22] If correct, this assumption would put the number of students for the fall 1925 term at about 90. However, these numbers may have been wishful thinking on the part of school officials, a little "puffing" for the public who might read the article. A more accurate enrollment during 1925-26 is reflected in the University of Tulsa *Kendallabrum* for that academic year which reports an enrollment of 59 students. Also, University records of graduates during the first years show a fairly level rate of graduation: 7 in 1926, 10 in 1927 and 9 in 1928.

If the student body grew over the first few years of operation, so did the faculty. Although no records exist concerning the size of the charter faculty, it is doubtful that it was much larger than the five men mentioned in the certificate of incorporation. By 1925, however, the University yearbook reflects a faculty of fourteen.[23] None of the faculty were full-time teachers. They were all practitioners who taught the evening classes the school offered. From the beginning, E.E. Hanson

ABOVE: A scene from a law class being held in Central High School. Classes were held in the evening four or five night a week. As this photograph indicates, women were always an integral part of the student body. *Courtesy of The University of Tulsa College of Law archives.*

combed the Tulsa County Bar to secure the best practitioners in each field to teach at the school.

One of the most enigmatic dates in the history of the school is the date law classes were first held in Tulsa. Was it 1922 or 1923? A few factors point to 1922 as the date. First, on March 11, 1925, the Oklahoma legislature authorized the granting of degrees by the law school.[24] If one assumes that this authorization occurred during the spring when students would first be graduating, one would be led to the conclusion that classes were first held three years earlier, 1922, because the program of study was three years in length at this time.[25] Second, the 1941-42 law school bulletin states: "The Tulsa Law School was founded and incorporated in 1922 by E.E. Hanson....". Although the incorporation date is in error, this statement could reflect the date of actual beginning.

However, a 1922 starting date would mean that classes were held an entire year before the enterprise was even incorporated. Would students and lawyer/teachers have participated in such an informal venture? There is no certain answer, although the optimistic, the-sky's-the-limit tenor of the times in oil-rich Tulsa could lead to such a possibility.

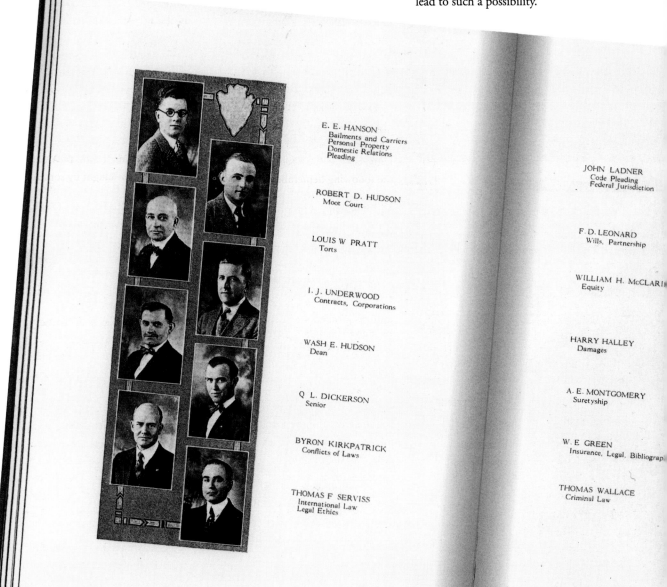

E. E. HANSON
Bailments and Carriers
Personal Property
Domestic Relations
Pleading

ROBERT D. HUDSON
Moot Court

LOUIS W PRATT
Torts

I. J. UNDERWOOD
Contracts, Corporations

WASH E. HUDSON
Dean

Q L. DICKERSON
Senior

BYRON KIRKPATRICK
Conflicts of Laws

THOMAS F SERVISS
International Law
Legal Ethics

JOHN LADNER
Code Pleading
Federal Jurisdiction

F. D. LEONARD
Wills, Partnership

WILLIAM H. McCLARI
Equity

HARRY HALLEY
Damages

A. E. MONTGOMERY
Suretyship

W. E GREEN
Insurance, Legal, Bibliograp

THOMAS WALLACE
Criminal Law

The faculty during the 1925-26 academic year, when the Tulsa law School was first affiliated with The University of Tulsa. The University of Tulsa Kendallabrum (1926). *Courtesy The University of Tulsa archives.*

On the other hand, a number of factors point to 1923 as the starting date for the school. First, the school was incorporated in May, 1923, which would make it reasonable for classes to begin the following September. Second, in the spring of 1926, the Oklahoma Supreme Court granted to graduates of the Tulsa Law School the privilege of admission to practice upon motion. Given the fact that the law school program was three years in length, that would put the start date of the school as 1923. Third, an unidentified 1966 newspaper article found in University archives states: "Several Tulsa attorneys, headed by Senator Wash Hudson, obtained a charter from the state in September of 1923 and opened the University of Tulsa School of Law the following September."[26] Fourth, the quotation from the 1925-1926 *Kendallabrum* indicates a 1923 starting date from a contemporary University source. Finally, the Minutes of the Board of Education of the City of Tulsa first refer to the Law School seeking to use rooms in the high school on September 10, 1923. As indicated earlier, the law school rented rooms in Central High School and dutifully appeared before the school board each fall and spring, requesting space. There is no reference in the school board minutes before September, 1923, reflecting such a request, yet there are regular requests thereafter. It would seem, then, that in order for classes to have begun one year earlier in 1922, either the school board minutes simply do not reflect a request to use the high school, or, else, another facility was used during 1922-23, although at this time the high school was commonly rented out to organizations and was the

logical place for classes to be held. Neither of these alternatives seems very reasonable.

So, we are left with something of an enigma as to the actual beginning date of legal education at the Tulsa Law School. Perhaps the date itself is not so important as the fact that the uncertainty shows the little-known origins of the Tulsa Law School. This characteristic stayed with the school during its early existence as the Tulsa Law School until it merged with the University of Tulsa in 1943.

Any uncertainty as to the details of the operation of this new school does not detract from its importance in launching legal education in Tulsa and northeastern Oklahoma. For several years, until 1925, this freestanding institution provided legal education taught by some of the finest lawyers in the city. The cost of this education to students was $5.00 per credit hour.[27]

On Again, Off Again (1925-27)

As indicated earlier, the University of Tulsa had first taught law courses beginning in 1910. But this effort was not permanent and by the mid-1920s there was a university in Tulsa without a law department and a law school in Tulsa without a university association. It was natural for each to eye the other and consider what advantages merger might bring. The University would obtain an established law school with a curriculum, students, teachers and location. The law school would obtain a continuing supply of students and the status of being associated with a university. In March, 1925, a contract was signed by the University of Tulsa and the Tulsa Law School providing for "reciprocal arrangements for the teaching of law courses and conferring degrees."[28]

In this same month the Oklahoma legislature granted authority to various educational institutions, including the Tulsa Law School, to grant the academic and professional degrees customarily granted to graduates of institutions of collegiate rank.[29] And, as was mentioned above, during the spring of 1926, the Oklahoma Supreme Court granted to graduates of the Tulsa Law School the privilege of admission to practice upon motion.[30] Thus, the University acquired a law school entitled to grant the professional degree and whose graduates would soon be enabled to practice law in Oklahoma upon graduation without the necessity of taking the bar examination. This relationship, which would last for only four short years, would prove to be both productive and troubled.

During 1925-26, the first full-year of university association, the law school enrollment hovered between sixty to ninety students, depending on the sources consulted.[31] The enrollment apparently grew rapidly during this period of university association, as reflected by graduation numbers. Students entering in the years before university affiliation graduated in numbers of ten or fewer;[32] while those students entering after 1925 began to graduate in numbers approaching twenty.[33]

By 1928 the faculty hired to teach these students had grown to twenty practicing lawyers.[34] E.E. Hanson, the secretary/treasurer of the law school, was in charge of recruiting both students and faculty. His downtown law office was the "office" of the law school where students would register, pay tuition and buy books. It originally was in the Pan American Building at 5th and Boulder, on the second floor above a drug store, and one block from the courthouse, then located at 6th and Boulder. He later moved his office to the Mayo Building at 5th and Main. These "administrative offices" of the law school consisted of a small outer reception area with a secretary and seating for students and others, and a larger room divided in half, one half providing the space for Hanson's office and the other half providing the space for the office of H.E. Chambers, who shared office space with Hanson, but who was not connected with the law school. A room elsewhere in the building was rented periodically to house law books sold to students.[35]

The law school attempted to expand its reputation by an interesting marketing approach during this period. School representatives gave lectures over the radio station KVOO during 1926-27 every Tuesday and Friday from 5:00-5:30 p.m.[36] E.E. Hanson even considered giving a credit course over the air if a sufficient number of applications were received.

Early in 1927 an academic milestone was reached in the form of a law library for the school. Prior to this time the school had no library of its own. Students were apparently relegated to using the libraries of their professors, the libraries of their employers, or, perhaps, simply not using a library at all. There was no county law library at the time. In February, 1927, Hanson announced that "the University will have a complete law library within the next few weeks. Twenty-five hundred volumes are on their way to Tulsa and the library will be in

The first Tulsa County Courthouse, located at the intersection of Boulder Avenue and Sixth Street, housed the law library on the third floor from 1927 to 1949. *Courtesy the Tulsa County Historical Society.*

the courthouse."[37] The library had a reported cost of $10,000.[38] It was open during both day and evening hours, and was staffed by two law students. The Tulsa County Bar Association expressed interest in securing library privileges for the organization.

This library continued to be housed in the Tulsa County Courthouse for over twenty years until it was moved to the new quarters of the law school at 512 S. Cincinnati. The library, housed in a room on the third floor of the Courthouse, was just below the county jail.

Students studying in these cramped quarters over the next twenty years would recall the smell of food being prepared for the jail inmates. The library housed a sparse collection of encyclopedias and treatises, the Pacific Reporter and the Oklahoma statutes.[39] The collection would not be catalogued for many years.

A University of Tulsa Bulletin of the day gives the first comprehensive look at the law school.[40] The Tulsa Law School is described as "the law department of the University of Tulsa."[41] The law school was

"swallowed whole" by the University and left intact in its existing downtown location, with its existing students, faculty and administration. The law school was, in essence, an "independent contractor" for the University.

Some of the terms of this "academic contract" shed light on the nature of the school at this time. There were two types of students admitted—regular and special. A student was required to have a minimum of one year of college credit to be admitted as a "regular" student, eligible for the LL.B. degree. However, the school "admitted also a class of students who have not had the preliminary education required for regular entrance, but can satisfy the Faculty

The law library located in the first Tulsa County Courthouse from 1927 to 1949. Paul Stithem Studio. *Courtesy The University of Tulsa College of Law archives.*

that they are qualified to pursue the course with profit."[42] Such students had to be at least 21 years of age. Upon graduation they received a certificate from the law school, unless they had obtained the minimum undergraduate education during their law course, in which case they also would be eligible for the LL.B. degree.

The symbiotic relationship desired by both the University and the law school is demonstrated by a "joint degree" program, which allowed a student to complete requirements for the A.B. and LL.B. degrees in six years. A student was allowed to enter law school after two years of undergraduate education, complete the three years of law school along with an additional year of undergraduate work and obtain both degrees.[43]

Students were tested by daily oral examinations (class recitation?) and unannounced written examinations, along with scheduled exams at the end of each semester. In addition, each senior student was required to submit a thesis of not less than 4,000 words upon some legal topic of his selection and approved by the dean.[44] Each student would be examined by the faculty upon his thesis.

Tuition is stated to be $75.00 per semester for a complete course of study.[45] This is a change from the per-hour tuition charged in the beginning and indicates an increase over the original tuition.

This optimistic period in the school's history was reflected in the public statements of E.E. Hanson and Wash Hudson. At the start of the 1926-27 school year, the second under University affiliation, Hanson stated that: "The subjects required for completion of the course are the same as those required by all standard university law schools, having a three year curriculum."[46]

At the same time, Senator Hudson reflected the public optimism of a dean and the prevailing local education philosophy: "In my opinion the University of Tulsa school of law is a better institution than the law departments of Yale or Harvard for the reason that it is conducted by teachers who are earning their living by practicing and who are not mere theorists."[47]

Underneath this progress and public optimism, however, tensions between the law school and the University existed very early which caused the association to be brief. During the middle 1920s, the University was essentially a liberal arts and science college. It expanded this core through "affiliation" with other existing educational entities. This was the relationship with the law school. Although the University and the law school were affiliated, they had little, if any, interaction with one another. The law school continued to operate as it had earlier, completely autonomous of the University.

Less than two years after the affiliation contract was entered into in March, 1925, the Committee on Affiliated Schools of the University of Tulsa Board of Trustees recommended to the Board that the contract be rescinded. The reason given was that:

[T]he fundamental and primary purpose of The University of Tulsa being the building up of a literary school and the preparation of its students for the professions and the various specialized activities of life, rather than the educating of them in such professions and activities, its efforts should be concentrated on the accomplishment of its primary and fundamental purpose until it shall have attained such success as will enable and justify it in the establishment of departments for professional and specialized training wholly under the management and control of its own officers and the tutorship of its own faculty.[48]

Why was this recommendation made, which was accepted[49] and implemented by the Board of Trustees during the spring of 1927? Why did the University and the Tulsa Law School go their separate ways after such a brief period of union? At least three reasons have been offered. First, the final portion of the above-quote statement by the Affiliation Committee points to University dissatisfaction with an academic component over which it had no administrative, academic or financial control. Further negotiations, discussed below, between the University and the law school during this time strengthens this conclusion.

Another view, held by some students in law school at the time, was that E.E. Hanson and Wash Hudson ended the law school's association with the University because it had not lived up to promises made to the school.[50] It is not known what such "promises" involved.

A third view, held by A. Allen King, the school's first full-time faculty member, and, later, dean of the law school (1958-62) was that the break was precipitated by a comment made by E.E. Hanson in reference to national prohibition [the Volstead Act] that "a law not popularly observed is not a law at all."[51] The University was staunchly Presbyterian and in favor of Prohibition, and the chancellor, so the story goes, "invited" Hanson to leave the University, which he did, taking the law school with him. This is the most colorful of the three possibilities, but, also the one most likely to be a smokescreen for the true reasons behind separation.

Although the break between the University and the law school would not be healed for another sixteen years, it was not for lack of trying by both sides. Soon after the University terminated the contract in the spring of 1927, Dr. John D. Finlayson became chancellor. Almost immediately Hanson approached Finlayson concerning establishing a satisfactory relationship between the University and the Tulsa Law School. Finlayson replied that the University would not be interested in any relationship other than one which would give the University "complete control over the Law School in all its activities and details."[52] Hanson responded that such a plan was possible. Officials of both institutions met several times and finally worked out an agreement which the Committee on Affiliated

Women have played an important role throughout the history of the law school, as this 1932 class photo illustrates. Paul Stithem Studio. *Courtesy The University of Tulsa College of Law archives.*

Schools recommended be adopted by the full TU Board. The terms of the agreement shed light on the relationship of Hanson to the Tulsa Law School—his involvement with it as well as his financial dependence upon it. Although not the founding dean, he surely was the principal in the enterprise during its early years.

The proposed agreement[53] provided:

1) that the capital stock of the Tulsa Law School and the property of the law library be transferred to the University;

2) that E.E. Hanson be retained in the Law School of the University

of Tulsa for a period of not less than six years;

3) that for the six-year period, Hanson's rank be that of full professor, and that for at least the first three years, he be the executive head of the school;

4) that the University pay Hanson an annual salary of not less than $4,500;

5) that Hanson shall "devote himself fully and conscientiously to the promotion of said Law School of The University of Tulsa and the best welfare of the University, and that he shall at

all times, maintain a conduct in keeping with the good name of the University and suitable to the position which he occupies";

6) that the University "shall pay E.E. Hanson a sum equal to the difference between the present cash value of the Law Library of the Tulsa Law School and the outstanding indebtedness of other obligations of said library, said sum to be paid within three years with interest at six percent (6%) on all deferred payments."; and,

7) that the present directors of the law school (Wash Hudson, Robert Hudson, E.E. Hanson, M.C. Rodolf, and I.J. Underwood) be given the privilege of using the law library at no charge and also an annual pass to University athletic events.

It is apparent from this proposal that much of Hanson's income was the product of operating the law school and he was trying to protect it in a University takeover. One can only speculate about his relationship to the law library. Does the fact that the agreement to pay him, rather than the corporation, the "equity" in it, indicate that he had paid for it and owned it, rather than the corporation? Ultimately, although the Tulsa Law School corporation was a not-for-profit entity, it is apparent that all its directors, but particularly Hanson, were attempting to benefit from the University association by way of income, free use of the law library and free passes to University sports events.

This proposal was never adopted by the University, and the original revocation of the operating agreement between the law school and the University in the spring of 1927 remained effective. However,

that revocation did provide that all students enrolled at the time of termination be granted a degree from the University upon successful completion of their work.[54] The last of those students graduated in the spring of 1929, and with their graduation, the last vestige of association of the law school with the University came to an end.

Thus, a relationship begun in 1925 with high hopes came to an end two years later and was moribund by the time the last students graduated with a TU degree in 1929. The Tulsa Law School was once again a fully independent educational institution. Not only would it have to succeed on its own, it would have to do so through a time of a great national depression and, then world war. Unknown to the participants at the time, the school was about to enter its "wilderness years" before coming back into the fold of the University.

operation was completely self-contained and continued as before.

Classes continued to be held in Central High School. About four classrooms were utilized in the basement of the building throughout the 1930s.[55] However, toward the end of the decade, classes were also held in two other locations. Beginning about 1939 some classes were held in the law library on the third floor of the county courthouse.[56] Dean Allen King speculated that economic necessity may have forced E.E. Hanson to give up classrooms in the high school and move to the cramped quarters of the library. Although the law school continued to operate throughout the Great Depression, it must have taken its toll on the operation of the school in ways like this.

Also, about the same time, some classes were moved to the Ault-Kirkpatrick Building, located at 5 East Third Street. In 1939, twelve years after the law school separated

The Wilderness Years (1927-43)

Just as association with the University in 1925 had produced no day-to-day changes in the operation of the law school, so disassociation in 1927, likewise, produced no immediate changes. The law school

A newspaper ad from the early 1940s, which describes the school's purpose, "accreditation," library, student organizations and entrance requirements. It lists E.E. Hanson's telephone number and address in the Mayo Building in downtown Tulsa as the contact. *Courtesy The University of Tulsa College of Law archives.*

THE UNIVERSITY OF TULSA
DOWNTOWN COLLEGE
NUMBER FIVE EAST THIRD STREET
TULSA, OKLAHOMA

**Make Your
Evenings Count**

RETURN POSTAGE GUARANTEED
POSTMASTER: IF ADDRESSEE HAS MOVED, NOTIFY SENDER

ON   FORM 3547   POSTAGE
FOR WHICH IS GUARANTEED

The University of Tulsa

DOWNTOWN COLLEGE

5½ EAST THIRD STREET

"A UNIVERSITY EDUCATION AT NIGHT"

REGISTER NOW

12 Noon to 9 P.M.

Phone 5-1107

FALL TERM 1943

A University flier from 1943, advertising the Downtown College, which provided evening education for the downtown work force. The law school utilized space in these University quarters before its association with the University in 1943, and after, until 1949, when the University built a new building on Cincinnati Avenue for the two downtown divisions of the University. *Courtesy The University of Tulsa College of Law archives.*

from the University, the law school began occupying, on a limited basis, University classroom space. It came about this way. The University of Tulsa opened a "Downtown College" in 1934.[57] During the Great Depression the University was looking for new sources of students and revenue; it found both in the downtown Tulsa work force. The Downtown College was basically a night school that offered a varied curriculum to downtown workers after business hours.

In 1938, James A. Chapman gave to the University the Ault-Kirkpatrick Building, located at 5 East third Street.[58] Space on the second floor was remodeled for the Downtown College, creating classrooms and offices, and was ready for the academic year 1938-39.[59]

The Downtown College shared the building with a variety of tenants. The basement of the building housed a billiard parlor, while the first floor housed a clothing store, a hatters, a barbershop, and the Fruit Juice Oasis, a popular hangout for students between classes. Going up the stairs to the second floor, a left turn would take one to the Seminole Hotel, a right turn, to the quarters of the Downtown College. These quarters consisted of several classrooms with long wooden desks and "soda fountain" chairs,

A classroom in the Ault-Kirkpatrick Building. The law school held classes in this building and in Central High School from the late 1930s until 1949. Paul Stithem Studio. *Courtesy The University of Tulsa College of Law archives.*

a small administration office and a small room used as a library. It was in these quarters that the Tulsa Law School held classes. Other businesses were located on the third floor. Ironically, when first associated with the University, the law school had never held classes in University classrooms; only after separation from the University were classes held in University space, nestled among a melange of downtown businesses.

The law school library continued to be located on the third floor of the Tulsa County Courthouse. The size had grown from 2,500 volumes in 1927 to approximately 8,500 volumes ten years later.[60] This increase spoke more to quantity than quality; acquisitions depended more on donations of unwanted books by attorneys than on a coherent acquisitions policy.[61] There was no classification system for the library except for the reporter series.[62] The school did not have a professional librarian, but, rather depended on a succession of individuals to serve as "managers" or "custodians." Between 1929 and 1943 there were at least six such managers.[63] In the early years of the library's existence, the managers were either faculty or students; later, employees were apparently hired to manage the facility.

The administrative office for the law school throughout this period remained the Mayo Building office of E.E. Hanson. From this office he continued to enroll students, hire faculty and conduct the affairs of the school. Thus, during the 1930s, as in the 1920s, the law school continued to have separate locations for classroom teaching, the library and the administration of the school. This situation would continue for another decade until the building at

512 S. Cincinnati Avenue pulled all of these operations under one roof.

It was during this period that the nucleus of a fine teaching faculty was formed. Although all teaching faculty were part-time, devoting themselves to their legal occupations during the day and coming to the classroom two to three times a week to teach at night, they were remembered by several generations of students as outstanding teachers. Attorney—teachers such as T. Austin Gavin, Roy Huff, Phillip Landa and Remington Rogers are representative of this group.[64]

Two individuals should be specifically mentioned. The first is Grace Elmore Gibson, who was both the wife of a Tulsa attorney and a practicing lawyer herself. She was the first woman to teach at the law school, teaching domestic relations, ethics, and practice and procedure. It would be more than thirty years before another woman would serve on the faculty. The second is John Rogers, who, at this time was attorney for James A. Chapman and vice-chairman of the University of Tulsa Board of Trustees. He taught contracts and, later, constitutional Law, at the law school. Mr. Rogers would later be instrumental in bringing the law school into the University fold once again. His dual connection with the Tulsa Law School and the University of Tulsa laid the groundwork for amalgamation of these two institutions in 1943. Ironically, during this period Mr. Rogers tried unsuccessfully to persuade the Board of Regents of the University of Oklahoma to move the OU School of Law from Norman to Oklahoma City in order to centralize the school and make it more accessible to students from Tulsa. The Tulsa Law

School might very well have failed had the regents followed Rogers' advice.[65] Thus, John Rogers' vision for legal education in Oklahoma in the 1930s could have sounded the death knell for the Tulsa Law School; his actions in the 1940s and after forever changed the course of its history and put it on the road to its current position.

Two types of faculty were hired to teach at the law school: older, experienced practitioners and young attorneys fresh out of law school. The first group was primarily motivated by a desire to share their knowledge and experience with law students; the second group were also motivated by the economic desire to supplement their income during the difficult days of the 1930s.[66] Hiring was done exclusively by E.E. Hanson, who would assess the Tulsa County bar, make decisions as to who he wanted to teach, and negotiate with and hire the attorneys over the telephone.[67] How teachers were paid during this period is uncertain; both a nightly basis[68] and a monthly basis[69] have been suggested. There was no organization among the faculty. They were practitioners who arrived for class, taught and then departed, never meeting as a group. These teachers used traditional teaching styles, such as the Socratic method, and used both textbooks and casebooks, bringing to their classes a combination of their own practice experience and the academic approaches experienced during their own legal education.[70]

Two traumatic events occurred in the life of the nation during this phase of the life of the law school—the Great Depression of the 1930s and World War II. Both events affected the law school. Enrollment in 1929 was

Grace Elmore Gibson, who taught during the 1930s and 1940s, was the first woman to teach at the law school. *Courtesy The University of Tulsa College of Law archives.*

Annual Review of Legal Education lists the law school as requiring two years of college to qualify for admission. What was needed, in fact, was a high school diploma, no college education being required, and the tuition in hand. Students who had completed the required college work would be awarded a diploma and the LL.B. degree upon graduation; students who had not attended college received a "Certificate of Graduation."

There were, in reality, few college age students in school during this period. Most students were older and working to support themselves and their families. They were intent on bettering themselves through education. Their teachers found them "mature"[74] and "committed."[75] All of the students were from Tulsa and surrounding communities in northeast Oklahoma. There were always women enrolled in school; ten of the fifteen graduating classes between 1929 and 1943 had female graduates. In contrast, no African-Americans would be admitted until the 1950s.

Despite the fact that most students were beyond college age and were busy supporting themselves and their families during the day and attending school at night, there was a need for some social interaction. This need was filled by several legal fraternities formed during this period. There were three legal fraternities open to men: the T. Austin Gavin Chapter of Delta Theta Phi, Phi Alpha Delta and Phi Beta Gamma, which "mavericks" joined.[76]

approximately 100 students; during the early-to-mid 1930s, when the country was mired in the depths of the Depression, enrollment declined to approximately one-half that number and less. It must have been very difficult for E.E. Hanson to keep the doors open. The decline certainly affected his approach to student finances. During the late 1920s he was seen as a generous man who worked with students who had difficulty paying the $75.00 tuition, allowing them to pay in installments.[71] Ten years later,

although tuition had decreased to $50.00 per semester, a darker picture emerges, one of a man who would insist on tuition "up front" and who would "lose" records of a student who was not completely paid up.[72] Because of this tendency, there were problems in assembling records of some students at the time of the acquisition of the law school by the University in 1943.[73] By the war years, tuition had once again risen to $75.00 per semester.

Entrance requirements were lax. During the late 1930s the ABA

Officers of Phi Delta Delta, a fraternity for women started in response to their inability to join men's fraternities. Their involvement continued after graduation, as this photo illustrates. Left to right: Elaine Dean Barnes ('36), Maurine Abernathy Howard ('38), Lillian Herndon, Dora E. Barnard ('38), Norma F. Wheaton ('27). *Courtesy The University of Tulsa College of Law archives.*

Although women were regularly admitted to the school, they were not admitted to these fraternities; therefore, they formed their own, Phi Delta Delta. It operated in the late 1930s and 1940s before merging with Phi Alpha Delta. These organizations would have rush parties, called "smokers," and seasonal parties. Over the years they developed an academic thrust as well which reached its peak in the 1950s and 1960s.

The three-year program of the 1920s had been expanded to a four-year program by the 1930s.[77] The curriculum was modeled on that of the University of Oklahoma Law School. E.E. Hanson had Charles Skalnik and, later, Charles Kothe,

review the OU curriculum for the purpose of improving existing courses and adding new courses to the curriculum.[78] By the late 1930s, the following four-year required curriculum was in place:[79]

First year: Agency, Contracts, Partnership, Personal Property, Torts

Second year: Bailments and Carriers, Bills and Notes, Common Law Pleading, Damages, Domestic Relations, Legal Bibliography, Sales

Third year: Evidence, Equity, Legal Bibliography, Municipal Corporations, Private Corporations, Real Property

Fourth year: Constitutional Law, Code Pleading, Conflicts of Law, Ethics, Indian Land Titles and Abstract Examination, Insurance, Suretyship, Wills

As in the 1920s, classes continued to be held Monday through Friday nights from 6:00 to 8:00 or 9:00 p.m. Legal bibliography would sometimes be taught on Saturday morning and teachers would regularly assign students to attend the motion docket held at the Tulsa County Courthouse each Saturday morning. This regimen would run for nine to ten months of the year during the fall and spring semesters.[80]

The fluidity of the situation at the law school was apparent in the varied commencement exercises held during this period. In 1940, commencement was held in the First Presbyterian Church, with exercises remarkably similar to contemporary commencement exercises. Most often, however, commencement during the 1930s was not so much an academic affair as a black-tie affair held at the Tulsa Club in downtown Tulsa. The entire student body was invited. E.E. Hanson served as master of ceremonies. The valedictorian of the graduating class, a prominent person in the community, and each class president, would speak. Wash Hudson, as dean, would award the diplomas and certificates. In contrast, in 1935, Wash Hudson simply called the five graduates into his office and presented them their diplomas and certificates with no ceremony at all.[81]

What of accreditation during this period? The 1941-42 Tulsa Law School bulletin makes this statement:

The school is approved by the Supreme Court of the State of Oklahoma, and Board of Bar Examiners. The school is also a member of THE NATIONAL ASSOCIATION OF LAW SCHOOLS, an organization whose purpose is the advancement of legal education in the United States. Membership in this organization is dependent upon meeting and maintaining high standards as to entrance requirements, faculty, library and curriculum.

The law school was not yet approved by the American Bar Association, limiting the eligibility of graduates to sit for the bar in other states, although approval by the Supreme Court of Oklahoma had allowed graduates to be admitted to the Oklahoma bar upon motion from 1926 until 1939, when the State Bar Act made it mandatory for applicants to pass an examination. Thereafter, the school's approval by the Oklahoma Board of Bar Examiners allowed Tulsa Law School graduates to sit for the Oklahoma bar. American Bar Association approval would not come until the 1950s, while membership in the Association of American Law School would come in the 1960s.

December 7, 1941, is the day that will "live in infamy" in American history. On that day the Japanese bombed Pearl Harbor and the United States quickly began its entry into World War II.[82] All facets of American life were affected by the war, including legal education.[83] As American men began to enter military service, law schools around the country

saw their enrollments dramatically decrease. Strong education institutions were able to withstand this situation and continue. More marginal institutions, like the Tulsa Law School, were more vulnerable. Following the stock market crash of 1929, the economic upheaval affecting the country was apparent in decreasing enrollment at the law school during the first half of the decade of the 1930s. Although there are no direct enrollment records for this period in existence, the Depression's impact can be seen on graduation rates, which steadily fell between 1929 and 1935.[84] During the second half of that decade and into the beginning of the 1940s, enrollments slowly rose again, as indicated by graduation rates, only to be dashed even more severely on the shoals of World War II.[85]

Adding to this strain was the fact that the leaders operating the school were now older men. Wash Hudson, who had been dean since the beginning, was 77 years old in 1943. Even more important E.E. Hanson, who had tackled the day-to-day responsibilities for securing students, faculty, classroom space, supplies and many other requirements for 20 years, was 54 years old in 1943. It is not known who approached whom, but E.E. Hanson, representing the Tulsa Law School and the past, and John Rogers, representing The University of Tulsa, and the future, met and worked out an agreement having momentous impact on the future of the school. The law school was about to come out of the wilderness and back home again to the University of Tulsa.

Early-day commencement exercises were often more social than academic, as this 1939 commencement dinner at the Tulsa Club illustrates. *Courtesy The University of Tulsa College of Law archives.*

THE TULSA LAW SCHOOL YEARS 31

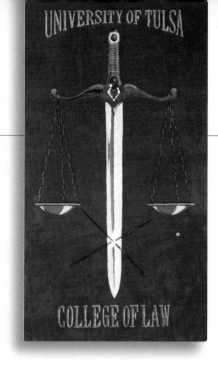

Chapter II

THE UNIVERSITY OF TULSA SCHOOL OF LAW— THE DOWNTOWN YEARS

(1943-1973)

A New Beginning (1943)

I n the summer and fall of 1943, the last act in the life of the Tulsa Law School was played out and the curtain was raised on its successor, The University of Tulsa School of Law. The University had already begun to lay the groundwork for legal education to once again be offered within the University. During the 1941-42 school year, the College of Business Administration began to teach a few law courses.[1] Within two years, this tentative effort was transformed into a new school at the University. The credit primarily belongs to the man who was the second founder of the law school—John Rogers.

Mr. Rogers was born in 1890 in Missouri and moved to Oklahoma in 1908 to work as a stenographer in the law office of his older brother, Harry. He attended the law school at the University of Oklahoma, graduating in 1914. After a year in the general practice of law he began an association with the Chapman, McFarlin and Barnard families which would last for the rest of his career and his life. He became an attorney for the McMan Oil Company, formed by Robert M. McFarlin and J.A. Chapman, and, later, the McMan Oil and Gas Company. Finally, beginning in 1930, he became general counsel for the Chapman-McFarlin-Barnard interests.[2] He joined the TU Board of Trustees in 1926 and, with brief periods off, remained an active trustee until 1964. Thus, by 1943, Mr. Rogers was a mature attorney, intimately involved in the affairs of the Chapman-McFarlin-Barnard interests and a powerful figure at the University. He was, at the time, the Chair of the Committee on Faculty and Curriculum of the Board of Trustees.

On August 23, 1943, Dean Paxson of the College of Business Administration proposed to this Committee the establishment of a law school as a separate school in connection with the Downtown College.[3] It was understood that the curriculum and library facilities would be established according to the requirements of the American Bar Association and the Oklahoma Bar Association and that the program of study would be approved by the Supreme

John Rogers was a guiding force behind the scenes at the law school from the 1940s through the 1970s. Hawkins Studio. *Courtesy The University of Tulsa College of Law archives.*

Court of Oklahoma.[4] The Tulsa Law School had never been approved by the ABA, but it was the early determination of Mr. Rogers to have an **approved** law school. It would take a decade, but his goal was ultimately accomplished.

Two days later, on August 25, 1943, Mr. Rogers presented the recommendation of the Committee on Faculty and Curriculum to the full Board of Trustees. After some discussion, a motion was made by Mr. Rogers and carried to approve the recommendation. The officers of the University were authorized and directed to proceed with the organization of a School of Law.[5]

Thus, in August, 1943, a law school was created by the University. But it was an empty vessel waiting to be filled.

The first move toward filling this empty vessel was to appoint a dean. On September 16, 1943, the Committee on Faculty and Curriculum recommended to the Board of Trustees that Judge Summers Hardy be appointed dean, "it being understood that the position carried no salary for the present."[6] The Tulsa Law School had enjoyed only one dean since its founding in 1923—Wash E. Hudson. The TU Board thanked Senator Hudson for his contributions

to the school over the previous twenty years,[7] turned from the past [8] and looked toward the future.

The Tulsa Law School had originally selected Senator Hudson, a non-academic, as dean because of the political and public-relations help he could provide. In like fashion the University now selected another non-academic lawyer to be dean because of the public image he could project for the school But the two men, although serving the same function for the school, were quite different individuals. Senator Hudson was highly political, a yarn-spinner and a feisty trial lawyer. Judge Hardy was judicial in career and temperament, much more conservative and a "gentleman."[9]

Summers Hardy, born in Arkansas in 1875, moved to Ardmore, Indian Territory in 1891. He later apprenticed with an attorney and was admitted to law practice in the United States Court for the Indian Territory in 1897.[10] He served as a delegate to the Oklahoma Constitutional Convention. He practiced law in Ardmore and Madill until 1910 when he was elected to the bench as a state district court judge. In 1914 he was elected an associate justice of the Supreme Court of Oklahoma and served in that office until 1918 when he became chief justice for one year. He resigned that office to become associated with the Sinclair companies, a position he held until 1942, when he retired to private practice in Tulsa with his son, Milton.[11] Thus, at the time of his appointment as dean, he had over 45 years of experience before the bar, on the bench and in industry. He brought a wealth of prestige to this newly created University law school.

Summers Hardy, second dean, 1943-49. *Courtesy The University of Tulsa College of Law archives.*

A poster promoting Summers Hardy during his campaign to be elected to the Supreme Court of Oklahoma.
He served on the Court 1914-19. *Courtesy The University of Tulsa College of Law archives.*

Since Judge Hardy would be a public figure who would not administer the school day to day, the University appointed an associate professor of law and economics on its own faculty, Harold Hughes, to become law school secretary to help administer the law program. What actual role Dr. Hughes played is unknown; what is better known is the continuing role of the true administrator of the law school— E.E. Hanson. "Dean" Hanson, as he had been known by students for the previous twenty years, would serve as the bridge between the old Tulsa Law School and the new School of Law of the University of Tulsa. He became assistant dean and professor of law.

In late September, 1943, there were two law schools in Tulsa, on paper at least. The Tulsa Law School was an existing entity about to merge into the University. The University's School of Law existed only on paper, an empty receptacle waiting to receive the substance of the Tulsa Law School. John Rogers and E.E. Hanson hammered out the agreement of transfer. On September 28, 1943, Hanson was present at the TU Board meeting at which Rogers presented the agreement of merger. Following is the agreement adopted by the TU Board of Trustees, and, later by the Board of Directors of the Tulsa Law School.[12]

AGREEMENT BETWEEN TULSA LAW SCHOOL AND THE SCHOOL OF LAW OF THE UNIVERSITY OF TULSA

1. Tulsa Law School is to make a gift of law library, including all book shelving, to the School of Law of the University of Tulsa which is to be evidenced by a written transfer of gift.

2. So far as it is agreeable with students, transfer all present students to the School of Law of the University of Tulsa.

3. Turn over to the School of Law of the University of Tulsa all cash and accounts receivable as of October 1, 1943.[13]

4. Tulsa Law School is to quit business and take the necessary procedures to dissolve the Tulsa Law School Corporation.

5. The School of Law of the University of Tulsa is to exert every effort possible to protect the legal fraternities now existing in the Tulsa Law School and have them transferred to the School of Law of the University of Tulsa.

6. All records of Tulsa Law School are to be delivered to the Registrar of the University of Tulsa.

7. Students enrolled in the Tulsa Law School who are beginning the study of law are to be requested to transfer to classes now being conducted by the School of Law of the University of Tulsa.

8. With the above exception, the classes now being taught by the Tulsa Law School are to be continued as classes of the School of Law of the University of Tulsa at the present location and with the present instructors for the remainder of this semester.

9. The University of Tulsa is to assume all current bills and obligations of the Tulsa Law School as of October 1, 1943.

10. The University of Tulsa is to employ E.E. Hanson as the Associate Dean of the School of Law of the University of Tulsa on the following basis:

a. His tenure is to be on the same basis as all other members of the faculty and evidenced by the University's regular employment contract.

b. His compensation shall be at the rate of $150 per month from October 1, 1943 to January 1, 1944.

c. Commencing January 1, 1944 his compensation shall be at the rate of $300 per month on a twelve-month basis and remain at this figure until a regular full-time enrollment of the School of Law equals 100 students. (By full-time enrollment is meant a student carrying 8 credit hours per semester.)

d. When regular full-time enrollment of the School of Law equals 100 students, then the future compensation of E.E. Hanson shall be mutually agreed upon by E.E. Hanson and the University of Tulsa.

For the second time legal education provided by the Tulsa Law School came under the auspices of The University of Tulsa. The first time this happened, 1925, the arrangement fell apart within two years.[14] There were similarities between the 1925 agreement and the 1943 agreement: the student body and the faculty remained intact; the location of classrooms, library and administrative offices remained largely intact; and the administration remained partially intact—although a new dean was appointed, E.E. Hanson remained the day-to-day administrator of the school.

However, Mr. Rogers insured that the basic problem of the 1925 agreement, lack of academic or financial control, would not recur. Thus, in 1943, the ownership and control of the basic aspects of the enterprise passed into the hands of the University: library ownership transferred to TU; cash and accounts receivable passed to TU; student records passed to TU; students transferred to the new School of Law; a new dean was appointed; and E.E. Hanson became a TU faculty member, responsible to the University. In addition, the dissolution of the Tulsa Law School prevented it from ever again resuming operation and becoming a competitor of the University.

With the implementation of the agreement in the fall of 1943, the Tulsa Law School passed into history and the University of Tulsa School of Law began its journey. Both the first founder, Emory Hanson, and the second founder, John Rogers, were principal participants in this new phase. This fact would initially cause conflicting pulls toward the past and the future. Ultimately, however, the future would win out.

The Drive for Accreditation (1943-53)

Just as association with the University in 1925 had not affected the day-to-day operations of the school, so this second association in 1943 produced no immediate changes. E.E. Hanson continued to administer the school from his office in the Mayo Building. The same faculty taught the same students in the same classrooms. A few classes were held in the Ault-Kirkpatrick Building at 5 East Third Street, site of the Downtown College of the University of Tulsa.[15] Most classes

were held in classrooms in the basement of Central High School. The law library continued to be located on the third floor of the county courthouse.

Students readily accepted the challenge of cramped physical facilities in those days. Edgar H. Parks ('50) described conditions in the Downtown College facility on Third Street and in the courthouse library this way:

It [the law school] had been part of an old hotel. Down below was a pool hall and domino parlor, and, if you turned the wrong direction inside the door, you ended up in the hotel. The courthouse library at Sixth and Boulder was in an attic room and you had to overcome the stench of restaurant garbage below and no air conditioning to get any studying done.[16]

Parks' classmate and long-time law partner, John Boyd ('50), described the school's small library maintained in the Downtown College facility on Third Street: "It was about 30 square feet and you can imagine how much studying could be accomplished with the dean's office in there also."[17]

During the first three years following the law school's affiliation with the University, there were forces pulling in two different directions. John Rogers and others wanted to begin to make changes necessary for ABA accreditation. But Mr. Rogers was involved in numerous business and civic activities and did not participate in the everyday operation of the school. He was more of an overseer. The day-to-day operation continued to fall on the man who had seen to the task for the previous

twenty years—E.E. Hanson. He apparently did not have the same vision as Mr. Rogers, being content for the school to continue as it always had.[18]

Then, as so often is the case, death allowed change to take place. E.E. Hanson died suddenly in the spring of 1946 and the brake to change was removed.[19] The first founder and the administrator of the law school for its first 23 years was gone; the path was open to the second founder, John Rogers, and others to begin the changes that would lead to ABA accreditation.[20] Dwight Olds, one of the instructors at the school, understood that change was now possible and needed and that John Rogers was the person to take the lead. In a 1946 letter to Rogers, shortly after Hanson's death, Olds outlined some of the changes he recommended and ended with the observation: "You now more than anyone else are in a position to direct our school toward ABA approval. High standards and worthwhile goals are in our grasp. We can and shall properly educate those in our school."[21] John Rogers came to understand what would be necessary to obtain ABA accreditation through a source close by—John Hervey. Hervey was an attorney practicing in Oklahoma City who had been dean of the University of Oklahoma Law School, and, equally important, was the advisor to the Section of Legal Education and Admissions to the Bar of the American Bar Association. He was helpful in communicating to Rogers and others what changes would be necessary to secure ABA accreditation. He indicated that the law school must improve in four areas if it hoped to achieve accreditation:

1) **Admissions**: Tulsa Law School had long had an admission requirement of 60 credits of undergraduate college work, but this requirement had often been ignored, especially after World War II when the school accommodated returning veterans by allowing them to enter with 24 credits if they made up the deficiency during the first two years of law school.[22] Not only would this practice need to end, but admission criteria would need to be increased.

2) **Program**: Since its beginning the school had offered only a part-time program, taught at night, aimed at educating men and women who worked during the day. But the press of World War II veterans seeking higher education caused the law school to begin a three-year program whereby students could take an overload and graduate in three years rather than four. This program violated ABA standards for part-time legal education.

3) **Faculty**: Heretofore all faculty had been part-time instructors, practicing during the day and teaching classes in the evenings. The ABA required that there be a minimum of three full-time professors for a school to achieve accreditation.

4) **Physical Plant**: Throughout its history the law school had never had its own building. Rather, functions had been scattered throughout downtown Tulsa: classrooms in Central High School and, later, the Ault-Kirkpatrick Building; library in the county courthouse; and the administrative office in the Mayo Building and, later, in the Ault-Kirkpatrick Building. The ABA required that these functions be consolidated physically for the school to achieve accreditation.

The University, John Rogers and a number of other people tackled these problems and, between 1946 and 1950, were remarkably successful in solving them. During this period there was a burst of activity and improvement. This burst, which led to American Bar Association accreditation, along with later, similar bursts of improvement, propelled the law school toward its current status of full integration into American legal education. The law school had offered quality legal education from the beginning, but for the first decades of its existence, it was not a part of the mainstream of legal education. The period of 1946-50 began the process of taking the school into that mainstream.

The admission and program problems were understandable in light of the law school's history. The school had always struggled financially, with enrollment seldom nearing 100 students and often being much lower. Then World War II brought the GI Bill which ultimately educated over seven million veterans.[23] Suddenly, following the war, the law school had an abundance of students for the first time, their tuition and expenses being paid, in part, by the federal government.[24] Enrollment in the spring, 1947 semester reached 123 students, the highest in the history of the school.[25] Dean Hardy stated that for the fall, 1947 semester: "[W]e will take all freshmen who wish to enroll this fall, regardless of number. We have a responsibility to those men and women who seek a legal education and must make space available to them. If one class

is filled, we'll offer the course at two different times."[26] It is little wonder that a small school which had always struggled financially bent its admission requirements in order to accommodate this tide of applicants. However, increased applications also brought the ability to be more selective and adopt admission criteria in line with ABA—approved law schools. By the 1950-51 academic year, the law school had ended its policy of allowing students to enter with only 24 college credits and had increased its entrance requirement to require 90-120 credits [3-4 years] of undergraduate college work.

The three-year program begun in 1947, aimed at meeting the GI Bill requirements of student veterans, was not a full-time program.[27] There were no requirements against a student working and taking the program. Seventy-five percent of the instruction was offered at night, with only twenty-five percent of the courses offered during the afternoon. No morning classes were offered. This program was phased out shortly after it began so as not to jeopardize the school's opportunity to obtain accreditation.[28]

Another important academic change was made during this period. Credits required for graduation were raised from 72 to 80. The curriculum for 1947-48 required a student to take 10 credits per semester. The first two years were composed of required courses. During the third and fourth years one-half of the courses were electives chosen by the student.[29]

An additional academic concern involved the law library. Mr. Rogers understood that an adequate library was essential to accreditation. He obtained $40,000 from James A. Chapman to buy law books and had

John Rogers, third dean, 1949-57. He was instrumental in the law school receiving accreditation by the American Bar Association in 1953. *Courtesy The University of Tulsa College of Law archives.*

individuals scout the area to obtain books from lawyers.[30]

Important personnel changes occurred as the decade of the 1940s came to an end. A. Allen King, who held B.A. and LL.B. degrees from the University of Tulsa and an LL.M. from the University of Michigan, was appointed the first full-time professor of law in the school's history in September, 1948. That year the illness of both Dean Hardy and Assistant Dean Franklin created a management crisis. To solve it, President C. I. Pontius appointed John Rogers acting dean

in June, 1949, and, six months later, dean of the law school. Allen King was appointed administrative dean in June, 1949. On the surface the administrator situation looked similar to the situation twenty years earlier when Wash Hudson was dean and E.E. Hanson was "administrative dean": a respected attorney in the community serving as titular head without compensation, while the "administrative dean" actually ran the school. In fact, the actual situation was quite opposite. Mr. Rogers, although an overseer, made the important decisions and King,

The law faculty at a University commencement, held on the "U", during the early 1950s. Left to right: James B. Diggs, Travis Milsten, Whit Y. Mauzy, Joye Clark (librarian), Remington Rogers, James E. Bush, John Rogers (dean), John W. Hager, A. Allen King (administrative dean), W. Preston Woodruff, Peggy Wilson (administrative secretary). *Courtesy The University of Tulsa College of Law archives.*

as the day-to-day administrator, carried them out. Bruce Peterson, a later professor and dean of the law school, put it succinctly: "You did not sneeze without Mr. Rogers' permission."[31]

In May of 1949, Mr. Rogers, still the Chair of the Committee on Faculty and Curriculum, recommended the appointment of Remington Rogers and Philip N. Landa as full-time professors of law. They both had been adjunct professors at the school for some time. A problem developed concerning the ability of Remington Rogers to serve "full time" because of his law practice. Therefore, John

Rogers hired a recent graduate of the University of Oklahoma Law School, John Hager, to become a full-time professor in the fall of 1950. The school now had the required three full-time faculty (Hager, King and Landa) necessary for ABA accreditation. The story is told that when Phil Landa became a "full-time" professor he scraped his name off the door of his downtown office where he practiced in order to comply with ABA requirements. The story may be apocryphal but it illustrates the very thin line that separated "full-time faculty" from "part-time instructors" at the law school. Classes were held only at night; thus, all of the early-

day full-time professors had much of the day to engage in the practice of law and still teach at night. John Hager served as an attorney in the City Attorney's office for several years before starting up a private practice, specializing in trial work. Allen King read title abstracts for title companies. Phil Landa had an appellate and insurance practice. None the less, the University had appointed three professors of law on full-time contracts, thus meeting this vital requirement for ABA accreditation.

The final requirement for accreditation was to bring all the functions of the enterprise together under one roof. John Rogers, in a newspaper interview in 1949 about pending ABA accreditation, indicated that the law school had not been accredited earlier because classrooms and library were in separate locations.[32] The unification came about in the following way.

The future site of the law school building would be 512 South Cincinnati Avenue in downtown

The law faculty, including additional personnel from the previous photograph, at another University commencement during the early 1950s. Left to right: Remington Rogers, Joye Clark (librarian), James W. Bush, Phillip N. Landa, W. Preston Woodruff, Roy M. Huff, John W. Hager, A. Allen King (administrative dean), Milton W. Hardy. *Courtesy The University of Tulsa College of Law archives.*

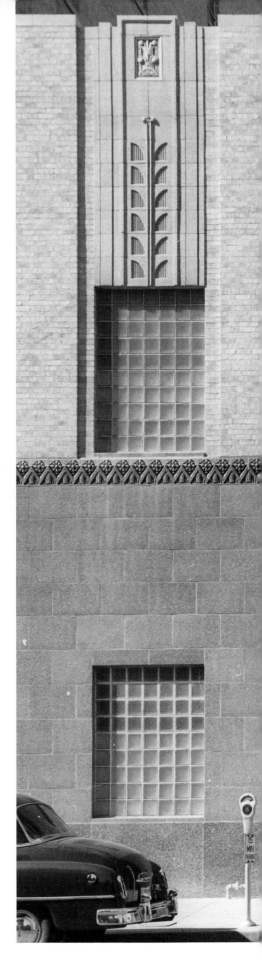

Beginning in 1949, the law school shared the building at 512 S. Cincinnati Avenue with the Downtown Division of the University. When the Downtown Division moved to the Kendall campus in 1962, the law school was the sole occupant of the building until 1973, when the school also moved to the Kendall campus and into John Rogers Hall. *Courtesy Bob McCormack Photographer.*

Tulsa. That site, on the west side of Cincinnati between 5th and 6th streets, was part of a larger tract of land along Cincinnati donated in 1935 to the University by Waite Phillips for the benefit of the College of Petroleum Engineering. The University had never used the property; the larger tract had earlier been occupied by the Barall Food Palace and the All Steel Coach and Trailer Corp., but was unoccupied by the mid 1940s.

After World War II Stanolind Oil and Gas Co., a subsidiary of Standard Oil of Indiana, decided to place its pipeline operations in a separate company, Stanolind Pipeline Company (later Service Pipeline Company) and place it in its own building near the parent company which was located on Boston Avenue. The only available land was that owned by TU. In 1948, TU leased the bulk of its land on Cincinnati Avenue to Stanolind, but retained the north 50 feet, known as 512 South Cincinnati Avenue, for the purpose of erecting a building to house the Downtown Division (the new name for TU's old Downtown College) and the School of Law. The term of the lease was 50 years at a rental of $7,500 per year. The lease contained the following salient provisions:

1) Stanolind agreed to furnish, at its expense, its architect who would draw up plans for the TU building, comprised of a basement and two stories, to be built on TU's remaining land during the construction of Stanolind's building. (Stanolind

paid sufficient rent in advance in cash to allow TU to erect its building.)[33]

2) TU would be allowed to use Stanolind's building wall as a party wall in the construction of its building.

3) Stanolind agreed to furnish TU's building with heat and air conditioning free of cost.

4) Stanolind granted TU an easement in its building to locate pipes and meters necessary to provide various utility services to TU's building.

The 512 South Cincinnati Avenue building was completed and occupied by the Downtown Division and the School of Law in September, 1949. The building cost $335,000 and its furnishings and equipment cost $75,000. It contained 20 classrooms, 4 private offices, a general office, a bookstore, a lounge with adjacent kitchen and, in the basement, the downtown athletic ticket office and a library comprised of 12,000 law books and 1,500 general academic books.[34]

That fall the building accommodated an enrollment of 205 law students; 1,518 undergraduate students; and 141 graduate students; (1,864 total.) Stated capacity was 2,400 students, a number for in excess of actual physical capacity.[35] It is little wonder that Professor John W. Hager once commented that, during class breaks, it was impossible to reach the bathroom or, even pick up a pencil which had been dropped![36]

ABOVE: John Rogers worked with officials of the American Bar Association to secure accreditation for the school. In this photo he gives a tour of the library to individuals attending the 1952 Oklahoma Bar Association convention, held in Tulsa. Left to right: C. Campbell McLaurin, chief justice, trial division, Supreme Court of Alberta, Canada; Robert G. Storey, president of the American Bar Association and dean of the S.M.U. Law School; John Rogers; Hicks Epton, president of the Oklahoma Bar Association; and, A. Allen King (administrative dean). *Courtesy The University of Tulsa College of Law archives.*

As the decade of the 1940s came to a close, far-reaching changes had occurred at the law school. Significant improvements had been made in the admissions requirements and in the program; the school had a full-time faculty for the first time; and finally, the school had a permanent home housing all operations, even if it was being shared with the Downtown Division. This burst of activity and improvement led to provisional accreditation by the American Bar Association on September 21, 1950, and final approval three years later

on February 27, 1953. A significant milestone in the history of the School of Law had been reached.

The Drive for Improvement (1953-73)

In the next twenty years following ABA accreditation, during which the law school occupied the downtown building, there were many improvements in the quality of the education offered. These improvements propelled the school toward the educational institution it had become at the start of the

BELOW: Roy Huff is seen here conducting a decedents' estates and trusts class in a classroom in the 512 S. Cincinnati Avenue building. Huff, the long-time head of the trust department at the National Bank of Tulsa, was typical of the many practicing attorneys who have taught at the law school over the years. *Courtesy Bob McCormack Photographer.*

twenty-first century. However, these improvements also created stresses that caused the school to move from downtown to the Kendall campus and be integrated into the University of which it had become a part.

THE JOHN ROGERS YEARS

Up to this point student organization had been through the fraternity system. For a number of years there had been three men's fraternities and one women's fraternity.[37] In the years following accreditation both students and alumni organized in other ways. A Student Bar Association was organized in late 1952.[38] Its purposes were to write a weekly news article about law school activities in the TU newspaper, conduct an orientation each fall for new law students, conduct information meetings with TU pre-law undergraduate students, and, obtain student discounts on

The law library in the lower level of the
building at 512 S. Cincinnati Avenue.
It served as the law library 1949-73.
Courtesy Bob McCormack Photographer.

TU football and basketball tickets. Sports provided the only meaningful integration between law students and the University.

Alumni also organized for the first time. In late 1951 the University of Tulsa Law School Association was chartered.[39] Three hundred alumni and students met and elected a twenty-seven-member board of directors. Officers included William G. Murchison, Max G. Feldner, Katherine Kile, William W. Biddle and Randall Glen West. Allen King, the administrative dean, was elected "resident agent." This organization would wax and wane and be revamped several times in succeeding years.

Only part-time legal education had been offered up to this time. The vision of both the Tulsa Law School and the early University of Tulsa School of Law was to allow working men and women a chance to advance by obtaining a professional education. Dean Rogers' vision for the school went beyond this, however. The most important advancement in the school in the years immediately following accreditation would be the establishment of a full-time division that would offer legal education in the same format as the best law schools in the nation. In early 1954, Allen King announced tentative plans for the law school to start a full-time division in the fall of 1956.[40] The reason given was that the school wanted to work toward admission into the Association of American Law Schools. Such admission would be a big step toward entering the mainstream of legal education. Although this target date was missed by one year, a full-time division was started in the fall of

1957.[41]   The full-time program was open only to entering students this first year. Fifteen students started the program, taking 14-16 credits, rather than the typical 10 credits taken by part-time students. These students had a work limitation of twenty hours per week, a limitation that remained constant over the years. Additional professors were being hired to meet the curriculum needs created by a full-time division. Ralph C. Thomas joined the faculty in 1956, Graham Kirkpatrick in 1957, and Bruce Peterson in 1959. Although it grew slowly, the full-time division ultimately surpassed the part-time division in size during the years that the school occupied the downtown campus.[42] During the balance of John Rogers' deanship (1949-1957), enrollments, remained low, going over 200 only occasionally.

The administration of the law library underwent change during this period. Prior to the law school occupying its own space in the building at 512 S. Cincinnati Avenue, there was no full-time librarian; rather, the library was managed by a series of "managers" who, often, were students. Only after the school moved into the building in 1949, was a true "librarian" in charge of the library. The first librarian was "imposed" on the law school by the University library in 1949, and did not work out.[43] The first "true" librarian was Joye Clark, who served from 1950 to 1957. Because the building housed the Downtown Division library as well as the 12,000 volume law library, she was the "Downtown Division" librarian who was in charge of both libraries. The law school would not have its own librarian until 1963, when the

Downtown Division moved out of the building, leaving the law school as the sole occupant. Before 1953, the library holdings had never been classified. Clark devised a classification scheme based on a Yale Law School system for small law schools.[44] Following Joye Clark, Pat Baker served as librarian between 1957 and 1959. She was followed by the woman who would ultimately become the first "law" librarian, Charlotte H. Highland. Highland began her duties in 1959, and served as "Downtown Division" librarian until 1963, and, between 1963 and 1970, as "law" librarian.

Up to this time no African-American had ever attended the law school in Tulsa. The University of Oklahoma had, however, already experienced the trauma of integration. In 1946, Ada Lois Sipuel (Fisher), a Langston University graduate, applied for admission to the University of Oklahoma Law School and was denied admission because of her race. She contested the denial of admission on such grounds in court, supported by the National Association for the Advancement of Colored People Legal Defense Fund and represented by Tulsa attorney Amos T. Hall and future United States Supreme Court Justice Thurgood Marshall. After three years and two trips to the United States Supreme Court, she was admitted to the law school in 1949.[45]

In contrast to the dramatic and traumatic events surrounding the integration of OU's law school, TU's integration was much quieter and much less dramatic. Kenneth Dones applied to the law school for the 1952-53 school year and was refused admission. Mr. Dones was the son-in-law of Edward

L. Goodwin, a respected leader in the Tulsa African-American community and publisher of the *Oklahoma Eagle*. Mrs. Goodwin went to her friend, John Rogers, to discuss the matter with him and an accommodation was reached: the law school would admit Dones as an auditor for one year, provided he agreed to transfer to another school at the end of that time.[46] At the end of the year, Dones transferred to Washburn University Law School. There are divergent views as to why he was admitted only as an auditor and only for one year. Was it because of his race or was it because he had graduated from an unaccredited undergraduate institution? [47] There are also divergent views about his treatment during the year. His wife remembered unequal treatment and isolation by administration and students, while the school registrar asserted that there was no discrimination during the year.[48]

Ironically, Kenneth Dones' father-in-law, Edward L. Goodwin, whose wife had played a role in Dones' entry into law school, himself attended the law school shortly after his son-in-law, and graduated in 1958. According to his widow, he experienced no hostility or prejudice during his years at the school.[49] A second African-American student, Theodric B. "Blue" Hendrix attended during the same years, also graduating in 1958. Thus, Goodwin and Hendrix became the first African-American graduates of the school. Over a twelve- year period, Oklahoma law schools had been integrated dramatically at OU and very quietly at TU. In ensuing years, African-American and other minorities would attend the law school, but in small numbers.[50] There would be later drives to

increase the minorities population at the school.

THE A. ALLEN KING YEARS

In December of 1957, John Rogers retired as dean. As a member of the TU Board of Trustees, he had earlier pushed through a requirement that all administrators must resign at age sixty-five. Turning that age himself, he honored the policy and stepped down.[51] The man who had been his long-time administrative dean, A. Allen King, was appointed dean in January 1958, serving in that capacity until May, 1962.

Allen King is singular among the law school's deans for being the first dean to hold a degree from TU (B.S. '34, LL. B. '41) and the first full-time dean in the school's history. Having been a student at the old Tulsa Law School and a faculty member at the successor school, he served as a bridge between the two institutions. After earning his law degree, he served in the U.S. Air Force in World War II. After the war, with the help of the G.I. Bill, he earned the L.L.M. degree from the University of Michigan in 1947. Returning to Tulsa, he practiced law with the Public Service Company of Oklahoma. In the fall of 1948, he became the first full-time professor

On the occasion of his retirement as dean in 1957, John Rogers received an honorary LL.D. degree from the University for his long service as trustee and dean. This photo shows him receiving the diploma from President C.I. Pontius and receiving the hood from Administrative Vice-President Ben Henneke. *Courtesy The University of Tulsa College of Law archives.*

Phil Landa, John Rogers, an unidentified
student and Peggy Wilson attending a
moot court argument at the Tulsa County
Courthouse. *Courtesy The University of Tulsa
College of Law archives.*

at the law school, accepting a job
offered by then administrative dean
W.C. Franklin. He, himself, became
administrative dean one year later,
in 1949. He served as dean of the
law school from 1958 until 1962.

He left the TU faculty in 1965
and taught for the remainder of his
career at American University in
Washington, D.C.

In saying that King was the
first full-time dean in the school's

RIGHT: A. Allen King, fourth dean,
1958-62, was the law school's first full-
time dean. *Courtesy The University of
Tulsa College of Law archives.*

history, the term "full-time" must be understood within the culture of the law school of that day. Until 1957, when the day division was started, the school and its faculty and students had always been "part-time," with both faculty and students splitting time between work and the law school. Thus, Dean King understood "full-time" to mean something different from what the modern-day dean understands it to mean. His field was property law; therefore, he examined abstracts for many clients. This

meant that he was absent from the school often during each week. Given the low salaries at the school during this period, many of the "full-time" faculty supplemented their income with outside practice.

BELOW: Dean King with William Fred Phillips ('60) in the library of the law school building at 512 S. Cincinnati Avenue. *Courtesy The University of Tulsa College of Law archives.*

In Dean King's case this meant that many of the day-to-day tasks of administering the school fell to the sole clerical person at the school, his secretary, Peggy Wilson, or, "Dean" Wilson, as she was called by students. For example, she was in charge of student recruitment and registration. She had a long-standing agreement with the president of the University, C. I. Pontius, that if she met the fall quota for entering students, he would buy her a steak dinner, but if she fell short, she would buy him one.[53] Wilson was, in essence, an early-day "associate dean for academic and student affairs."

This does not detract, however, from Allen King's major accomplishment as administrative dean and, then, dean—the start-up of the full-time division. Both King and Rogers had a goal for the law school of membership in the Association of American Law Schools. They understood that having a full-time division and a full-time dean were important components of achieving that goal. The realization of this goal,

The student lounge in the 512 S. Cincinnati Avenue building consisted of a canteen located in a small room on the second floor. *Courtesy The University of Tulsa College of Law archives.*

set in motion by King, would be completed by his successor, Bruce Peterson.

The school took its first steps toward what would be called today "clinical legal education" during King's deanship. This was in the form of a "Legal Aid Clinic." The program was set up as a one credit-hour course wherein

students would work for the public defender program and the legal aid society. Students performed case investigation and legal research, but did not give advice to clients or try cases.[54] This program operated for several years, but was finally replaced by the Legal Internship Program operated by Professor Ralph Thomas.

Another "practical skills" program that was growing during this time was the Moot Court Program. Prior to 1959, the competition had always been intra-school. That year a team traveled to Houston to compete for the first time in the regional competition.[55] Another first occurred in 1960, when a regional moot court competition was held in Tulsa and drew participants from nine schools.[56] The law school was finally becoming part of the larger legal education community.

Two interrelated factors were beginning to simmer during this period which would reach a flash point during the administration of Bruce Peterson. The first involved the physical facilities downtown. The downtown building was such a vast improvement over the makeshift and scattered facilities used before that few minded sharing it with a large number of undergraduate students in the Downtown Division. But, over the years, competition between these two components of the University grew. The law school slowly occupied more and more of the building. James Poe ('59) described the evolving building-use situation this way:

> By the time I was in school in the mid-50's, the law school occupied the basement and most of the street level of the building place. A laboratory

had been moved from the basement and the library had taken its place. When I graduated in 1959, it was spilling over onto the second floor where some of the fraternities had offices.[57]

The second factor related to the very fact of being downtown, rather than on the TU campus. The school had always been downtown and had a symbiotic relationship with the practicing bar, all of whose offices were downtown. Law students worked downtown for lawyers and various businesses and went to school at night, while the bar took advantage of the law library, which was the best in the city. This had always been John Rogers' vision for the school. But Allen King chafed under this arrangement. His view was that the law school was the "forgotten" division of the University.[58] He would frequently learn about University events by the grapevine and have to call campus to confirm. King wanted to see the law school integrated into the rest of the University. It would be another ten years before this vision would prevail, during which time there would be unrest on the part of students, faculty, administration and trustees.

THE BRUCE PETERSON YEARS

The dean during most of this remaining period was Bruce Peterson. Peterson had grown up in Tulsa, graduating from Will Rogers High School. Like so many of his generation, he joined the U.S. Army immediately after graduating from high school and served in World War II. He later served in the reserves in the Judge Advocate General's Corps, retiring as a colonel in 1984. Returning from World War II,

Peterson earned a law degree from the University of Oklahoma, and, at the outset of his career on the TU faculty, he earned an LL.M. degree from New York University. Peterson served on the TU faculty from 1959 until 1979. After leaving the faculty, he was in private practice, served as associate district judge in Haskell County, and ended his legal career as a referee with the Oklahoma Court of Civil Appeals in Tulsa.

Peterson became dean in the following manner. In the spring of 1962, Allen King came to President Ben Henneke and asked for immediate release from his administrative duties because of the grave illness of his wife, who suffered from cancer.[59] Henneke conferred with John Rogers, who still played a central role behind the scenes at the school. Rogers suggested that Henneke offer the deanship to Graham Kirkpatrick, who refused because of his own battle with cancer, and then, to John Hager, who declined because of his involvement in outside legal practice. Peterson, the third alternative, accepted Henneke's offer of the deanship.[60] Peterson would prove to

ABOVE: Bruce Peterson and Allen King enjoying a light moment at an annual Gridiron, the most important all-school event during the 1950s and 1960s. *Courtesy The University of Tulsa College of Law archives.*

RIGHT: Bruce Peterson, fifth dean, 1962-69, worked to secure law school membership in the Association of American Law Schools. *Courtesy Bob McCormack Photographer.*

be the last dean to date drawn from the internal faculty ranks.

His deanship, from May, 1962 until August, 1969, saw substantial improvement in the school in a number of areas, but would also witness growing tension between students and administration concerning the downtown physical facilities. Peterson had one paramount goal during his administration—membership in the Association of American Law Schools, one of the two fundamental pillars indicating the quality of a law school. The first pillar, accreditation by the American Bar Association, had been achieved during the deanship of John Rogers. These two men could not have been more different—John Rogers, the dignified and courtly leader in civic and church affairs; and Bruce Peterson, the rumpled and profane fellow often seen with a cigarette or pipe in one hand and a drink in the other. Each, in his own way, accomplished marvelous things for the school during this period.

The law school had always operated on an economic shoestring.

The great value of Dean Peterson was his resourcefulness and ability to effect improvements with little expenditure of money. This was a time in the life of the school before fundraising from friends and alumni. Peterson accomplished objectives in other ways, for the most part.

One method Peterson used was to increase enrollment, and, thus, tuition revenue, in innovative ways. He created a new admission program that allowed students to begin in the spring semester as well as the fall semester. The first mid-year class of 26 students registered in January, 1963.[61] He and the faculty carried this idea further several years later, creating, in the fall of 1966, a trimester system at the school, which had heretofore always been on the semester system. Under this system the academic year was divided into three terms ("trimesters"), each 14 weeks in length, stretching from September through July.[62] This did away with a long summer period with few classes; rather, the summer was a part of the regular academic year. This program was popular

with working students because they were available for class anyway and because they could graduate in less than the traditional four-year period. Full-time students liked the program because they could graduate in less than three years. Enrollment was maximized because students were admitted at the beginning of each of the trimesters, expanding on the "mid-year admission" program. The program was popular with faculty because it provided for employment throughout most of the calendar year. This resulted in a "raise" in salary for faculty at a time when salaries lagged far behind most law schools and the dean had little money for direct raises. And, every nine semesters, a faculty member would be eligible for a paid sabbatical to engage in scholarship. Dean Peterson had adroitly found a way to meet the needs of two constituencies at no direct cost.

Dean Peterson was interested not only in increasing the quantity of students and, thus, income, but he was also desirous of increasing the quality of the student body. He

During the 1960s, the law school clerical staff was small. In 1965, it was composed of Sylvia Hatfield and Vena Nipper, shown here. *Courtesy The University of Tulsa College of Law archives.*

Gridiron, the annual spring social /
academic get together by the entire student
body, was very popular during the King and Peterson
years. Students lampooned the faculty in skits, such as the one
represented here. Left to right: Ronald Ricketts ('69) as Professor Jim Thomas;
Sam Graber ('67) as Professor John Marvin; William Douglass ('67) as "The Colonel," Professor
Graham Kirkpatrick; Gene Mortensen ('68) as Professor Ralph Thomas; Mallie Norton ('68) as Professor
John Te Selle; and, Glenn Brokaw ('67) as Professor Dale Searcy. *Courtesy Bob McCormack Photographer.*

During its heyday, Gridiron was as popular with faculty as with students. Faculty participated with skits and song numbers, such as the one represented here. Left to right: A.F. (Tony) Ringold (adjunct); Roy Huff (adjunct); "The Colonel," Graham Kirkpatrick; Bruce Peterson; Ralph Thomas (with head turned); Allen King (with back to photographer, leading the song); John Hager; Richard McGee (adjunct); and Thomas Landrith (adjunct). Monroe Studio. *Courtesy The University of Tulsa College of Law archives.*

approached this goal in two cost-effective ways. First, beginning in the fall of 1963, all entering students were required to take the Law School Admission Test (LSAT).[63] Although this may not have had much immediate effect on a school striving to increase the size of the student body, it set the school on the road to a regular process and objective measurement of the qualifications of entering students. Second, one year later, in the fall of 1964, the school required all entering students to either have an undergraduate degree upon entering or to be in a combined-degree program and have earned three-fourths of the credits necessary for the undergraduate degree.[64] These requirements were strengthened still further three years later when, as of the fall, 1967 term, the combined-degree program was eliminated and all entering students were required to have an undergraduate degree.[65] These changes allowed Peterson to seek related changes that would affect the status of the school in the eyes of students, the public and the profession. Now that all graduating students had an undergraduate degree, Peterson proposed that the degree granted be changed from the LL.B. to the J.D. (Juris Doctor.) This trend was sweeping through law schools across the country in the 1960s; the University followed suit in first granting the J.D. degree to graduates in the spring of 1965.[66] The Board of Trustees placed prior graduates on a parity by allowing

those who held an undergraduate degree when they obtained their law degree to exchange their (Bachelor of Law) LL.B. degree for the J.D. degree.

In addition, Peterson wanted to change the status of the institution by making it a "college" with the University system, because it was freestanding and not a part of any other college within the University. He presented the idea to John Rogers, who supported it and engineered the change through the Board of Trustees. The institution became the College of Law in the fall of 1965.

Over a period of four years, Dean Peterson had presided over an enhancement in entrance requirements, and changes in the nature of the degree awarded and the status of the institution within the University. He had adroitly effected a "make-over" of the institution at almost no direct cost.

Academic changes were occurring during this time. New full-time professors were expanding the traditional curriculum. James C. Thomas, joining the faculty in 1963, brought expertise in the areas of labor law, anti-trust law and legislation. Charles W. Linder brought land use controls into the curriculum, and W. Paul Gormley introduced international law and admiralty into the curriculum. By 1968, when the number of academic credits needed to graduate was raised from 84 to 88, only 39 were required, while 49 were elective.

The law school environment, as exhibited by class schedules, was also changing. Even though full-time students were limited to working no more than twenty hours per week, this limitation was honored as much in the breach as the observance and the schedule had accommodated this breach by offering mostly morning and evening classes. By the mid-1960s, more afternoon classes were being scheduled in an effort to stem

this breach. Also, part-time students, after having attended class five nights a week, Monday through Friday, for years, finally saw the schedule change to a Monday-through-Thursday format. And, the number of credit hours that a part-time student could take was reduced from ten to nine hours.

Several non-classroom academic programs developed during this period. Moot court was the oldest of

these programs. As an appellate-court-argument exercise, it had traditionally been organized and run by the legal fraternities. In 1959, it was taken over by Ralph Thomas and expanded from a intra-school program into one in which TU students fielded teams on a regional and national basis. Thomas and others expanded this type of mock practice experience into mock-trial and client-counseling programs in the mid-1970s.

By the early 1960s, the Legal Aid Clinic was attempting to expand under the direction of Professor Graham Kirkpatrick. He, Dean Peterson and U. S. District Judge Allen Barrow were working to see that students in the program would be allowed to appear in state and federal court, something heretofore denied them. Kirkpatrick and Peterson were working with the Oklahoma Bar Association and

the Oklahoma Supreme Court. Upon Kirkpatrick's death, Ralph Thomas took up the cause. In 1964, Thomas was appointed to the OBA Internship Committee which created a state-internship program allowing Oklahoma law school students to intern with practicing attorneys. In 1967, the Oklahoma Supreme Court approved the program. There were important differences between the old "Legal Clinic" program and the new Legal Internship program. First, under the old program, students could not "practice law" by advising clients or appearing in court; under the new program, such was possible. Second, under the old program, students received academic credit only; under the new program, students both received academic credit and were paid as interns by their supervising attorney. Ralph Thomas served as administrator of the program, working with the students and their supervising attorneys for over twenty years. The receipt of academic credit and monetary compensation was unique to the Oklahoma program and required periodic American Bar Association dispensation because it was at variance with ABA accreditation rules. During the 1970s, 1980s and 1990s, as in-house clinical education became more common in the country's law schools, TU's legal internship model came under more and more scrutiny by the faculty and was ultimately replaced by an in-house clinic, as discussed in a later chapter.

Perhaps the capstone of Dean Peterson's drive for membership in the Association of American Law Schools was the creation of the *Tulsa Law Journal*. Although there had been a number of informal informational publications by students over the years, there had never been a scholarly journal edited by law students. One problem was the lack of funds for such a publication. Peterson set about remedying that problem by fund-raising, something not done by previous deans. He solicited door-to-door among the area banks, which, along with the Tulsa Bar Foundation and the Oklahoma Bar Foundation, contributed about $5,000, enough to pay for the first issue.[67] That first issue was published in January, 1964, with Stan Doyle as editor-in-chief, and Professors Charles Linder and Jim Thomas as faculty advisors. In an introduction, Maurice H. Merrill, Research Professor of Law at the University of Oklahoma and one of Oklahoma's most distinguished legal scholars, wrote: "One of the axioms of law school administration is that the law review provides one of the most effective adjuncts to the basic teaching program. With the inauguration of the *Tulsa Law Journal*, legal education in Oklahoma takes one more step forward."

One other initiative by Dean Peterson marked his deanship and aided in admission of the law school into the AALS. Since 1949, the law school had shared the building at 512 S. Cincinnati Avenue with

TU's Downtown Division, which, by the time of Peterson's deanship in the 1960s, was called the Evening Division.[68] In the fall of 1962, the beginning of Peterson's deanship, there were 823 undergraduates occupying the building each evening, along with 209 law students,[69] all in a three story building of only 21,000 square feet. Peterson argued to the University administration that if the law school was to grow and prosper, it must have the building to itself. In addition to his own resources, Peterson often used the influence of John Rogers. This combination resonated with President Ben Henneke, who was interested in bringing the academic program of undergraduate evening education to campus. As a result, the University decided to move the Evening Division to campus, effective fall, 1962, leaving the law school as the sole occupant of the building. Peterson immediately created a plan for improving the facility. For a cost of $10,000,[70] renovations to the building were made which resulted in (1) expanding the law library into the entire basement ("lower floor") of the three-story building, thereby accommodating up to 30,000 volumes; (2) consolidating smaller classrooms to create larger classrooms on each of the two upper floors, which also had the effect of creating additional faculty offices that could hold up to 11 faculty; (3) creating a faculty conference room; and, (4) creating an improved student lounge. The goal was to create a facility capable of handling

The 1969 National Moot Court team for the law school. Top, left to right: John B. Farr, Tommy L. Holland, William D. Nay, and Ronald K. Olsen. The judges selecting the team appear bottom, left to right: Judge Hez Bussey, Oklahoma Court of Criminal Appeals; Judge Tom Brett, Oklahoma Court of Criminal Appeals, and Professor Hugh V. Schaefer (coach). *Courtesy The University of Tulsa College of Law archives.*

around 300 students, a number which would be exceeded within three years.[71]

Peterson was not content with a physical improvement; he wanted an image improvement as well. He created the idea of a "Tulsa Law Center" at the building, which would be comprised not only of the law school, but also offices for the Tulsa County Bar Association, and, the "Lawyer Reference Service," his term for the law library. He also envisioned the Tulsa County Legal Aid Society, which was housed in the courthouse, moving to the building. On October 4, 1963, a dedication of the University of Tulsa Law School Building and Tulsa Law Center was held in front of the building.[72] Present at the ribbon-cutting ceremony were Oklahoma Supreme Court Justice Harry L. A. Halley, Oklahoma Bar Association President Robert Blackstock, Oklahoma Bar Foundation member T. Austin Gavin, Tulsa County Bar Association President Richard Bert, Tulsa Mayor James Maxwell, TU Board of Trustees Chairman R. K. Lane, Northwestern University Law School Dean John Ritchie, and John Rogers, who cut the ribbon. This was the largest collection of dignitaries for the most formal affair in the history of the school. In the media, at least, Dean Peterson had transformed a law school sharing facilities with undergraduates into a "Law Center." This was, largely, smoke and mirrors. The Tulsa County Bar Association occupied space in the building for only a short time before moving into the Beacon Building downtown. The Tulsa County Legal Aid Society never occupied the building. The law library continued to do what it had always done, serve as a resource for students and practicing attorneys. The name of the school was never formally changed and the term "Law Center" never caught on. But, for one brief moment, Dean Peterson created a "Camelot" on a shoestring. His talent was to create improvements, both real and imaginary, at little cost.

Dean Peterson's efforts worked. In December of 1966, the law school was admitted into membership in the Association of American Law Schools. The image and status of the law school rose and dovetailed into a time of increased national interest in legal education. Enrollment would rise during the 1960s to over 300 students[73] and would set the stage for increasing student dissatisfaction with the law school's physical facilities and propel the institution toward a break with its historic mission of educating students downtown.

In the twenty years the law school had been in the downtown building since occupying it in 1949, fundamental changes had occurred in the student body. In 1953, for example, the enrollment was 160 students, all attending part-time;[74] by 1963, the enrollment had grown to 220 students, 52 of whom were full-time;[75] whereas, by 1968, the enrollment had swelled to 312 students, 204 of whom were full-time. In this period the enrollment had almost doubled, but, more important, the "full-time" student had emerged at the school and become the majority. This student, unlike the part-time student who appeared each night for class and went home, was in the building much more during each day, using the facility for both academic and extra-curricular purposes. The building, with bare-bones classrooms, a tiny and spartan library, a cramped student lounge, and no space for any student organizations, was increasingly viewed as inadequate by a majority of students. Add to this the fact that parking consisted of plugging parking meters hourly or paying downtown prices to park in a lot, and the students' sense of inadequacy boiled over into action.

In November of 1968, Dean Peterson and the Student Bar Association (SBA) arranged for the new young University president, J. Paschal Twyman, to attend a SBA luncheon. At that lunch the students presented their grievances concerning the facility and the program to Twyman. President Twyman was non-committal at the luncheon, but, within a month, the University announced that a number of physical improvements to the building would be made.[76]

The strong personalities of President Twyman and Dean Peterson would dictate that they could not work together. Paschal Twyman had been appointed president only a few months before the luncheon. At 34, he was one of the youngest presidents in the nation at the time, and, over the next twenty-two years, would prove to be a forceful, almost overwhelming presence within the University. Peterson ran the law school as if it were detached from the University, and when necessary, would go over the head of the president to John Rogers, who was still a powerful force with the Board of Trustees. Twyman wanted to establish his presidency and felt that he had been blindsided by law school students, with the acquiescence of, and, perhaps, at the instigation of, the dean. Peterson was forced to resign at the end of the 1968-69 academic year. President Twyman would later comment that, at the time, he considered the law school to be not only physically separated, but, also, socially separated from the University, and considered it to be headed, not by a collegiate dean, but, a "czar."[77]

THE EDGAR H. WILSON YEARS

That November, 1968 luncheon led all parties to understand that the law school had come to a crossroads: remain downtown, either at the present facility, adding floors, or, moving to another location close to the courthouse;[78] or, alternatively, move to campus. The vision of John Rogers, shared by Bruce Peterson, was the law school as a downtown institution close to the courts where students could observe and work and where the bar had easy access to the law library. Paschal Twyman's vision was of a college more closely connected with the University. This vision was shared by another relatively new player on the stage—William H. Bell, Mr. Rogers' partner and successor as attorney of the Chapman/McFarlin/Barnard interests and trustee of the Chapman Trusts. Bill Bell was a 1954 graduate of the law school who had first gone to work for Mr. Rogers as a law clerk, staying on as an associate and later a partner in Mr. Rogers' firm. More importantly, he became Mr. Rogers' protégé and, ultimately, successor in University affairs. Mr. Rogers, increasingly aged and infirm, was moving off-stage with his vision of the school, to be replaced by Bill Bell and the vision he and President Twyman shared. The remaining years of the law school downtown would be taken up with the preparation for moving to campus.

With the resignation of Bruce Peterson in 1969, the law school had its last dean drawn from the ranks of its own faculty. President Twyman desired, and the faculty approved, the hiring of an academician from another school. All previous deans had, effectively, been presidential appointments, with little faculty involvement. This appointment broke that cycle, with the faculty actively conducting the search and the final appointment being subject to the president's approval. All parties settled on Edgar H. Wilson, a member of the University of Florida faculty at the time, but with strong ties to Mercer University in Georgia.

Dean Wilson had a background in academia, administration and government that impressed the faculty, President Twyman and the alumni. He held three law degrees from Duke University (LL.B., LL.M and the J.S.D.). This, alone, was considered as giving him insight into what "good legal education" was all about and was very important to the decision-makers at TU. He had served for twenty years, 1948-68, on the faculty of the Walter F. George School of Law, Mercer University. During a part of this period he had also served as mayor of Macon, Georgia, and as a member of the Georgia General Assembly. During the year before his appointment at TU, he was a professor of law at the University of Florida and executive director of the Florida Law Revision Commission. After serving as dean at TU from 1969 to 1972, he returned to Mercer University as dean of the law school for several years and completed his career as a professor of law there.

Ed Wilson became dean in September, 1969 and set out to achieve four goals:[79]

1) change the graduation ceremony from an informal "party" atmosphere, present in the Gridirons held each spring, to a more formal affair that would instill pride and a sense of academic accomplishment in the graduates and their families;

2) move to a more business-like method of administering the daily financial life of the school;

3) obtain a knowledgeable, qualified and cooperative librarian for the library; and

4) conduct a fund-raising program for a new law school facility.

The first two goals say something about the general atmosphere of the school at this time. Under Dean Peterson the atmosphere was not always that of a formal, professional academic institution. Graduation had a "party" flavor to it more than a sense of academic recognition; school finances were operated out of an old cash register, and records were sparse and rather informal. Wilson wanted to bring a more business-like atmosphere to the school. He did achieve some success in bringing about a more formal graduation experience for students and in setting up a more formal record-keeping system, but true improvement in these areas would come only after the school moved to campus and took full advantage of the University's atmosphere and offices for finance and financial aid.

The third goal resulted in a change in the law librarian. Charlotte Highland had been the librarian since 1959 and enjoyed autonomy under Dean Peterson. She had a library science degree, but not a law degree. Dean Wilson wanted his own team, including a law

The Phi Alpha Delta fraternity in the late 1960s. In the front row are the faculty advisors, Professors Bueford (Boots) Herbert and Jim Thomas. *Courtesy Bob McCormack Photographer.*

Edgar H. Wilson, sixth dean, 1969-72. He was involved in the decision to move the law school to the Kendall campus and in the fund-raising for the construction of John Rogers Hall. *Courtesy Bob McCormack Photographer.*

librarian with a law degree. Highland was replaced in the summer of 1970 by Imogene Harris, a 1958 graduate of the law school. Harris' tenure spanned the planning for the move and the actual move from downtown into John Rogers Hall. Also, her tenure marks a turning point in the type of librarian serving the library. All subsequent librarians have had law degrees as well as library science degrees.

By far and away the most important contribution Dean Wilson made was in the shaping of the institutional decision on whether the law school should stay downtown or move to campus, and once the decision was made, to organize and execute the fund-raising effort needed to carry the decision out. In the fall of 1969, President Twyman instructed him to engage in a study and forward to Twyman recommendations regarding the proper location of a law building. Wilson conferred with the faculty and students and with law school deans around the country,[80] sending out a questionnaire to the 118 fully accredited schools and receiving responses from 103 of them. From the views received he assembled eight reasons for a downtown location and nine reasons for a campus location.[81] He proceeded to rebut each argument in favor of a downtown location and support each argument in favor of a campus location. In the process, he pointed out that all but one of the Tulsa faculty favored a campus location and that " the overwhelming majority of them [legal educators] and the great weight of the arguments, indicate that a location on the main university campus is far superior from the point of view of legal education."[82] The new dean had

thrown his weight behind a move to campus.

All of the important forces of the day were lined up behind this historic decision in the life of the law school. The dean had

cast his lot behind the move, recommending it to the president. President Twyman probably needed very little persuading. His presidency, from beginning to end, showed a desire for strong central

William H. Bell, left, protege and successor to John Rogers, right, as attorney for the Chapman / McFarlin / Barnard interests. Both men played important roles in building a new law school building on the Kendall campus of the University. *Courtesy Rogers and Bell Law Firm.*

administrative control. In the case of the law school, that could be better exercised on campus than off. The new vice-president for academic affairs, John Dowgray, also favored moving the school to campus.[83] Objectively, there was precedent for this decision. There had been a long-standing campus plan calling for consolidation of the three University locations (Kendall campus, housing arts and science, business administration and music; North campus, housing engineering; and, the downtown law school) on the Kendall campus.[84] (This plan was ultimately accomplished.) The other important decision-maker in this situation was Bill Bell, who had taken over management from an aging John Rogers of Chapman/McFarlin/Barnard and Chapman Trusts affairs, including those which involved the University. Although there is no direct information on his attitude, the fact that the major funding for the new law school building on campus came from Chapman money, as will be seen shortly, and in the same year as Wilson's memo to Twyman, would lead one to believe that Bell was aligned with Twyman in wanting the law school to be on campus.[85]

The timetable for the decision on the school's future was this: the fall semester of 1969-70, Wilson's first semester as dean, was taken up with obtaining information and views from a variety of sources; the spring semester of that year and the fall semester of 1970-71 was taken up with behind-the-scenes decision-making on the location and nature of a new building and arranging the lead gift to pay for it. This activity culminated in November, 1970, with a University announcement that a

$1 million anonymous donation had been received that would allow the construction of a new College of Law building on TU's Kendall campus.[86] After forty-seven years of operation and twenty-seven years of connection with the University, the law school was leaving downtown Tulsa and moving to campus. The next two and one-half years in the life of the school would be dominated by this impending move.

Ed Wilson and the University organized a drive to raise the additional $500,000 needed for the building. Wilson was aided by Edwin M. Schmidt, who had joined the faculty as a professor and assistant dean in the fall of

1970, the first true assistant dean in the school's history. He had been hired because of his experience as the director of academics (dean) of the Judge Advocate General School in overseeing that school's move from the general campus of the University of Virginia to its law school campus.[87] College of Law and University personnel fashioned a fund-raising drive called the "College of Law Advancement Program." The drive was headed by Paul E. Taliaferro and Judge Royce H. Savage. The library in the new building (the Taliaferro - Savage Library) would be named for these two men in appreciation for their efforts. Taliaferro was a 1930 graduate of the law school who had been chairman of the TU Board of Trustees and CEO of Sun Oil Company, DX Division. Savage was a former United States District Court judge and general counsel of Gulf Oil Corporation. Both men had impeccable credentials and standing within the business, legal and philanthropic communities in Tulsa. They headed a "Fund-

Raising Cabinet" of fourteen leading citizens.[88]

Taliaferro and Savage headed up the drive for large donations. They were well suited for the task because of their close connection to the corporate and oil communities. Savage would later comment that, "It was an easy job."[89] Claude Rosenstein and others solicited the business community, while Floyd Rheem, Ed Hieronymous and others did the same with the Tulsa County Bar. Ed Wilson and Ed Schmidt, along with LeRoy Blackstock and others, raised funds from alumni. A collateral benefit of their activity was a revitalization of the Alumni Association. As a result of efforts to contact alumni, records were created

for the first time and a first-ever Alumni Directory was published for 1971-72. Royce Savage's comment could be applied to the over-all fund drive - - it was completed in less than one year.[90] Undoubtedly, it was helpful that the new home of the school would be named for John Rogers, who was highly esteemed by all the constituencies involved.

There had been speculation as to the location of the new building from the time of the announcement that it would be located on the main University (Kendall) campus. Three locations were mentioned: 1) the TU Oval, in front of McFarlin Library (President Twyman played down the likelihood of this location, stressing the need to "preserve grass and open

areas" there; 2) Harwell Practice Field, behind Harwell Library and between fraternity and sorority rows; and 3) "the northwest corner across from Westby Student Center on land TU already owns near some campus religious organizations."[91] This third speculated- location proved to be remarkably accurate. The University had been acquiring property in the College Addition Subdivision, located north of Fifth Street. In May of 1971, the University announced that John Rogers Hall would be located on the north border of the campus on Fourth Place between Florence Place and Gary Avenue. The University had acquired all but three lots in the area bounded by Fourth Place and Fifth Street, and Florence

Paul Taliaferro ('30), left, and Judge Royce Savage, right, served as co-chairs of the fund-raising drive for the new law school building. Here, they are seen during the fund drive, flanking Dean Wilson and looking at a fund-raising brochure. *Courtesy The University of Tulsa College of Law archives.*

Place and Gary Avenue. Because the remaining lot owners had refused to give easements in the alley running down the middle of this tract, the decision was made to place the building on the north half of it, with the north boundary being Fourth Place and the south boundary being the alley.[92] This ultimately resulted in John Rogers Hall being a rather long rectangular building, rather than more square in shape.

Construction of John Rogers Hall actually began in October, 1971, although formal groundbreaking did not occur until November of that year. The building was described as designed "to complement the overall campus architecture while retaining a contemporary look of its own. It will be built on three levels and will feature a student lounge built a half-level down from the ground level offices and classrooms, with

Paul Taliaferro ('30) and Judge Royce Savage, co-chairs of the fund drive, received plagues in appreciation for their efforts at the conclusion of the drive. Left to right: Paul Taliaferro, John Rogers, Judge Royce Savage, and President Twyman. *Courtesy Judge Joseph W. Morris.*

the library on the lower level."[93]   It would be built of native Arkansas crab orchard stone (often called "TU" stone because so many campus buildings utilize it), cement and glass and contain 50,000 square feet (as compared to the downtown building's 21,000 square feet). The size of the building would be sufficient to handle 350 full-time and 75 part-time students, 22 faculty, and a library of 120,000 volumes. This was the first law school building that McCune, McCune & Associates had designed; therefore, the firm surveyed law schools around the country to come up with a suitable plan. The design was said to be a scaled-down version of the Texas Tech Law School building, which caused Eugene L. Smith, an ABA inspector from Texas Tech, to comment, during the first inspection held shortly after the building was occupied, that John Rogers Hall seemed "vaguely familiar."[94]

An incident occurred in the spring and summer of 1971 that some feared would affect the fundraising drive for the new building and others saw as an assault on the concept of academic freedom at the school. Although it stirred intense controversy at the time, it ended without violence to either the financial or academic life of the law school.

At the time, Professor Jim Thomas was chair of the Tulsa County Democratic Party. In that capacity he became involved in two hotly-debated issues of the day in Oklahoma.[95] The first involved the state's oil and gas industry. Governor David Hall had proposed additional taxes on that industry, a proposal which the industry was vigorously opposing. In March of 1971, Thomas sent telegrams to the Oklahoma Congressional delegation, the Federal Trade Commission and the Antitrust Division of the Justice Department, suggesting that the industry may have violated federal antitrust laws in their attempts to thwart Hall's proposal. That action riled many industry supporters, including members of the University's Board of Trustees.[96]

The second action Thomas took involved the controversy over the Vietnam War. War protestors had wanted to demonstrate outside the downtown Assembly Center where a Governor's Ball was being held for area governors in town for the dedication of the Tulsa Port of Catoosa. The city commission refused a permit and the rally was held in Woodward Park, instead. At that rally, Thomas addressed the protestors, criticizing the city commission's refusal to grant the permit. His action was controversial, supported by some and condemned by others, including those who had been offended by his earlier telegram.[97]

Soon after Thomas engaged in these actions, President Twyman called Thomas into his office and told him that several members of the Board of Trustees were very upset and calling for his dismissal. Twyman followed up his indication of displeasure with a letter to Thomas in June 1971, " . . . to express my concern and displeasure regarding the degree of professional responsibility exercised by you in recent weeks." After referring to Thomas' actions at issue, Twyman stated, "If you find it impossible to reconcile your role as Professor of Law at The University of Tulsa with your roles as Chairman of the Tulsa County Democratic Party and social critic in such a manner as to do injustice to neither, it seems to me that you have no alternative but to make a choice between the two efforts." Twyman ended the letter by stating, "A copy of this letter will be made a part of your personnel file."[98]

Thomas released the letter to the public and controversy immediately erupted.[99] Both the *Tulsa Tribune* and the *Tulsa World* ran articles and editorials about the issue, the *World* calling Thomas the "Popoff Professor." The University of Tulsa Alumni Association backed Twyman, while a "Tulsa Committee for Free Speech" circulated a petition in support of Thomas, calling Twyman's criticism a "heavy-handed disregard for constitutional rights." Thomas filed academic freedom complaints with the Association of American Law Schools (AALS), the American Association of University Professors (AAUP) and the local AAUP chapter at the University. Both Dean Wilson and the faculty indicated support for Thomas privately, but never offered public support.

President Twyman appointed an ad hoc committee, composed of representatives of the faculty, student body, administration and Board of Trustees, to investigate Thomas' complaint of the University's violation (through President Twyman) of its academic freedom and tenure policies. The local AAUP chapter, headed by Professor Allen Soltow of the Economics Department, also appointed an investigatory committee. Both committee reports were ambivalent, recognizing rights in both Thomas and Twyman, but neither concluded that Thomas's academic freedom had been abridged.[100] There is evidence that, although Twyman was critical of Thomas's actions, he worked behind the scenes to insure that the

Board of Trustees did not take action against Thomas.[101]

The controversy was soon resolved by negotiation. Al Soltow got Thomas and Twyman together. They met at a bar, each "spoke his mind,"[102] and they drafted a joint statement that was, however, never released. Instead, the local AAUP chapter issued a statement on August 24, 1971, that the parties " . . . . agreed that the matter could and should be resolved within the local academic community," and that they ". . . . consider this matter closed."[103] Thomas withdrew his complaint to the AAUP, the fundraising for John Rogers Hall

continued and nothing subsequently came of the matter.[104]

At the end of the 1971-72 academic year, Ed Wilson resigned as dean to accept the deanship at the Mercer Law School, where he had earlier taught. During his tenure at Tulsa there had been little change in the academic nature of the school. The same faculty, plus one, were teaching the same curriculum to a similar student body. The organization of the faculty and student body remained the same. What had changed? Two important administrative changes had occurred in the hiring of the first assistant dean and the first

Joseph W. Morris, seventh dean, 1972-74, presided over the move of the law school from downtown Tulsa to John Rogers Hall on the Kendall campus. *Courtesy Jurick Photography.*

law-trained librarian in the school's history. Tuition had increased 40%, increasing from $30 to $42 per credit hour, still a bargain among law schools of the day. What had really changed, however, was where the future of the school would play out—on campus, not downtown.

THE JOSEPH W. MORRIS YEARS

The dean who would oversee this physical transition was Joseph

W. Morris, who served as dean from August, 1972 through April 1974. Dean Morris came from a distinguished career in the oil industry, having been an attorney for Shell Oil Company and an officer and counsel for Amerada Petroleum Corporation both before and after its merger with Hess Oil and Chemical Company. Earning his law degree from Washburn University and a S.J.D. from the University of Michigan, he had been an adjunct professor at the law school since 1950, teaching oil and gas law and future interests law. Because of the high esteem with which he was held by the Tulsa bar and business community, he raised the status of the school in the eyes of these groups. This was an important consideration in his appointment.[105]

The move was set to occur in April, 1973, at the end of the second trimester of the 1972-73 academic year. It was carefully planned so as to cause minimum disruption. Except for the library, the move was a relatively simple affair because the new building was fully furnished; only school records and personal materials of law school personnel had to be moved. The library was a different story.

At this time the library had over 59,000 volumes placed in three separate locations:1) the downtown library; 2) Harwell Library, on the main campus; and, 3) on the North Campus in an unheated/unair-conditioned building. Because of the uncontrolled climate conditions at this third location, many of the books were damaged beyond repair and had to be discarded; others had to be treated for silverfish and other damage before being moved to the new building. The plan was to consolidate all of these holdings in John Rogers Hall. The library staff analyzed and diagrammed the existing facilities' shelving and the new building's shelving to determine where and how to put all volumes to be moved. The decision was made not to use University equipment or personnel, but to hire an outside mover, Tulsa-Federal Storage, because it could provide "90 movable bookracks to transport books, packed by students as trucks move. Ample float of bookracks to prevent delay in truck time while students load and unload racks. Advantage: Library inoperable only 3 days. Eliminates cost of student help packing and unpacking boxes, and the cost of boxes."[106] As this memo indicates, students and library staff were used to make the move.

The move began on a Friday evening at 10:00 p.m., after the library in the building at 512 S. Cincinnati Avenue had closed for the day. The movers, students and library staff moved books all Friday night and all day Saturday. They took Saturday night off and, then, moved all day Sunday, ending at 10:00 p.m.[107] On Monday morning the law library opened as usual, except that it was now located in John Rogers Hall, on the main University campus.

With the library moved, and law school and personnel documents in the new building, the law school started the third trimester of the 1972-73 academic year, in April of 1973, in John Rogers Hall. A new era in the life of the law school was beginning. It nicely coincided with the fiftieth anniversary of the founding of the school. There could have been no better golden anniversary gift.

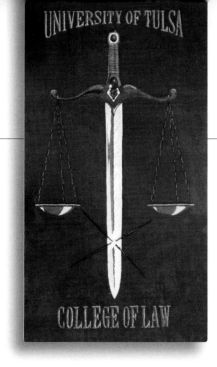

THE UNIVERSITY OF TULSA COLLEGE OF LAW ENTERS THE MAINSTREAM OF LEGAL EDUCATION *(1973-1980)*

Home at Last (1973-74)

THE JOSEPH W. MORRIS YEARS COMPLETED

Wednesday, January 23, 1974, dawned clear and cold. At 10:00 a.m. about 250 people gathered on the south plaza and lawn of John Rogers Hall for the presentation ceremony. Though frail at age 83, John Rogers, the man who had contributed so much to the school and for whom the building was being named, was present. Also present was Justice William H. Rehnquist, at the time the newest member of the United States Supreme Court, who was to give the dedicatory address. On behalf of the donors, William H. Bell presented the building to the University with these words:

> On behalf of Mrs. Leta M. Chapman, a friend of this University, and Royce H. Savage and Paul A. Taliaferro, who represent the hundreds of lawyers, their firms and companies, who contributed to this College of Law, I am pleased to present John Rogers Hall to the University of Tulsa.

> The hallmark of freedom is the law, and the servants of the law are the bench and bar. May the bench and bar be served by those who teach, learn and work in this magnificent building for legal education.

> With deep pride, on behalf of all the donors, I present John Rogers Hall, to be a continuing beacon of excellence to the bench and bar, and a cornerstone for freedom under law, for us all.[1]

This presentation was the culmination of two days of activity. On the preceding day the law school had sponsored a symposium on the law of

Leta McFarlin Chapman and James A. Chapman. The Chapman Trusts created by this couple transformed the University of Tulsa from a financially-struggling institution into a well-endowed university. *Courtesy Rogers and Bell Law Firm.*

ABOVE: Mrs. Chapman, center, made the lead $1 million gift to the University for the law school in honor of her long-time business adviser and friend, John Rogers, left. Bill Bell, right, was beginning to assume Mr. Rogers's responsibilities with the Chapman / McFarlin / Barnard interests and with the University. *Courtesy Rogers and Bell Law Firm.*

RIGHT: Justice William H. Rehnquist, speaking at the dedication of John Rogers Hall. The platform party, seated left to right: William Bell, representative of Mrs. Leta M. Chapman; William Wiseman, pastor of the First Presbyterian Church of Tulsa; President Paschal Twyman; Dean Joseph Morris; and, Robert Kelly, University Chaplain. *Courtesy The University of Tulsa College of Law archives.*

comparative negligence. W. Page
Keeton, dean of the University of
Texas School of Law had given the
dedicatory lecture, with responses by
Floyd L. Walker, James D. Foliart,
and the Honorable William H.
Means. Justice Robert E. Lavender,
of the Supreme Court of the State of
Oklahoma, a 1953 graduate of the
law school, served as moderator.

There had been a nine-month
delay between the time John Rogers
Hall had been occupied and its
formal dedication. Dean Morris
strove mightily to obtain Justice
Rehnquist as the dedicatory speaker.
Even with the assistance of two
Tulsans who had been classmates of
the Justice, James Ryan and Maynard
Ungerman, Rehnquist kept declining
because of scheduling difficulties.
Finally, Morris issued a "challenge"
to him that the school would hold

the dedication whenever he could
come.[2] That, finally, turned out to
be January of 1974.

Although the dedication of John
Rogers Hall may be considered
the symbolic high point in the
deanship of Joe Morris , other
events occurred, some of which
presage the changes that would turn
the law school into a true university
institution. Student enrollment
continued to grow, continuing
a trend begun in the Peterson
administration. In the 1973-74
school year, enrollment exceeded
400 for the first time. Heretofore,
growth had brought problems
related to the physical plant, along
with positive benefits. Now, the
new building was "an empty vessel
waiting to be filled," which had
implications, not only for the size
of the student body, but also for the

faculty, administration and library. The school now had a facility that could accommodate the growth that would come in these areas.

There was some faculty growth during Morris' deanship. Two members were added in 1972-73, including Rennard Strickland, who was and would continue to be an important scholar in the area of American Indian law and history. Although there had always been scholarship by faculty members,[3] the primary emphasis had been on classroom teaching. President Twyman and Vice-President for Academic Affairs John W. Dowgray believed that it was the right time in the life of the University to encourage faculty to focus on scholarship as well.[4] In the future, the faculty would, more and more, be expected to be productive scholars as well as good classroom teachers.

The following year three more faculty members joined the faculty, including Georgina B. Landman, who was the first woman to teach full-time at the school.[5] Dean Morris asked her to teach a course in "Women and the Law." This was the first time such a course had been taught at the school. Out of it sprang the idea for the Women's Law Caucus.[6] Beginning in the 1970s, and coinciding with the move of the school to campus, the number of women attending steadily increased.[7] This organization continued to play an important role in the life of the school.

In the fall of 1973, the beginning of the first full year on campus, the law school abandoned the trimester system and switched to the semester system, which was what the rest of the University was on. The thought was that, by being on the same system as the University: 1) there could be more interdisciplinary activity between the law school and other colleges in the University; 2) students and faculty would have options to do other things in the summer, such as attend or teach at other schools, clerk or work in Tulsa or elsewhere; and, 3) professors at other law schools could be brought to Tulsa to teach in the summer.[8] All of these possibilities came about in varying degrees. This was one of the first indications of a change in the nature of the school to integrate more closely with both the University and the larger law school world. This integration would accelerate as the decade progressed.

LEFT: Justice Rehnquist and Professor John F. Hicks at the reception following the dedication of John Rogers Hall. *Courtesy The University of Tulsa College of Law archives.*

BELOW: John Rogers and Professor John F. Hicks at the reception following the dedication of John Rogers Hall. *Courtesy The University of Tulsa College of Law archives.*

Another important event in the deanship of Joe Morris was the American Bar Association inspection of the law school, held in May, 1973. It had been postponed until after the school had moved into John Rogers Hall. The final report said something about the recent past and augured something for the future. All of the changes and improvements made in the last few years paid off in a finding that the law school was in "full compliance" with the ABA standards. The report "...commended the university and the law school on the new building...and great progress in faculty accomplishment and university support ...."[9] The report, however, also indicated that "...as additional resources become available, consideration should be given to directing them toward needs specified in the report, including an expansion of the administrative staff, continued improvement in the size of the faculty and the library staff, and additional secretarial aid for the faculty...."[10] These needs would be addressed by future administrations.

During this time the federal judgeship for the eastern district of Oklahoma opened up. United States Senator Dewey Bartlett nominated Joe Morris for the position in the fall of 1973. Dean Morris resigned his position and was appointed by President Richard Nixon as a United States district judge in April, 1974. Morris served as a federal judge until 1978, when he left the bench to become vice president and general counsel of Shell Oil Company. He held that position until 1983, when he joined the Tulsa law firm of Gable & Gotwals, where he practiced law and served as an arbitrator for the remainder of his career.

Professor Rennard Strickland, who had joined the Tulsa faculty in 1972, was selected to serve as acting dean, following the resignation of Dean Morris. He served in that position until Frank

T. Read assumed the office of dean in December, 1974. Strickland, who had earned his bachelor's degree from Northeastern College in Tahlequah, Oklahoma, and his J.D. and S.J.D. degrees from the University of Virginia, was becoming recognized as a scholar of American Indian law and history by the time he joined the TU faculty. With a brief interruption to serve on the faculties of the University of Washington and the University of New Mexico between 1975 and 1977, he would remain on the TU faculty as John Shleppey Research Professor of Law and History until 1985. Following his years at Tulsa,

he would serve on the faculties of Southern Illinois University (as dean), Arizona State University, the University of Wisconsin, the University of Oklahoma, Oklahoma City University (as dean), and, the University of Oregon (as dean, and, later, professor). During his career he became preeminent in the field of American Indian law and history.

ACTING DEANSHIP OF RENNARD STRICKLAND

Strickland set two goals for his acting deanship, which spanned the spring, summer and fall of 1974.[11] The first was to work on improving front-office relations

with students. Dean Morris, coming from a corporate background, had set up a more structured style of management. Strickland, in a more relaxed and informal manner, cultivated students and student organizations in a variety of ways. His second goal was faculty recruitment. Two members had resigned in the summer of 1974. Thus, faculty numbers were down at the very time when: 1) student enrollment was rising;[12] 2) the new building would accommodate a larger faculty; and, 3) the University administration was beginning to provide money for more positions in anticipation of the coming

John Rogers Hall in the 1970s. *Courtesy The University of Tulsa College of Law archives.*

Rennard Strickland served as acting dean in 1974, between the administrations of Joseph W. Morris and Frank T. Read. He later served as the John Shleppey Research Professor of Law and History from 1977 to 1985. *Courtesy The University of Tulsa.*

deanship of Frank Read. Six faculty
positions, plus the librarian's post,
were open and needing to be filled.
The faculty, Acting Dean Strickland
and Dean-Designate Read recruited
and hired a large group of new
faculty members, who would begin
in the fall of 1975.[13]

Imogene Harris had resigned as
librarian in the summer of 1973,
following the move into the new
building. A very competent long-
time assistant librarian, Wilma
Thrash, served as acting librarian for
a two-year period, from 1973 until
1975. It was she and her library staff
who organized the library and set it
on its course in its new home.   Joel
Burstein replaced Thrash as librarian
in 1975.

One other faculty development
of note occurred during this time.
Judge Leah Brock McCartney, a
municipal judge from Missouri,
served as a visiting professor during
the spring term of 1975. She was
the first African-American to serve
on the faculty. The law school
continued to struggle to include
minorities in its student, faculty and
staff populations. Although there
were, occasionally, African-American
students at the school since the
1950s,[14] there had never been any
institutional effort at recruitment.
In 1972, at a time when no African-
Americans were at the school, a
group of students, led by Tom W.
Tannehill ('74), organized an effort
to recruit minority law students.
The student committee contacted
alumni, legal firms, and individual
lawyers in an attempt to locate
prospective minority students. The
students even set up a scholarship
fund. But these worthwhile efforts by
students were overshadowed by the
activity surrounding the relocation of
the school. Two years later, in one of

the first newspaper interviews Dean
Read gave after being appointed,
he called for an increased effort to
recruit and admit students from
"those groups who, traditionally,
have been unable to get in."[15]

In December, 1974, Frank T.
Read became the first dean to begin
his deanship at the on-campus law
school. The next four and one-half
years would see a burst of activity
that would transform the school into
a "university" law school.

Entering the Mainstream (1974-80)

Frank T. Read, the new dean,
at age 35, was one of the youngest

Frank T. Read, eighth dean, 1974-79.
Courtesy The University of Tulsa College of Law archives.

deans in America. He had earned his bachelor's degree from Brigham Young University and his law degree from Duke University. After serving as dean at Tulsa between 1974 and 1979, he would go on to serve as dean at the University of Indiana, Indianapolis; the University of Florida; the University of California, Hastings College of the Law; and, the South Texas College of Law. In the process he became one of the longest-tenured deans in the last half of the twentieth century, serving over 25 years at these various schools.

At the dawn of his decanal career, Tom Read, as he was known, came to the law school with energy and fresh ideas about improvement. He knew what good education was, having attended and having taught at Duke University Law School. He was also lucky in that he arrived at a time of unprecedented demand for entrance into legal education. TU was sharing in that demand. In 1975, enrollment stood at 556; in 1978, it peaked at 728, before falling back to 669 in 1979, Read's last year in office.

ACADEMIC PROGRAM

The new dean and faculty immediately undertook a series of changes to the academic program. The first-year experience was altered somewhat. First-year courses had traditionally all been large enrollment where theory was emphasized. Application would come only in courses taught later. In 1975, this pattern was altered for the contracts course. Small-enrollment sections of contracts were created that allowed more personal interaction between professor and student and among students. In addition, the course incorporated the legal writing and moot court programs so that students would apply contracts law in a series of exercises.

The dean and faculty took up the issue of which second and third year courses would be required and which would be elective. A middle path was taken—students were required to take three of seven designated courses.[16] This became the law school's solution to the long-term trend across the country of reducing the number of required courses in the curriculum. This trend finally overcame this requirement, which was eliminated in 1979.

A similar approach was taken concerning "enrichment" courses. Up to this point the curriculum had always focused on the every-day practice of law. Although perspective courses, such as jurisprudence, had been offered, they had never been required. A third change required all second and third year students to take one of four enrichment courses.[17] This requirement still existed in modified form at the time this history was written..

A final change required each student to take a seminar and complete a substantial written research paper. The purpose was to insure that all students, not only law journal students, had the experience of in-depth research and writing. All of these requirements were causing the curriculum to become more modern and complex.

Another change during this period shows the impact both of curriculum development and the law school's move to the main campus. In 1977, the school approved four joint-degree programs with other colleges in the University: JD-MA (History), JD-MA (English), JD-MA (Urban Studies) and a JD-MBA (Business Administration). With alterations in the specific disciplines involved, joint degree programs were continuously offered thereafter.

NATIONAL ENERGY LAW AND POLICY INSTITUTE

All of these changes were implemented to accomplish Dean Read's vision of creating a law school with a "strong regional and growing national reputation."[18] One of the most important programs developed during Read's deanship with the purpose of realizing this vision was the creation of the National Energy Law and Policy Institute (NELPI.)

Kent Frizzell served as the first Director of the National Energy Law and Policy Institute from 1977 until 1992. *Courtesy Kent Frizzell.*

In the early 1970s, the University embarked on an ambitious fund raising campaign—the "Decade Fund". A part of this process involved the development of a ten year academic plan for the various colleges. The University hired the consulting firm of Cresap, McCormick and Paget (CMcP) to undertake a study which would lead to a plan. The study concluded that primary emphasis should be placed on the development of professional and graduate programs with the purposes of improving the quality of education, increasing research activities and enhancing the regional and national reputation of the University.[19]

At Dean Read's urging, the CMcP Report recommended the establishment of a "National Energy Law Institute" at the law school in order to capitalize on the University's reputation in the petroleum industry and the city's waning reputation as the "Oil Capital of the World." The Institute would have three missions: 1) to advance knowledge of energy law and promote sound energy policy through publication and research by legal scholars resident at the law school; 2) to provide training in the field of energy law to students at the school; and, 3) facilitate communication among the many individuals and entities interested in energy law.[20] In the ensuing years NELPI carried out these missions through funded and unfunded research; publishing scholarly articles by staff members and others; publishing, in conjunction with the Federal Energy Bar Association, the *Energy Law Journal*; publishing, on behalf of the ABA Section of Natural Resources, Energy and Environmental Law, the *Year-In-Review*; publishing the Oklahoma

Bar Association *Mineral Law Section Newsletter*; teaching an extensive energy-related curriculum at the school; conducting symposia and CLE programs; and, giving speeches to a wide variety of groups.

The Institute was to be administered by a director and two associate directors. Read secured Kent Frizzell as director. Frizzell had a background in government in Kansas and in the federal government as solicitor and, later, under-secretary of the Department of the Interior in the Nixon Administration and acting secretary in the Ford Administration. He joined NELPI in January of 1977. NELPI benefited from a number of fine associate directors during its early years. Professor Patrick Martin secured the first large grant and administered the fledgling program from its creation in June,1976, until the arrival of Frizzell. Professor Gary Allison was responsible for a number of early grants as well as producing scholarship in the area. Professor John Lowe was involved in securing grants, producing scholarship, and teaching continuing legal education courses.

JOHN W. SHLEPPEY INDIAN LAW AND HISTORY COLLECTION

If NELPI was the product of careful planning, the obtaining of the John W. Shleppey Indian Law and History Collection and the return of Professor Rennard Strickland to the law school was serendipitous. Strickland had left the law school soon after his acting deanship ended to develop an Indian law program at the University of Washington at Seattle. Within two weeks of his arrival in Seattle in the fall of 1975, President Twyman called and asked him to examine a

trove of materials bequeathed to the University by John W. Shleppey. Shleppey had attended the University and thereafter collected what Strickland soon determined to be one of the finest collections of Indian law and history materials of its kind in the country.[21] The collection was placed in McFarlin Library and, due to the efforts of President Twyman and Professor Thomas F. Staley, dean of the Graduate School, Strickland returned to the law school in January, 1977, as the John Shleppey Research Professor of Law and History. He spent the following years organizing the collection and filling in gaps, as well as heading the revision of the Cohen Handbook on Federal Indian Law.

FACULTY

Another important development occurring during Read's deanship was the growth in the size of the faculty and changes in its nature. When he arrived at the law school, the faculty size stood at thirteen. One impact of his negotiations with the University administration and the Chapman Trust money that was flowing into the University was felt the following fall, when six new members, plus a librarian, joined the faculty.[22] The following year, 1976-77, six additional faculty came on board.[23]

The nature of the faculty was also changing in that under-represented groups were starting to appear. Although Judge Leah Brock McCartney became the first African-American person to serve on the faculty when she visited in the spring of 1975, her appointment was exceptional. No other African-Americans served on the faculty until Taunya Lovell Banks joined

In 1973, Georgina Landman became the first woman to serve on the faculty as a full-time member. She followed in the footsteps of Grace Elmore Gibson, who had served as a part-time faculty member at the Tulsa Law School in the 1930s and 1940s. *Courtesy Tulsa Tribune.*

Distinguished Visiting Professor during the spring of 1976. For several years, the University of Tulsa and Brigham Young University swapped professors during the summer. During the summers visiting faculty came from such schools as the University of Arkansas, the University of California at Davis, Case Western Reserve University, Duke University, Emory University, the University of Houston, Mercer University, the University of North Carolina, the University of Oklahoma, Toledo University and Wake Forest University. This interaction helped bring the law school into the mainstream of legal education.

In addition, the use of adjunct faculty grew. This was necessitated by the growth in the number of specialized courses in the curriculum and, also, by the need to cover courses normally taught by permanent faculty who were on leave. From this point on, the use of practicing lawyers as adjuncts became a two-edged sword; on the one side, they brought expertise in specialized areas to the curriculum; on the other side, the questions of their over-extensive use and use in core courses created continuing tension with the students and faculty. Ultimately the faculty limited the use of adjuncts to advanced and practice-oriented courses.

LAW SCHOOL GOVERNANCE

Under Read's leadership, the faculty created a modern system of governance at the school. Theretofore, the law school had operated on an older model wherein the dean played a much more dominant role. Although there had been faculty administrative

in the mid 1980s. What became unexceptional, however, was the presence of women on the faculty. Georgina Landman had joined the faculty in 1973 as the first full-time female faculty member.[24] Carol Potter joined the faculty in 1975; Edna Ball joined in 1976; and, in 1978, Margaret Potts and Sue Titus Reid joined the faculty.[25] Since that time the law school has been one of the leaders in legal education in the number of women on the faculty.

This period also marks the first extensive use of visiting faculty. Dean Read wanted to expose the Tulsa students and faculty to professors from other law schools and to have his faculty teach at other schools. Also, rising expectations of scholarship meant more of the faculty would be away from the school periodically, engaged in research, necessitating replacements. Alan Polasky, of the University of Michigan, served as the first committees for many years, they had operated on a more ad hoc basis, with the dean managing the school from day to day. In the spring of 1975, the faculty and dean created task forces to examine this approach. By the end of the term, two important documents had been approved. The first, the College of Law Governance Document, created a standing committee system through which all routine law school policy matters would be handled, with the full faculty and dean acting on a matter only after committee consideration. This document served as the cornerstone in the evolution of the role of the faculty in law school governance. The second document, the Tenure and Promotion Document, defined the criteria for a faculty member's promotion and tenure and the role of the faculty and dean in the process. These documents, although modified, remain in place at the time of this writing.

STAFF

The general staff of the law school had grown also. Counting both non-academic administrative staff and academic staff with administrative duties, the administrative personnel of the law school tripled between 1975 and 1979, going from five to fifteen individuals. There were more assistant deans, secretaries, admissions and placement personnel, and NELPI personnel.

STUDENTS

As with the faculty and staff, there were changes in the size and nature of the student body during this time. In the new John Rogers Hall, the school had the space to take advantage of high demand for

entrance into law school. Enrollment rose from 534 students in 1974 to 669 students in 1979. Interestingly, during this period, the long-term trend of an increasing full-time division and decreasing part-time division reversed; the part-time division grew at the expense of the full-time division.[26]

One dramatic change in the nature of the student body during the last half of the seventies was the growth in the number of women in the school. Although there had always been women attending law school, their numbers were consistently low. Many a graduate from the 1960s and earlier can remember the sole woman in class. By 1974, women accounted for 13% of the student body; by 1979, the percentage had grown to 25%.

In contrast, ethnic minorities had not attended the school until the 1950s,[27] and then, only sporadically and in small numbers. Dean Read indicated the importance of recruiting minorities in a newspaper interview early in his deanship: he pointed out that law schools must recruit and admit qualified students from "those groups who have been traditionally unable to get in."[28] The number of minority students grew, but remained relatively low during this period, going from 3% in 1976, the first year statistics on minority populations at the school were kept, to 6% in 1979. Native Americans were the largest minority population, followed by African Americans and Hispanics in relatively equal numbers, with Asians being the smallest minority population.

The desire to create both a high-quality and inclusive student body was the reason for two student recruitment programs of the day. Beginning early in the Read era, the

faculty fanned out across the country to recruit good students at colleges and universities. The purpose was to interest good students in attending the law school and cultivate pre-law and other advisors who influenced students. This effort continued for several years before being taken over by the admissions office at the school. The combination of innately high demand for entrance during this period and the recruiting efforts by the faculty and Velda Staves, the newly-appointed admissions officer, resulted in entering classes with higher academic credentials.

High demand has always been a two-edged sword at any law school. On one side, it produces a more qualified entering class with higher credentials; however, it also excludes many applicants who are qualified to succeed in law school but who may not be admitted because their credentials are not competitive with the admitted group. The law school dealt with this latter situation in an innovative way—the Summer Admission by Performance Program.

The Summer-Admission-by-Performance Program was begun in the summer of 1975. Benefiting from the national bulge in applications, the law school had received 1,000 applications for the 225 available seats for the 1974-75 school year. Dean Read and the faculty created this special admission program for those students who had marginal college grade point averages and/or Law School Admission Test scores, which were the prime criteria for admission, but, who had other factors, such as graduate work, work experience, or military experience, which indicated the potential for success in law school. Thirty students were admitted to a summer contracts course and

Velda Staves served as the first admissions director at the law school. *Courtesy The University of Tulsa College of Law archives.*

subjected to rigorous analytical and research and writing training under the close supervision of a faculty member. Those who successfully completed the course with a grade of "C" or better were admitted to the fall entering course. This course ran for several summers under Professors Tom Holland, Eric Jensen and Martin Frey and resulted in a number of success stories among those admitted.

Students were active at this time in ways that both confounded and pleased the dean and faculty. The Student Bar Association created a minor tempest in the spring of 1977 when it announced its public support of legislative efforts to decriminalize the use of marijuana. Although Dean Read, in a memo to the faculty, characterized the controversy as "perhaps more humorous than serious," he found it necessary, in a community as conservative as Tulsa, to declare in the media that the students "do not speak for the school."[29] One year later, in the spring of 1978, students were receiving media attention in ways about which the dean was more pleased to comment. William J. Wenzel ('78) was named International Graduate of the Year by Phi Delta Phi, one of the recognized national legal fraternities, and Kay Bridger-Riley ('79), Student Bar Association president, received the O'Brien Award as National Law Student of the Year from the California State Student Bar Association.[30] And the TU Student Bar Association for 1977-78 was named the Most Outstanding Student Bar Association in the 500-1,000 student category by the

American Bar Association, prompting Dean Read to call it the "runaway SBA."[31]

ADMISSIONS PROGRAM

Dean Read started two administrative programs which quickly became important and fundamental to the operation of the school. One dealt with the admission of students. Through the deanship of Bruce Peterson, admission was handled by the dean, or his designate, on a rather informal basis. Each dean was concerned about "making the class," and would use his own methods to accomplish that goal. The first shift in this model occurred during the Wilson and Morris deanships in the late 1960s and early 1970s, a time when applications to law schools around the country were growing. These two deans turned to Assistant Dean Edwin Schmidt and, later, to Assistant Dean Georgina Landman to handle admissions. Dean Read wanted someone to devote full time to the admissions process in order to maximize the school's potential, and, in the spring of 1975, asked his secretary, Velda Staves, to assume the job as "admissions officer."[32] The first year on the job, 1975-76, she worked out of a desk in the front office of John Rogers Hall. In 1976

she moved the operation to the first "Little House on the Prairie," located at the corner of Fifth Street and Gary Avenue.[33] Formally known as Law Annex 1, it was one of the few residences remaining on the block after John Rogers Hall was built. It was renovated and used for the admissions office, the placement office, and two faculty offices. Little more than three years had passed since the dedication of John Rogers Hall and the school had already run short of administrative and faculty office space. Admissions would remain in the Annex until the early 1980s.

The admissions office focused on three tasks during the balance of the 1980s. The school had never recruited students through visitations to feeder colleges and universities. Dean Read started such a program. Velda Staves organized faculty trips by geographic location and about one-half the faculty fanned out over the country for multi-day trips, meeting with students and pre-law advisors to inform them about and interest them in the University of Tulsa. In addition, Staves herself began attending pre-law forums organized by college pre-law advisors, meeting students and advisors. For the first time the school was getting its name out in the region and across the country. These trips continued for the balance of Read's deanship.

The second task of admissions was to work with the faculty admissions committee, one of the standing committees created in the faculty administrative organizational structure, as discussed earlier, in selecting each year's entering class. At this time, the applicant pool was growing each year, peaking in 1978. This model for handling the admissions process, compared to the older model under Peterson and earlier deans, gave the faculty much more input.

Finally, the admissions office participated in the annual spring Pre-Law Day organized by the Student Bar Association. Individuals accepted for the following fall and other interested persons were invited to campus to learn about the school, talk to students, faculty and administrators and tour the building. Admissions worked with the SBA in this way for the rest of the 1970s, before taking over the organization of the event during the deanship of Frank Walwer.

PLACEMENT PROGRAM

The second administrative program that Dean Read developed was a placement service, whereby the school would aid graduating students in locating employment. Before 1975, the law school had no formal

mechanism for aiding students in finding work after graduating. It was the student's total responsibility. This situation traditionally prevailed in most law schools, ameliorated only by the help that faculty could provide from time to time. Professor Georgina Landman, then the assistant dean, having an interest in the area, started a "job placement service" for students in her office.[34] Another assistant dean, Professor Ray Yasser, continued this service, with student help. When the first "Little House on the Prairie" was renovated in 1976, as discussed above, the placement office occupied it, along with admissions. Two years later Dean Read hired Anthony Bastone, II to become the first full-time placement director at the school. Bastone had been executive director of "On the Bricks," a post-release treatment center for ex-offenders. Bastone would quip that, "If I can find jobs for ex-cons, I should be able to find jobs for law students!"[35] The placement office then moved to a house adjacent to Law Annex 1, thereby creating the "Little Houses on the Prairie."[36] This structure, Law Annex 2, like the first one, was shared with faculty who officed in it. Bastone

Anthony (Tony) Bastone, II served as the first placement director at the law school. Courtesy Anthony L. Bastone, II.

set about to build a legal career resources library, implement an on-campus job-interview program, hold legal-career workshops and symposia, and advertise the program in print, radio and television.

ALUMNI

Dean Read also worked to develop an alumni program. The law school had done little over the years to develop such a program. There had been an Law Alumni Association in existence since 1951,[37] but there had been little development of it except during the time of the John Rogers Hall Fund Drive. The problem had always been money. Development funds had been used to contact alumni during the campaign. Once the campaign was completed, there was once again no money. Acting Dean Strickland had looked into the situation, but was not in a position to do much about it.[38] Dean Read did take some steps in developing a program. His main purpose was to "energize" alumni and instill pride in them in their law school. He did attempt to lay the groundwork for fund raising. He appointed a development council to work with the University's development office to assist in fund raising activities for the school. He made a start toward organizing alumni by appointing a class agent for each class. Any real attempt at fund raising during this period, however, foundered on the University's policy of keeping all meaningful fund raising efforts on the University level and out of college hands. But Read was able to start an annual TU Law Alumni Day, bringing alums to the new building and making awards to distinguished alumni. The first such awards went to Judge Allen Barrow,

chief United States judge for the Northern District of Oklahoma, and Justice Robert Lavendar, of the Oklahoma Supreme Court.[39] In 1976, the school first published an alumni newsletter, the *Law Alumni Brief*, which ran for several years.

LIBRARY

One of the other priorities established in the Cresap, McCormick and Paget Report was growth in law library holdings. This, in fact, occurred in both general holdings and in the energy and Indian law areas. In 1975-76, library holdings stood around 70,000 volumes. In 1976-77, holdings had grown to 75,000, with a ten-year plan for future growth, specifically in the energy and Indian law areas. Money was forthcoming under the plan, and, by 1778-79, the library had grown to 100,000 volumes, plus a downtown library. The downtown library, which operated for a number of years, arose out of happenstance. A group of lawyers, who had been operating a for-profit law library downtown, were about to close it. Learning about it, Read acquired the library, concluded that it could serve a number of purposes for the school: 1) provide some money to the library from subscriptions, while aiding the downtown bar; and, 2) provide the potential future benefit of serving student needs if a downtown law school clinic were ever opened. During its years of operation, the first purpose was served, although the second one never was.

The law library had two librarians during this period. Joel Burstein started in the fall of 1975 and served for three years. In 1978, Alan Ogden became the law librarian and served until 1982.

The size of the staff about doubled during this time, going from four in 1975 to seven, plus the downtown librarian, in 1979. Only the librarian was law trained, but both the librarian and assistant librarian held library science degrees. It was during Ogden's tenure that the law library became a part of the University library system. The library, having originated at a school unaffiliated with the University and located downtown, had never been a part of the University system, even though the library had moved to campus with the school. The library now became an administrative part of the University system in the areas of finance and personnel. This was never popular in the law library or the law school, and the school worked for years to bring the library back under the jurisdiction of the school, a feat finally accomplished in 1992.

PHYSICAL PLANT

What were the implications of all the foregoing changes in the faculty, student body, academic and non-academic programs, library and administrative staff in the last half of the 1970s? First, the salary budget, always the largest budget at the school, had grown appreciably. Second, space in John Rogers Hall had grown very scarce. Assistant Dean Tom Holland, in a memo about space usage to Dean Read, dated October 2, 1978, stated that: "At the present time, we are using all the space in John Rogers Hall and the two additional buildings [Annex 1 and Annex 2]...." How did the school respond to a growing budget and shrinking space in the law school building? Or, more directly put, what financial actions did the school take, what avenues of resources were available?

Would alumni contributions be a possible source? As mentioned earlier, Dean Read tried to reach out to the alumni, trying to bring them into the life of the school and organize them. At this time, however, alumni were not a viable source of contributions. It would take personnel and money to accomplish the task, and Read had elected to spend his resources elsewhere. In addition, the stringent controls the University placed on the ability of the college to fund raise made this avenue for raising money unrealistic.

A second and obvious source would be student tuition. This was the source that Dean Read tapped. In 1973, just before the Read deanship began, tuition stood

at $52 per credit hour. Each year thereafter it increased anywhere from 6% to 19% each year, [40] so that, by 1980, tuition stood at $90 per credit hour, an increase of 73%. Students were getting more for their money and they were paying more for it. This was ameliorated for some students by increasing scholarship money coming from Chapman funds, but, for the average student, the tuition bill had risen considerably between the first part of the decade and decade-end.

Tuition increases could cover the rise in salary and other internal costs, but could not raise, in addition, the funds necessary to expand John Rogers Hall. Only five years after first occupied, the building was filled to capacity.[41] Dean Read and the faculty had developed a "Ten Year Development Plan" in conjunction with the University's "Dimensions for a New Decade Campaign." The Plan describes the school's personnel, building and library needs. Under "Building Needs," the document states: "We propose a high-rise building on the lot to the east of the present law building. The

lower level of the present building would be extended under the new addition. At ground level, there should be an open area between the present building and the new addition."[42]

Read lobbied hard to have the building included in the University's fund drive but did not succeed. However, thanks to the efforts of Dean Read, as described below, Bill Bell made the decision to use $929,000 of Chapman/Barnard/McFarlin Trust funds to finance the first phase of an expansion of John Rogers Hall.[43] The concept at the time was that an addition would be built in two phases. The first phase would add a "lower level" (basement) and ground floor level. This would allow the law library to expand by 20,000 square feet, providing space for 40,000 additional volumes. It would also increase student seating in the library and bring seating up to ABA accreditation standards, important in that the school was facing a re-accreditation inspection in 1980 and was currently below ABA standards.

The announcement of the building expansion and its financing was made jointly by President Twyman and Dean Read in the fall of 1978. Earlier in the week, President Twyman had announced the launching of the $43 million "Dimensions for a New Decade Campaign" to fund a ten-year plan of physical and academic development. As mentioned earlier, the law school was not included for building expansion in this campaign.

William H. (Bill) Bell, the successor to John Rogers as trustee of the Chapman Trusts, worked with Dean Read to fund the construction of the first major addition to John Rogers Hall, which came to be known as the East Wing. *Courtesy Rogers and Bell Law Firm.*

Tom L. Holland served as acting dean during 1979 and 1980. *Courtesy Tom Holland.*

How did this "restricted gift" to the law school, as it was called, come about? The securing of this gift provided an interesting story around the law school for decades. Tom Read told it this way.[44] Earlier in 1978, Read presented the case to Twyman for inclusion of a law school building expansion in the "Decade Campaign", but Twyman was "cool" toward the idea, telling Read that the project would not be a part of the University's plan, but "if you can get the money, fine." Read "liberally" construed Twyman's words to give the green light for Read to seek the money himself, although large donors were normally off-limits to college deans. Read went to Bill Bell and presented the proposal and justification. One month later, Bell called Read to his office and presented him a check for $929,000. Read took the check to Twyman, not knowing what the reaction would be. Twyman told Read that he had not followed University protocol, but, ultimately smiled, congratulated Read and said,

"never do this to me again." Read never did during his remaining year in office.

In the fall of 1979, the construction of the expansion to John Rogers Hall, known thereafter as the East Wing, began.[45] For some time there was uncertainty as to the scope of the project. The initial gift covered only the cost of a ground floor into which the existing library could expand.[46] It was understood by everyone that additional space was needed for uses in addition to library expansion. For example, the University wanted to raze Law Annex 1 and Law Annex 2, creating a need

The East Wing, on the right in this photograph, provided much needed space for the expansion of the library and a variety of academic and administrative functions of the law school. In the center of the photograph is John Rogers Hall (1973), flanked by its two major expansions, the East Wing (1980) to the right and the Mabee Legal Information Center (2000) to the left. *Courtesy The University of Tulsa College of Law archives.*

for a new location for the admissions and placement operations, as well as additional faculty offices. Ultimately, additional Chapman/McFarlin/Barnard Trust funds were secured, allowing the expansion to be two floors, with the capability of a third floor to be added later.

The lower level would be devoted to library expansion, while the ground floor would originally be an empty shell which could eventually house a variety of administrative and academic functions and would ultimately be available for library expansion. A top floor could be added later that would allow further expansion of administrative, academic and library uses. The East Wing was completed in the summer of 1980, during the acting deanship of Tom Holland. The final cost of the project was $1,945,459.[47] It consisted of a lower level, into which the library expanded, and a ground floor, which was vacant. The utilization of that space, and the reconfiguration of that utilization, would occur over the next two decades and involve the next three deans. A top floor was never added. Rather, John Rogers Hall was expanded years later in another direction, as will be discussed in a subsequent chapter.

A few months before the construction of the East Wing began, Tom Read resigned to accept another deanship. He had accomplished much of what he had set out to do and, in the East Wing, had provided for quite a going-away present for the law school.

ACTING DEANSHIP OF TOM L. HOLLAND

Tom Holland, who had been associate dean under Tom Read, became acting dean in August, 1979, and served in that capacity until Frank K. Walwer arrived the next August.

During Tom Holland's acting deanship, the law school sponsored a reception for graduates in conjunction with the summer 1980 state bar admission ceremony in Oklahoma City. Left to right: Acting Dean Holland, Acting Associate Dean Sue Titus Reid, Bobbie Callahan-Frieburg ('81) and Caroline Pulice Vadala ('81). *Courtesy The University of Tulsa College of Law archives.*

A graduate of Friends University in Wichita, Kansas, Holland had earned his J.D. from The University of Tulsa and his L.L. M. from the University of Illinois. An expert in the field of commercial law, he had joined the Tulsa faculty in 1973, and would remain on the faculty long after his tenure as acting dean.

Holland's tenure was primarily taken up with preparing for and hosting the American Bar Association (ABA) inspection in 1980. He and the faculty had to prepare the Self-Study Report required in the inspection process. The purpose of the Self-Study Report is to have the institution engage in introspection, determining what are its current strengths and weaknesses and deciding where it

would like go in the future. The Report is very useful to both the institution and to the inspectors and the ABA in determining whether the institution is meeting the standards of accreditation and what areas of operation need to be improved. This is the most basic function of the Report. There is a second purpose, however, for which it is often used by a law school: to point out weaknesses in the institution and use the inspection and following ABA accreditation process as leverage to extract concessions from the University administration. It is this use, of which both the law school and University administration are aware, which provoked sparks in the 1980 inspection.

The Self-Study Report contained

some negative material, especially in the library section. The librarian, Alan Ogden, was frustrated with the budgeting process. Now that the library was under University supervision, the process mirrored the larger budgeting process at the law school. The University provided a "bare bones" budget that usually was not realistic or adequate for yearly needs. This necessitated the librarian going to the University and requesting additional funds before the end of the fiscal year. Often, private funding would be used as a supplement to the regular acquisitions budget. President Twyman used this approach for years to control the flow of funds around the University and, thus, exercise control over the various components of the University. This was frustrating to the law librarians because it made planning for publications continuations and collection development very difficult. These problems were placed in the Self-Study Report. When President Twyman and Vice-President Dowgray learned of the content, they demanded of Holland that the material be removed. The Self-Study Report was rewritten, but Holland kept a copy of the original version and both were provided to the inspection team. The issue became somewhat moot in that, the following year, the incoming dean, Frank Walwer, obtained a good package of economic benefits for his first years in office.

One other issue arose during Holland's acting deanship, an issue that continued during the Walwer years - - tension within NELPI and between NELPI and the faculty. The issue that faced Holland was a disagreement between Kent Frizzell, the director, and Gary Allison, an associate director, relating to the publication of a report written by Allison which was critical of the energy industry. Frizzell was very supportive of the energy industry; Allison was far less so. A more fundamental issue underlay the specific disagreement: was NELPI intended to be neutral or energy-industry oriented in its work? Before the dispute between Frizzell and Allison was resolved, Holland had to bring in President Twyman and Vice-President Dowgray to broker a solution.[48]

Physical enhancements to John Rogers Hall occurred during Tom Holland's acting deanship. These enhancements were the physical manifestations of efforts by Dean Read and the faculty to build a deeper sense of pride in the institution. During his deanship Read had created an ad hoc Committee on History and Institutional Traditions, chaired by Professor John F. Hicks, to foster pride in and understanding of the law school's history and mission. The Committee's work resulted in two gifts intended to advance these purposes.

Mark and Terrie Ernst donated a trophy case and plaque cabinet which was placed in the student lounge ("the Pit") and which allowed public view of the many trophies, plaques and faculty publications at the school. The Ernsts made this donation in memory of Michael D. Erwin ('73). These improvements were followed by others in later years, all allowing the accomplishments of students and faculty to be displayed.

About the same time Martin Stevens, a noted Oklahoma rug designer and father of a law student in the school at this time, Laurie Lyons, designed and crafted a tapestry containing a legal motif ("The Balance of Justice") that hangs in the atrium of the student lounge in John Rogers Hall. The tapestry was donated by Mrs. Lee Harrington in memory of her son, Lee Harrington, Jr., who attended the University in the 1930s. As any artwork might, it has elicited a range of opinions over the years, from admiration to John Hager's acerbic comment, in response to a request for faculty suggestions for name, that it should be entitled, "Essence of Fraternity Row #1"!

In August of 1980, Frank K. Walwer assumed the deanship at the law school. His administration would run throughout the entire decade and see the fortunes of the school ebb and flow with internal and national circumstances.

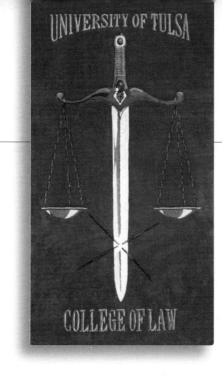

PROGRESS DURING A TIME OF INTROSPECTION
(1980-1991)

F rank K. Walwer came to the law school from Columbia University, where he had spent his entire career up to that time. Having earned both his undergraduate and law degrees from Columbia, he had been a long-time associate dean at the Columbia School of Law. In addition to his decanal duties at Tulsa, described in this chapter, he was much involved in American Bar Association activities, including the Law School Admission Council, the Section on Legal Education and Admission to the Bar, the Council on Post-Secondary Accreditation, and the Standing Committee on Lawyer Competency. Later, after his tenure as dean had ended, he moved to Texas Weslyan University School of Law as dean of that law school.

The decade of the 1980s, during which Walwer was dean, had a different feel to it than did the previous decade. During the previous ten years, the move to campus to occupy a new building and the subsequent development and improvement of the law school in almost all areas had created a sense of optimism, a belief that today was better than yesterday, and that tomorrow would be better still. That spirit did not continue through the 1980s. Both external and internal events created a more somber and introspective era. The feel of this decade is captured in Dean Frank Walwer's introduction to his Annual Report for 1984-85:

> The 1984-85 academic year was characterized by both movement and introspection in the College of Law. Although legal education is not and should not be immune from the dynamics of "outside forces," our intention is to move forward as part of a design governed by our own mission and not by the happenstance of other influences. Accordingly, we initiated a structured effort at self-examination by the introduction of a series of faculty colloquies dealing with the underpinnings of our overall program.[1]

UNIVERSITY EVENTS AFFECTING THE COLLEGE OF LAW

What were these "forces" which caused this self-examination? They are best understood by starting at the University level. First, the demographics

Frank K. Walwer, ninth dean, 1980-91.
Courtesy The University of Tulsa College of Law archives.

of student population was changing: the number of college-age students was decreasing each year during this period.[2] This shrinking population reduced the law school's numbers during the first half of the decade, as will be discussed later.

Second, a change in the University's academic emphasis had a profound effect on the law school. John Dowgray, who had been vice president for academic affairs and provost for many years, retired in 1983 and was replaced by Thomas F. Staley. Staley had been an important figure at the University for years and was about to play an even more important role. A long-time English professor and authority on James Joyce, he had served as dean of the Graduate School, 1969-76, and dean of the College of Arts and Sciences, 1981-83. Upon becoming provost, he directed the focus of University energy and resources toward undergraduate education.[3] The law school was on the fringes of University concern for the balance of the decade. During this period, Staley's drive to build up the undergraduate program was often summed up as a drive to make TU the "Harvard of the Southwest." Although the University's undergraduate program was greatly strengthened, it came at a price. Undergraduate attrition rates increased and the number of non-traditional and part-time students, long an important factor in University enrollment, decreased. University enrollment declined from about 6,300 students at the start of the decade to about 4,300 at its end.[4]

Declining University and law school enrollment meant declining tuition revenue, a fact that haunted the law school during this period. Budgets in the law school remained

static at a time when various constituencies were pushing for improvements. The other important source of revenue during this period was income from the Chapman Trusts. This money was widely viewed at the time as the revenue that would "make the difference" in the University becoming the "Harvard of the Southwest." These funds did increase greatly during the early 1980s and were used by Provost Staley to improve the quality of the undergraduate programs and selected graduate programs, but, by and large, the law school did not share much in them.

Apart from student enrollment trends and revenue trends, a third factor on the University level that affected the law school at the end of the decade was disruptive and continuing changes in leadership. Theretofore, the University had enjoyed stability in its administration. President Tyman and Provost Dowgray had been in office since the late 1960s. The only change that had occurred was the replacement of Dowgray by Staley in 1983. Then, in 1988, a set of tragic circumstances arose that created administrative instability until 1991. First, Twyman and Staley, who had enjoyed a long, successful and amicable academic association at the University, had a bitter falling out, and Staley left the University, and Joe Middlebrooks replaced him as provost. One year later, in 1989, Twyman, who had led the University for twenty-one years, died of cancer. Michael W. Davis, the vice president for administration, who had been at the University since 1969 and who had worked directly with Twyman for the previous eight years, was appointed acting president in May, 1989. Shortly after assuming office,

he, too, was diagnosed with cancer. However, he remained in office until his death in January, 1990. Provost Middlebrooks was then appointed acting president and served in that capacity until Robert H. Donaldson was appointed President in July, 1990. After twenty-one years of stable presidential leadership, the University experienced four presidents in a little over one year. To compound the instability, the office of provost changed hands frequently during this period. Middlebrooks had taken over from Staley in 1988 and, by 1990, had been thrust into the acting presidency. Roger Blais, a long-time physics professor, became acting provost in 1990 and served in that capacity until George Gilpin, Jr. was hired from the University of Miami by Donaldson in the summer of 1991. Thus, between 1988 and 1991, when Frank Walwer resigned as dean of the law school, the University had seen four presidents and four provosts.

These external and internal events, as well as other factors, took a toll on the law school. Dean Walwer, in an interview in the student newspaper at the end of his deanship, upon being asked to describe the changes throughout the law school during his eleven year tenure, said this: "If I were to describe the 11 years in which I served as dean, I would say they were contraction years for the University. The student enrollment throughout the [U]niversity had declined considerably. The University had priorities which were separate from the enhancement of the professional schools. They were mainly focused on the undergraduate curriculum."[5]

Despite these constraints, the law school did enjoy progress in a number of areas. Even with a decline in size, student activities, organizations and accomplishments continued. The faculty grew in size and the nucleus of the faculty in place at the time of this writing arose. The curriculum continued to develop, especially in the area of professional skills; new academic publications joined the *Tulsa Law Journal*, which heretofore, had been the only academic publication at the school. Library holdings and technology increased. The physical plant was rearranged and improved. And, alumni were more organized and active than ever before. The decade of the 1980s was, indeed, a time of both introspection and progress.

STUDENTS

This decade witnessed a struggle by the school to maintain the size and quality of the student body. During the last half of the 1970s, applications ran over 1,000 per year, but by 1987, they had fallen to one-half that number.[6] A slow growth in applications occurred each year thereafter. This decline in applications forced the school to accept ever higher percentages of applicants in order to make a class.[7] These facts affected the academic profile of entering classes. Unlike the school of years gone by, the object was no longer simply to "make a class" by having the appropriate number of students in their seats on the first day of school; the faculty now desired to have the most academically qualified class possible. Beginning in the 1970s, the two-objective criteria of academic promise—undergraduate grade point average and Law School Admission Test score—became very important. During the 1980s, the

school struggled to maintain the academic profile of each previous class, and ultimately, accepted a slight decline.[8] In this environment, it is no wonder that the Summer Admission by Performance Program ("Summer Contacts"), which had been launched in 1975 during a period of high optimism, was ended in 1982. Times had changed.

The school responded in a number of ways to the demographics of the 1980s. First, to protect the academic profile of each entering class, fewer numbers of students were enrolled. Student body size had grown dramatically in the 1970s; it now shrank during most of the 1980s.[9] A reduction in tuition revenue was one result, placing strain on the budgets of the various programs of the school. Even in this environment, due to the efforts of Dean Walwer and the faculty, many of the programs of the school did grow and improve, as will be discussed later.

Where would the necessary revenue come from, with fewer tuition-paying students enrolled and Chapman money largely going elsewhere? The school turned to higher tuition for those students in school. During the decade of the 1980s, tuition tripled, increasing from $105/credit hour in 1980 to $325/credit hour in 1990.

This increase in the price of legal education led, in turn, to the second method employed to protect the academic profile of the student body—scholarships. The law school had historically enjoyed very low tuition, placing it close to the bottom in cost among private schools. As tuition rose, it became increasingly necessary to award scholarships on a merit basis to appropriate students. Dean

Walwer and the faculty began a scholarship program that, by 1990, was awarding over $500,000 to over twenty percent of the student body.[10]

Students were involved in an expanding range of interests during the 1980s. This is illustrated by the new student organizations formed. Added to the traditional organizations such as the Student Bar Association, moot court, law journal, and the law fraternities, were the American Indian Law Organization; the Black American Law Organization; the International Law Society; the Communication, Entertainment and Sports Law Club; and the Law and Medicine Society. These new organizations indicate not only the expanding interests of students, but also expanding interests of faculty members which also show up in a more diversified curriculum. The *Briefly*, the law student newspaper which had been produced for a number of years, gave way in 1988 to the *Baculus*, a larger, more professional publication that was still being published in 2003.

New student intraschool and interscholastic competitions were added to the traditional moot court competition. In line with the increasing interest in developing "lawyering skills," a negotiation competition and a client counseling competition were started. Also, the evolving emphasis within NELPI on natural resources, as well as energy, was evident in the start-up of a natural resources law moot court competition. Up to this point, competitions had been managed solely by faculty members. With the increasing number and complexity of competitions, students began playing a much more important roll. In 1989 the student-run Board of Advocates was created, charged

Faculty regularly attended the annual spring Alumni Dinner Dance which Dean Walwer began. Left to right: Professor Charles Adams, Maureen Adams, Professor Catherine Cullem, and Professor Dennis Bires. *Courtesy The University of Tulsa College of Law archives.*

with the task of promoting and organizing all competitions at both the intramural and interscholastic levels.

The Student Bar Association remained very active during the decade. Joining the 1977-78 SBA , which had won the American Bar Association's Outstanding SBA award a decade earlier, the 1986-87 SBA won the award again. In giving the award to the Tulsa group, the ABA cited the organization's active public lecture series and community service activities during the year.[11]

Student advising on both academic and life issues was evolving during this period. Academic counseling had historically been done by the faculty on an informal basis. In the 1970s, with the creation of a more complex dean's office, involving a dean and associate/assistant deans, the office

of associate dean for academic affairs had evolved. The faculty member in this position provided academic counseling to the entire student body. In 1986, an effort to improve the academic counseling program was begun by assigning groups of students to specific faculty members, who would be their academic counselors throughout their law school career. It was hoped that this program would bring a more personal touch to the counseling effort. The program, with various modifications over the years, has remained in place as of 2003, supplementing the work of the associate dean for academic affairs.

There had never been anyone formally designated to aid students in life counseling. What life or personal issues or problems students might face while in school had to be dealt with on their own initiative by, perhaps, going to a respected faculty member. The problem with this approach was the faculty member's lack of training in this area, and, often, a reluctance to become involved. No other resource being available within the law school, a student might go to the University chaplain's office or counseling office, or, seek help outside the University. In 1981, Dean Walwer set about to improve this situation by creating the office of assistant dean for student affairs. Deborah R. Cunningham-Fathree was hired to fill the position. In addition to dealing with the life concerns of students, this office was responsible for certain areas of law school administration, continuing legal education and community service. Up to this point, "front office deans" had always been faculty members who devoted only part time to administration.

continued to evolve. Women continued to come to the school in ever-increasing numbers. In 1966, only 3% of the student body were women. By 1971, the percentage had doubled to 6%. Just two years later, in 1973, the percentage had doubled again to 12%. By 1978, the percentage had again doubled to 24%. By 1982, the percentage had gone up to 32%. The percentage remained over thirty percent for the rest of the decade, reaching a high of 39% in the1987-88 school year.

Enrollment by minorities [12] fluctuated during the 1970s and 1980s, rising during times of strong student demand to enter law school and decreasing

BELOW: Taunya L. Banks was the first African-American to serve on the permanent faculty. *Courtesy The University of Tulsa College of Law archives.*

With this position, Walwer created a non-academic decanal position involved in various aspects of the administration of the school.

During the 1980s the composition of the student body

when demand was lower. In 1976, the percentage stood at 3%. For the next three years, a period of strong student demand, the percentage doubled to the 7% range. As general student demand weakened in the

LEFT: A number of professors on the faculty in the 1980s went on to hold important positions elsewhere. Two such individuals are shown here, attending the Alumni Dinner Dance in 1988. Left to right: Professor Daniel Morrissey, who later served as dean at St. Thomas University School of Law and Gonzaga University School of Law; Professor John Lowe, who later became the George W. Hutchinson Professor of Energy Law at Southern Methodist University, Dedman School of Law; Phyllis Frey ('81), wife of Professor Martin Frey. *Courtesy The University of Tulsa College of Law archives.*

early 1980s, minority enrollment fell back, dropping to 2% in 1982. From 1988 on, when general demand for entrance into school increased again, so did minority enrollment, rising once again to the 6% level.

Full-time versus part-time enrollments show a pattern of gradual growth in the full-time division. In 1960, only 25% of students were attending full time. But, by 1966, a majority, 53%, of all students were full-time students. The percentage of students attending full time reached an all-time high of 83% in 1974. After that, for the rest of the 1970s, and for the entire decade of the 1980s, the full-time division remained constant at about two-thirds of the student body.

FACULTY

Despite the general tone of the decade as one of contraction, such was not the case with the faculty. Progress was made. Dean Walwer engineered a significant growth in faculty from 23 at the beginning of the decade to 30 at its end. There was not only a growth in numbers, but also a change in nature. Many more women joined the faculty during this period, so that by decade-end, the law school was a leader within the University in both the number and percentages of women on the faculty. Of eleven women hired for full-time, non-visiting positions during Walwer's deanship, seven remained on the faculty in 2003.[13]

BELOW: The spring Alumni Dinner Dance often brought together past and present faculty. Left to right: Dean Frank Walwer, former Dean Allen King, Professor John Hager, and Professor Ralph Thomas. Hager and Thomas would soon retire from the faculty. *Courtesy The University of Tulsa College of Law archives.*

LEFT: Professor John Hager, left, striking a familiar pose at his retirement program. In the center background is Dean Walwer, and, to the right background, Mayor Roger Randle ('78), who declared the day to be "John Hager" day in Tulsa. *Courtesy The University of Tulsa College of Law archives.*

ABOVE: President Twyman, Professor Hager and Dean Walwer at Hager's retirement reception. *Courtesy The University of Tulsa College of Law archives.*

LEFT: For decades of students at the law school, Professor Hager was "the King of Torts"! *Courtesy The University of Tulsa College of Law archives.*

Likewise, there was a significant number of men joining the faculty during this period. Of eight men hired for full-time, non-visiting positions, six remain on the faculty as of the time of this writing.[14] These two groups of women and men formed a core of the faculty in 2003.

Minority representation on the faculty grew during this decade. Taunya Lovell Banks became the first African American to hold a permanent position on the faculty when she joined in 1985. Winona Tanaka became the first Asian American to hold a faculty position when she joined in 1987. Vicki Limas became the first person with a Native American heritage to hold a faculty position when she joined in 1989.

A shift toward a stronger research orientation among the faculty had begun during the 1970s. This trend accelerated during the 1980s.

Continuing research on a wide array of topics by most of the faculty became the norm. The faculty's 1987 ABA Self-Study Report, written in anticipation of the up-coming ABA inspection, cited a report, "Senior Law Faculty Publication Study: Comparisons of Law School Productivity,"[15] which pointed out the TU faculty's scholarly productivity. The Report also listed the eighty books, articles and other publications which had been produced by twenty-two faculty members during the 1984-87 time period.

While the faculty hired during the decades of the 1970s and 1980s were becoming the core of the faculty, the original full-time faculty from the Downtown years were beginning to pass off the scene. Ralph Thomas retired in 1986, after having served thirty years on the faculty, and John Hager retired in

1989, after having served thirty-nine years on the faculty.

A significant development during the decade was the establishment of the Chapman Distinguished Professorship. It had its origins in the 1970s "Dimensions for a New Decade Campaign," discussed in the previous chapter. Dean Read had lobbied hard for a building addition to be placed in the fund drive. The University had refused this request,[16] but President Twyman had promised the law school one of the Chapman Professorships that were to be created in various departments across the campus. This Professorship came on line in the law school in 1985. The faculty decided that the Professorship should have two characteristics: 1) it should be a visiting position, not a permanent one (this characteristic was changed in the 1990s, as will be discussed later); 2) it should be held by an older, established scholar, not a "rising young star." During the balance of the decade, the law school benefited from a series of visiting scholars from around the country:

James W. Ely, Jr. (Vanderbilt University) [Spring, 1985]

Walter Ray Phillips (University of Georgia) [1985-86]

Peter Maxfield (University of Wyoming) [1986-87]

Richard Delgado (University of California - Davis) [1987-88]

Reid P. Chambers (Law firm of Sonosky, Chambers & Sachse, Washington, D.C.) [Spring, 1989]

R. Dobie Langenkamp (Tulsa attorney, deputy assistant secretary for Oil and Gas,

Department of Energy, 1978-81; Department of Energy Liaison for National Petroleum Council; Cherokee Operating Company) [1989-90 and 1990-91] (Langenkamp also served as associate director of NELPI during these two years)

A larger number of adjuncts taught at the law school in the 1980s than had been the case before. This need arose because the curriculum was expanding, with more courses being offered, while the faculty were increasingly teaching in more focused areas of expertise. This necessitated the use of a growing number of adjuncts to fill in coverage gaps. The faculty became concerned about the inappropriate use of adjuncts and passed a rule requiring full-time faculty to teach first-year required courses and seminars, while the adjunct faculty would cover upper-division elective courses, specialized courses and practice-oriented courses.

The evolving scholarship-bent of the faculty was evident in the creation of a program of regular faculty presentations, beginning in 1984-85. The faculty began meeting regularly for the first time to discuss members' works in progress. Topics ranged from President Ronald Reagan's "Star Wars" proposal to the emerging Critical Legal Studies Movement. This program evolved into the Faculty Colloquy Program. This idea of discussing scholarly topics of interest was expanded upon to include guest speakers. In 1988-89, for example, Professors Morton J. Horwitz and Duncan M. Kennedy, both of Harvard Law School, and founders of the Critical Legal Studies Movement,

were invited to campus to give presentations to students, faculty and the public.

ACADEMIC PROGRAM

The curriculum was the subject of re-examination during the decade. With a few exceptions, the law school's curriculum had been a traditional one, focused on the theoretical and analytical, teaching students to "think like lawyers." Two fundamental issues threaded their way through the decade: the need to teach "lawyering skills" of various types and the quest to find how best to do it. This is illustrated in a statement found in the 1987 ABA Self-Study Report:

In addition to a continuing commitment to provide high quality education in the traditional substantive areas of the law, the College is analyzing the current status of lawyering skills education in the curriculum. At the request of the Dean, Professor Chris Blair has prepared a comprehensive report to the Curriculum Committee identifying sixteen specific skills that could be considered necessary for the practice of law. He has analyzed our current curriculum to determine which of these skills are taught and how well they are taught. He also has made recommendations for improving our teaching of lawyering skills. . . . In the last several years the College has, in fact, been placing increased emphasis on skills training.[17]

What was this "increased emphasis"? Primarily, it was in the areas of training in legal research,

Rick Ducey, law library director, sports a class of 1999 Dog Law T-shirt. *Courtesy Mabee Legal Information Center archives.*

writing, reasoning and advocacy during the first year, although there were other areas of emphasis as well. Toward the beginning of the Walwer deanship, in 1981-82, the faculty had engaged in a general review of the legal research and writing program. The ideas generated were put into place the next year in the form of the time of one faculty member, Catherine Cullem, whose time was devoted entirely to teaching an introductory legal writing course to all first-year students and an advanced legal writing course as an upper-class elective. Toward the middle of the decade, these areas continued to be strengthened by (1) hiring a supervisor of the program, Judith Finn; (2) using practicing attorneys as adjuncts; (3) increasing the number of topics included; and, (4) increasing the credit hours of the courses.

In the fall of 1985, first-year students were required to arrive one week before the start of the regular fall semester and take an intensive legal research course taught by the library director and student assistants. Thus began the infamous "Dog Law" week, (named after the dog-bite cases used to train students) which has evolved and continued down to the time of this writing.

Beyond the first year, the faculty put in place other lawyering skills courses. Over the decade, at least five courses in this area were added to the curriculum.[18] One of these courses, Alternative Methods of Dispute Resolution (ADR), brought the law school into the significant national trend of finding ways to handle disputes more expeditiously and efficiently. The law school's involvement arose out of activity in the City of Tulsa. In the early 1980s, the Tulsa municipal court system

started "Project Early Settlement." Terry Simonson, the Program's director, sought space in the law school for training of personnel, and Professor Martin Frey, then the associate dean, became involved and was trained and, ultimately, headed the ADR Program at the school. Because of the city's work in the area, the American Bar Association chose Tulsa as one of three cities for a "Multi-Door Resolution Center" which conducted a program that would screen individuals with legal problems and direct them to appropriate paths, such as litigation or mediation. Also, the federal district court, under Chief Judge Dale Cook, became involved, and U.S. Magistrate John Leo Wagner was instrumental in implementing the concept in the federal court system in Tulsa. The synergy between the programs in the city and the work of Professor Frey and the faculty resulted in a number of ADR courses coming into the curriculum,[19] and, ultimately, the creation of a certificate program in the area. As discussed in chapters five and six, the law school created programs whereby students who took courses in designated areas and met other criteria were awarded a certificate in the appropriate legal field, indicating their concentrated study in the area. This was as close as the law school came to recognizing "specialties" in the curriculum.

Over the years the "workhorse" of the lawyering skills program at the law school had been the Legal Internship Program. Started by Professor Ralph Thomas in the 1960s, the concept was that second and third-year students could qualify to obtain a limited license to practice law that would allow them to work under the supervision of a licensed attorney. The work involved could be both office work and court appearances. During the 1980s, there was increasing faculty concern over the adequacy of this program, centering on questions such as: 1) was there adequate student supervision by their attorney-employers, i.e., did the quality and quantity vary too much from employer to employer; 2) was there a larger "learning" process going on, apart from the short-term meeting of client needs; and, 3) was there more than simply legal research for a lawyer going on, i.e., were students receiving adequate training in client handling and court appearances?

An additional concern about the Legal Internship Program was the fact that students were receiving both academic credit and monetary compensation for their work. Although this was very popular with the students, it raised concerns in the accrediting process and required a variance from Standard 306(a) of the ABA Standards for Approval of Law Schools.

These concerns by the faculty resulted in tighter requirements being imposed on the program, beginning in 1986.[20] More fundamentally, debate concerning the necessity and desirability of an in-house legal clinic began in earnest. Faculty debate occurred within the confines of the faculty and in the public arena.[21] Students and local attorneys discussed the topic in the law school newspaper.[22] All of this concern would lead to the creation of an in-house clinic at the law school during the next administration.

Lawyering skills may have been the dominant area of curriculum

development during the decade, but it was not the only one. An important development in the first year curriculum occurred in 1990. The faculty altered the traditional first-year curriculum of contracts/criminal law and administration/legal reasoning, research and writing/property/torts by reducing torts from a six-credit, two-semester course to a four-credit, one-semester one and adding a new course, legal thought, a jurisprudence-type course. This was a harbinger of change that, over the next few years, would led to a reduction in credit hours assigned to most the traditional substantive first-year courses and the placement of other courses in the first year.

In addition to changes in the first-year curriculum, a number of courses were added to the upper-class curriculum. These additions show both development of the traditional curriculum and expansion into new areas of the law.[23]

One final change in the curriculum over the decade involved the enlargement of the joint-degree program. Three new joint-degree programs were added: J.D./M.S. in Accounting, J.D./M.S. in Biological Science and J.D./M.S. in Taxation.

NATIONAL ENERGY LAW AND POLICY INSTITUTE

The 1980s was a decade of discussion, controversy and changing directions for the National Energy Law and Policy Institute (NELPI). During this time NELPI's course offerings remained constant at first and then expanded toward the end of the decade. What proved to be controversial was not its course offerings, but its research activities. The controversy appears in the school's 1987 ABA Self-Study Report:

NELPI Self Critique. There is a belief that there is some danger of NELPI losing its reputation as an energy law and policy research center or institute. Concern has been expressed that NELPI is imperceptibly moving toward being an "Energy Law and Policy Institute" in name only, i.e., a "program" *** which merely encompasses a core of energy law related courses in its curriculum, incidentally offers/sponsors some continuing education programs from time to time, and supervises the editing of certain journals and publications.[24]

NELPI's mission from the start had been three-pronged: 1) the training of law students and others, 2) engaging in publication and research, and 3), facilitating communication on energy topics. The second mission—publications and research—proved to be the controversial one. It had always been assumed that its status as an "institute" meant that NELPI would engage in research, preferably funded research. That, indeed, happened between 1976 and 1983. During that period NELPI received seven grants, totaling $313,950.[25] The work on some of these grants had provoked tension within NELPI during Tom Holland's acting deanship, as was mentioned in the preceding chapter. Beginning in 1984, however, funded research gave way to other activities, which, in itself, created tension within the faculty. NELPI turned its focus to writing articles in law reviews and other publications; organizing conferences; speaking at academic and other programs; and, most directly in substitute for funded research, publishing energy-related publications. Over the decade NELPI began to publish:

Energy Law Journal, edited at the law school under a contract with the Federal Energy Bar Association in Washington, D.C.

Natural Resources Law Monograph Series, edited at the school under a contract with the Natural Resources, Energy and Environmental Law Section of the American Bar Association.

Year-In-Review, edited at the school under a contract with the Natural Resources, Energy and Environmental Law Section of the American Bar Association.

Mineral Law Newsletter, edited at the school under a contract with the Mineral Law Section of the Oklahoma Bar Association.

Annual Mineral Law Symposium in the *Tulsa Law Journal*.

Concern within the faculty over this change in focus by NELPI exhibited itself in controversy over the NELPI staffing level and over the teaching loads of the staff. NELPI was originally envisioned as having a director and two associate directors. The continuance of two associate directors became an issue. Kent Frizzell served as director through the 1970s and 1980s. The organization benefited from a series of able associate directors during this period. Patrick Martin served in the mid-1970s. Gary Allison served in the late 1970s and early 1980s. He was joined in the late 1970s by John Lowe, who was a prolific scholar and program presenter for NELPI

through the mid-1980s. In the mid-1980s, Rex Zedalis and David Pierce served as associate directors. In the late 1980s, Dobie Langankamp was both Chapman Distinguished Visiting Professor and NELPI associate director. He was joined in the late 1980s by Marla Mansfield, who continued to serve as associate director into the 1990s.

The more intense controversy centered on the teaching load of the NELPI faculty. It had originally been set as a one-half load (six credit hours per year), compared to the regular teaching load of twelve credit hours per year for the rest of the faculty. There had been few exceptions to this normal teaching load; for example, Rennard Strickland, as Shleppey Research Professor, had a light teaching load. The question of increasing the teaching load for the NELPI faculty was the manifestation of controversy over NELPI no longer engaging in significant funded research, but engaging in traditional scholarship and administrative duties associated with the publications. This work was alleged to be the type of work expected of all faculty while carrying a normal teaching load. These concerns were manifested in a recommendation of the 1985-86 curriculum committee that "unless prevented by major funded research or an unusual need, the collective teaching loads of the NELPI faculty in a given academic year not average significantly below two-thirds of a full course load.[26] NELPI responded to these concerns. In an "Advance Planning Document for 1987-88," referred to in the school's 1987 ABA Self-Study Report, NELPI agreed that "all three of the professional staff (director and two associate directors) will assume increased

teaching loads, i.e., a three quarter yearly teaching load ...."[27]

At the end of the day, however, when the smoke from these controversies had cleared, the faculty affirmed its support for NELPI and its program. A planning document, containing the conclusions of the faculty from a series of meetings held to plan the direction of the school after the 1987 ABA inspection, indicates this support:

At its special meetings, the law faculty addressed the concerns raised by the evaluation team. The faculty voted in favor of the following two proposals:

1. The faculty reaffirms its support and commitment to the goals, objectives and continuing existence of NELPI, including the retention of the three (3) NELPI positions of one (1) Director and two (2) Associate Directors.

2. The faculty recommends that the Director of NELPI be assigned a one-half teaching load and that the Director's release time shall include the additional duty of working toward the prompt completion of funding for an endowed Chair in the area of Energy Law.[28]

Sufficient funds were never raised and a Chair was not obtained.

AMERICAN INDIAN LAW PROGRAM

Just as the direction of NELPI changed over the decade, so did the direction of the American Indian Law Program. It will be recalled that the University acquired the Shleppey Indian Law Collection

in the mid-1970s, and Rennard Strickland returned to the law school as the Shleppey Research Professor of Law and History. In the first half of the decade, Strickland guided the program in a research direction, cataloguing and expanding the Collection, as well as engaging in research and writing. When he left the school in 1985 to become dean at the Southern Illinois School of Law, the program took a more instructional turn. In the middle of the decade, Ray Sanford, an attorney with expertise in the area, taught in the program as an adjunct. Toward the end of the decade, Gloria Valencia-Weber joined the faculty and further developed the program. Reid Chambers, an Indian Law expert from Washington, D.C., served as Chapman Distinguished Visiting Professor at the end of the decade. During this period additional Indian Law courses were added to the curriculum and an American Indian Law Certificate Program was started.

This Certificate Program was the first of its kind at TU and a harbinger of future programs. The law school, like all American law schools, had always offered an "generalist" education, preparing students for the general practice of law without specialty. In the 1970s the school had created a "tract" or "area of concentration" system of organizing and advertising courses along general subject themes in order to help students in their

The Native American Law Certificate

At The University of Tulsa College of Law

The law library staff stand behind the old card catalog on its last day of use in 1986. It was being replaced by the on-line LIAS-TU Catalog. Left to right: Kathy Kane, Chuck McKnight, Katherine Tooley, Linda Burris, Karen Kevil, University Libraries Director Robert Patterson, Carol Schultz Arnold, Sue Sark, Law Library Director Rick Ducey. *Courtesy The University of Tulsa College of Law archives.*

curricular planning, but had never held out a graduating student as having special expertise in any area. The idea of indicating that a graduating student has some special knowledge in a given field was a product of the 1990s and began with the American Indian Law Certificate Program.

LIBRARY

The Law Library illustrates the progress and contraction that characterized this decade. Between 1980 and 1991, the span of Frank Walwer's deanship, library holdings more than doubled, from 120,000 volumes to 254,000 volumes. Computerized legal research grew, with the installation of LEXIS and WESTLAW and automated technology caused the card catalog to finally be replaced in favor of the online LIAS-TU Catalog. The opening of the East Wing in 1980 insured adequate study and work space. Amazingly, this progress was made in an era of inadequate budgets that did not reflect increasing costs due to inflation. A November, 1987 faculty planning document indicates the conditions under which the library operated :

The ABA Site Evaluation Report was critical of the Law Library's acquisitions budget, both as to its amount and as to the procedure by which it is set and supplemented. In amounts budgeted, the Law Library ranked 174 (last) out of the 174 reporting U.S. law schools in both 1984-85 and 1985-86. Inadequate budgeting has forced cancellations of serials and prevent[ed] any attempt at collection development.

A pattern of eleventh hour supplementation of Law

LEFT: Former Dean Allen King and Dean Frank Walwer at a spring Alumni Dinner Dance. *Courtesy The University of Tulsa College of Law archives.*

BELOW: The Alumni Dinner Dance was popular with alumni from all eras during the 1980s. left to right: John Boyd ('50), Edgar Parks ('50), Dean Walwer and Neil Bogan ('70). *Courtesy The University of Tulsa College of Law archives.*

ABOVE: Alumni and faculty mingle at an Alumni Dinner Dance during the 1980s. Left to right: Dean Walwer, Barry Epperson ('68) and Professor Martin Frey. *Courtesy The University of Tulsa College of Law archives.*

Library funds has enabled the College of Law to rank 154 out of 174 in 1984-85 and 153 out of 174 in 1985-86, in amounts actually expended (versus budgeted) on acquisitions. Far from providing encouragement, this erratic supplementation results in cancellations and resumptions of serials which could be subscribed to continuously if actual expenditures could be planned.[29]

These budget problems continued even after the Law Library budget was taken out from under the University library system and placed within the law school.

The Law Library and the College benefited from a number of able directors who served during the decade of the 1980s. Alan W. Ogden had taken over from Joel Burstein in 1978 and served until 1982. He proved to be a good administrator, but was limited by a tight budget. Sue Sark, who was assistant law librarian for acquisitions, served ably as acting law librarian during the 1982-83 academic year. Marian F. Parker served as director between 1983 and 1986. It was during her tenure that cataloging became automated with the introduction of the online LIAS-TU Catalog. The old card catalogue, which had been brought to the Talaiferro Savage Law Library in John Rogers Hall from the downtown building in 1973, was removed in the fall of 1986, during the first year of the directorship of Richard (Rick) E. Ducey. Starting in October, 1986, Ducey continued to serve as director as of 2003. During Ducey's first year, the library budget was tight, as described in the faculty planning document above. In response to the 1987 ABA inspection, $280,000 was poured in to retrospective collection development and current collection development. The growth areas in the collection were the energy law and American Indian law areas. Automation increased - the LIAS-TU Catalog was joined by LEXIS, WESTLAW and the first library computers, which were needed to work CALI exercises and for word processing. The size of both the professional and staff personnel grew by the end of the decade. Finally, Ducey and the library staff further developed the pre-semester legal research orientation week ("Dog Law" week) for entering students, as a part of the enhanced "lawyering skills" program described earlier.

PHYSICAL PLANT

The physical plant was upgraded by improvements to the East Wing which were planned and carried out by Dean Walwer. Upon arriving in 1980, he was aghast to find that the two offices where the public most interacted with the school—admissions and placement—were located outside of John Rogers Hall in two small frame houses, the "Little Houses on the Prairie." The East Wing had just been completed. The lower floor was being occupied by expansion of the library; the upper floor was a "blank slate," a bare and open expanse of concrete floor from wall to wall. Walwer planned and executed the in-filling of part of this space. The admissions office and the placement office were moved in; six faculty offices were created; two secretarial offices were created; a seminar room was created; a student SBA office was created: and, an *Energy Law Journal* office was created. The periphery of the East Wing was completely filled-in; the interior was the scene of holiday

parties and graduation receptions throughout the decade.

Decorative enhancements were made to John Rogers Hall in the form of Native American artwork which was hung in the faculty corridors. Due to the efforts of Professor Martin Frey and his wife, Phyllis ('81), Warren L. McConnico donated a number of paintings and prints to the school in memory of his father, William B. McConnico. Additional artwork was donated by the artist, John Walkabout, and by the Chibitty family in memory of Charles J. "Sonny" Chibitty, Jr. ('76).

STAFF

Important changes occurred within the staff during the decade of the 1980s. In 1981, a new full-time administrative position was created—assistant dean of students—and first occupied by Deborah R. Cunningham-Fathree, who served in that position throughout the decade. This position was created to handle many of the non-academic matters that students might face. This is one indication that the law school was becoming more pro-active in assisting students in their lives as law students.

Also in 1981, the placement director's position was upgraded to assistant dean status. By 1985 the title had been changed to assistant dean/director of placement and alumni affairs, an indication that alumni matters had been added to the responsibilities of the office. Anthony L Bastone, II, who had occupied the position since its creation in the 1970s, left in 1986 and was replaced by Mary N Birmingham, a 1977 graduate of the law school. Since this time the position has been filled by a person holding a law degree.[30]

ALUMNI

The additional duties given to the placement director in the area of alumni affairs is indicative of the renewed emphasis Dean Walwer placed on alumni affairs. Although the Law Alumni Association had existed for decades, it was rather inactive when Walwer became dean. He reinvigorated it. The first annual Alumni Reunion Dinner Dance was held in June of 1982 and was held each spring/summer thereafter. Walwer started the first annual Alumni Fund Drive in the Fall of 1986. Although the results were, at the start, rather modest, establishing the principle was important because the effort to raise money from law alumni had always been hampered by the University's insistence, under President Twyman, that fund raising be done on a centralized basis. It ultimately took a change in University presidents to change that system and free the dean to raise large amounts of money.

Increasingly over the decade, students were coming to the law school from states other than Oklahoma and, after graduation, practicing in other states.[31] Over the years, the nature of the law school had been changing from a "state" institution to a "regional" and "national" institution, drawing students and faculty from around the country and sending them out to far-flung places.

A DECADE OF CHANGE CONCLUDES

The decade of the 1980s had started with a well-established University administration in office; it ended with the president having died in office, along with the successor acting-president, and the University being administered by a second acting president.[32] These events may symbolize the turbulence of the decade. Robert Rutland, a history professor at the University, wrote an editorial in February of 1990, stating that: "TU is in the process of choosing a new president, and it's possible that the chosen educator will play a greater role in Tulsa's future than any short-term mayor or governor."[33] The search process resulted in Robert H. Donaldson being selected and becoming the University president on July 1, 1990. The University had begun a long-term planning process in 1988; President Donaldson enlarged and refocused it into a new strategic planning process. With the new decade, changes were on the horizon. One of them would be a change in the administration of the law school. In October of 1990, Dean Walwer announced his resignation, effective at the end of the academic year. A search committee was appointed and a search conducted which led to the appointment of John Makdisi, professor and associate dean at Cleveland State University, Cleveland-Marshall College of Law, as dean on July 1, 1991. Frank Walwer had served as dean for eleven years, longer than any previous full-time dean in the school's history. Always the gentleman, Walwer ended his report on his years as dean in the *Baculus* this way:

> I have many, many people to thank for their support over the decade. President Paschal Twyman and Trustee Bill Bell played special roles prior to their passing. My very deep and warm appreciation goes to all those of our law school student body, faculty, administration, staff, alumni, the university and Tulsa community, the Tulsa County Bar, the Oklahoma Bar Fellows, the American Bar Association, who have contributed so positively this past decade to the development of our College of Law. I look forward to the great and good in the years to come.[34]

Indeed, the decade of the 1990s would bring much of the "great and good" to the College of Law.

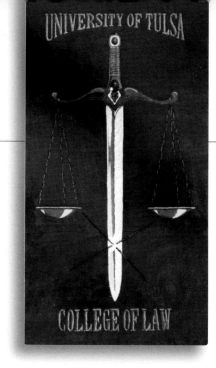

Chapter V

PROGRESS DURING A TIME OF CONTROVERSY
(1991-1995)

John Makdisi, the new dean as of July 1, 1991, arrived from the associate deanship at Cleveland-Marshall College of Law full of energy and ideas about how to improve the University of Tulsa College of Law. His own background was instrumental in forming those ideas. Holding law degrees from the University of Pennsylvania and Harvard University, he had engaged in graduate study at the University of Paris and the American Research Center in Cairo, Egypt. His interest was in Islamic law, and he would bring an interest in comparative and international law with him to Tulsa. But his paramount interest was in improving the national status of the law school.[1]

Soon after his arrival, the dean and faculty created a Strategic Plan for 1992-97 which listed the areas of focus for the immediate future:
- improve the quality of the student body by bringing the academic profile of entering students up to the national median;
- attract, encourage and retain a superior faculty;
- improve the diversity of the faculty, staff and student body;
- enrich existing programs at the school and begin selected new programs;
- improve the quality of the library by developing its holdings and staff;
- develop a strong alumni program.

Most, although not all, of these goals were realized over the next three years. But, they were realized in an atmosphere of controversy that obscured them to some extent. Progress was made in an atmosphere charged with controversy.

There were two reasons why these goals were realized to a large extent. First, Dean Makdisi secured the necessary financial commitment from Provost George Gilpin that would make these goals realistic.[2] Second, the goals of the University's Strategic Plan 1991-96 would aid the law school. There proved to be a synergy between the goals of President Donaldson for the University and the goals of the dean and faculty for the College of Law. This is a case where a rising tide of program direction at the University lifted the law school with it. However, there was a price to be paid. A number of factors, including a combination of the cost of the President's aspirations

John Makdisi, tenth dean, 1991-94.
Courtesy The University of Tulsa College of Law archives.

and the impact on tuition of a declining student body,[3] caused a continuing financial struggle at the University in which the law school became enmeshed. What started as progress at the beginning of Dean Makdisi's administration turned into controversy at its end.

UNIVERSITY EVENTS AFFECTING THE COLLEGE OF LAW

What were the University's program directions which made the start of Makdisi's deanship so promising? The story begins several years before Makdisi's arrival, at a time when the University was searching for a replacement for President Twyman. As the University launched its search for a new president following Twyman's unexpected death in 1989, Acting President Mike Davis appointed a task force to begin the process of long-range planning. This was thought to be an appropriate time for such an endeavor. When President Donaldson was appointed in 1990, he re-focused the effort into a strategic plan, which resulted in The University of Tulsa Strategic Plan 1991-96, adopted by the Board of Trustees in May and June, 1991. The Plan's "Evaluation of Programs and Services" called for the development of five new emphases,[4] the first two of which were:

A. **Globalization Program**.[5] Such an emphasis, which would cause programs to focus on the "global community," was near to the heart of President Donaldson, a political scientist specializing in Russian issues. This initiative was to have an important impact on the comparative and international law programs at the law school.

B. **Environmental Studies Programs**.[6] This initiative would have an important Impact on the future direction of the National Energy Law and Policy Institute at the law school. A new director and a new direction for NELPI would come out of a confluence of the goals of the University and the law school in the environmental studies area.

Dean Makdisi's emphasis was always on quality - - quality of people, programs, and activity - - with the goal being an enhanced national reputation for the school. This emphasis, often in the areas of international and environmental law, but also in other areas, produced both improved quality and change at the law school.

STUDENTS

An improved academic profile for entering students was a goal Dean Makdisi set out to achieve during his first year. The admissions office, under Velda Staves, and the admissions committee worked hard to increase the number of applications so as to be able to be more selective. The budget enhancement the provost had promised translated into more and better promotional literature and an award-winning video to interest more and better applicants in the school. Also, a slowing economy helped to increase applications.[7] It is counter-intuitive but true that a poor economy often results in increased applications for admission to law school. For the years of Makdisi's deanship, applications increased each year: 830 ('91); 1,146 ('92); 1,478 ('93); and 1,570 ('94.) This was combined with a deliberately smaller entering class: 238 ('91); 204 ('92); 216 ('93); and 224 ('94.) This gave

the school the luxury of accepting a lower percentage of students in order to make the entering class: 55% ('91); 39% ('92); 40% ('93); and 39% ('94.) All of these figures resulted in entering classes during this period which had improved grade point averages and Law School Admission Test scores.[8] What do all these numbers say about modern law schools? At a minimum, they point out that schools play a "numbers game." On the positive side, law faculties and deans are convinced that, to some degree, the numbers do, in fact, translate into quality differences in the academic potential and performance of students. On the negative side, numbers take on an exaggerated importance in an era of ratings and rankings, best exemplified by the annual U.S. News & World Report "Best Law Schools" rankings.

Not only did the student body change in academic profile during this period, it also changed in composition in other ways. The percentage of women grew only slightly, from 33% of the student body in 1991, to 36% of the student body in 1995. However, the dean and faculty were accomplishing their goal of increasing minority representation in the student body; it doubled during this same period, from 6% to 12%. Increasingly, students were coming to the school from out of state. For example, in the class entering in the fall of 1992, 55% came from 30 states outside of Oklahoma.

The Student Bar Association continued to be active and garner awards. As it had in the 1970s and 1980s, the SBA once again was selected by the American Bar Association as the outstanding student bar association in the country. The ABA commended the 1992-93 SBA for its pro bono work and high percentage of student participation in SBA activities.

The position of assistant dean for student affairs changed hands during this time. Martha Cordell took over from Deborah Cunningham-Fathree in the early part of the decade. Later, Dana Lamb served in the position toward the end of John Makdisi's deanship, during the acting deanship of Tom Arnold, and during the first part of Martin Belsky's deanship.

FACULTY

Important changes in the composition of the faculty occurred in the first half of the 1990s. First, the nature of the Chapman Distinguished Professorship changed from a visiting position to a permanent position when the noted constitutional law scholar, Bernard Schwartz, became the holder in the fall of 1992. Dean Makdisi secured additional funding from the University to make the position permanent and the dean and faculty set out to find a highly qualified holder. Bernie Schwartz surpassed everyone's hopes. During his five and one-half years on the faculty, he produced a large body of scholarship[9] and organized important retrospectives on the Warren Court and the Burger Court.

The synchronized direction of the law school and the University toward internationalism and environmentalism is apparent in a number of hires during the Makdisi deanship. Kent Frizzell, the first and long-time director of NELPI, retired in 1992 and was replaced by Lakshman Guruswamy, a recognized expert in international environmental law and biodiversity. Nicholas Rostow brought a national

security law perspective when he came to the law school from the position as special assistant to President George H.W. Bush for national security affairs and legal advisor to the National Security Council. Larry C. Backer came from

Bernard Schwartz, holder of the Chapman Distinguished Professorship position from 1992 to 1997. *Courtesy Mabee Legal Information Center.*

Students enjoy a day with the Supreme Court of Oklahoma in Oklahoma City. Students met with the Justices in the courtroom and at lunch. Members of the Court present, left to right: Hardy Summers, Rudolph Hargrave, Robert Lavender ('53), Ralph Hodges, Yvonne Kauger and Joseph Watt. Justices absent from the photograph are Robert Simms ('50), Alma Wilson and Marian Opala. Members of the faculty and staff present include Dean John Makdisi, left, and, next to him, Professor John Hicks, and, on the extreme right, Professor Martin Frey and Mary Birmingham, director of alumni relations. *Courtesy The University of Tulsa College of Law archives.*

Lakshman Guruswamy, the second director of NELPI, brought an environmental and international focus to the Institute. During his tenure the name was changed to the National Energy-Environmental Law and Policy Institute. *Courtesy The University of Tulsa College of Law archives.*

private practice with an interest in criminal law, legal history and comparative and international law. He would play an important role in the comparative and international law program and the study-abroad programs. Juraj Kolesar, professor of criminal and international law at Comenius University in Bratislava, Slovakia, visited in the fall of 1992 and taught a course entitled, "Czechoslovakia in Revolution."

American Indian law was also a hiring focus at this time. Gloria Valencia-Weber left the faculty in the early 1990s, leaving Vicki Limas as the person most interested in the area. Judith Royster, who combined an interest in American Indian law with natural resources and environmental law, joined the faculty in the fall of 1992. James Anaya, whose area of interest was the international law of indigenous peoples, visited from the University of Iowa in the fall of 1993.

Wider ethnic representation on the faculty continued to be a goal. In the 1980s, Winona Tanaka, of Asian American heritage, and Gloria Valencia-Weber, of Mexican/Native American heritage, had joined the faculty. This trend continued in the 1990s. Johnny Parker and Lundy

Langston, both of African American heritage, joined the faculty in the early 1990s, as did Larry Cata Backer, of Cuban American heritage. Lakshman Guruswamy, a Sri Lankan by birth, became director of NELPI during this same period.

In his efforts to "attract, encourage and retain a superior faculty," to use the words of the law school's strategic plan, Dean Makdisi focused on scholarship. He not only believed in its innate importance, but also saw it as a vehicle to raise the national status of the school. In 1992 the faculty, by and large, did not have computers in their offices. Makdisi secured money from the University his first year to provide the faculty with computers. Over and above this, he secured additional money to complete the computerization of staff offices. He saw this technological advance as a way to enhance the scholarship capabilities of the faculty.

In addition, he secured money from the University his first year to fund summer research grants for the faculty. Heretofore, the faculty had always faced the choice of teaching in the summer for additional income, or foregoing that income in order to engage in research. Dean Makdisi was able to fund summer research grants in amounts comparable to summer teaching income at the school, allowing faculty to have an economically-equivalent choice of summer activity.

Finally, he secured a commitment from the University to raise faculty salaries to the national average over a three year period. This occurred and caused controversy across campus during the third year when, in that year of financial-stringency campus-wide, law faculty were the only University faculty to receive raises.

These raises were also at the heart of an internal controversy within the school. Rather than spreading the raises faculty-wide, Dean Makdisi, gave disparate amounts to various faculty, based on a formula he devised that gave heavy weight to certain types of scholarship. This created lingering tension among the faculty.

This period saw emerging areas of faculty teaching and scholarship. For example, Professor Marguerite Chapman moved into the areas of health law and bioethics. She lectured and wrote extensively on such contemporary topics as the right to die. Professor Ray Yasser increasingly focused on sports law. He wrote one of the most widely-used casebooks in the area and began consulting and advising in various types of NCAA and Title IX disputes.

NATIONAL ENERGY—ENVIRONMENT LAW AND POLICY INSTITUTE

A number of important developments in various academic programs occurred in the first half of the 1990s. Kent Frizzell, who had served as Director of the National Energy Law and Policy Institute (NELPI) since its founding in 1976, retired at the end of the 1991-92 school year. Marla Mansfield, then associate director, served as acting director during 1992-93 while the school searched for a new director. Up to this point, NELPI had focused exclusively on energy law and policy. Now, the faculty made the decision, consistent with the goals of the University and law school, to expand the mission statement of NELPI to include environmental law and international law. In the spring of 1993, NELPI became the National Energy-Environment Law and Policy Institute. The faculty

also made the decision to hire, as director, an expert in environmental and international law. The school found such a person in Lakshman Guruswamy, who became director in the July of 1993. Having been educated in Sri Lanka and Great Britain, and having taught in Great Britain and the United States, he came with the credentials and the outlook necessary for this new phase in the life of NELPI. He brought with him from the University of Arizona, where he had been teaching, Brent Hendricks, as research coordinator for the research in the environmental and international arenas in which NELPI would be engaged for the next few years. Hendricks was later followed by Jason Aamodt in 1996, who served as research fellow at NELPI and as a legal research, writing and analysis instructor.

NELPI activities moved in the direction of environmental and international law. In 1992, the law school held an international energy law symposium, attended by speakers and attendees from around the country. In 1993, NELPI sponsored a conference on "Energy and Environmental Law in Slovakia and Neighboring Eastern European Countries," in conjunction with the law school's summer Bratislava program, which will be discussed later. In 1994, NELPI and the University of Arizona co-sponsored a major conference on "Biodiversity: Exploring the Complexities."

Over the next few years, NELPI scholarship moved in the same direction.

Guruswamy and others produced works such as *International Environmental Law and World Order* and *Strategies for Preserving Global Biodiversity*.

A Society of NELPI Fellows was created in the spring of 1995. It was composed of fifteen scholars in different disciplines around the University whose aim was to exchange ideas and engage in interdisciplinary interaction, leading to interdisciplinary research, teaching and public service. This type of cross-fertilization took on international scope when a visiting Fulbright Scholar, Ambrose O. O. Ekpu, associate professor (lecturer) of law at Edo State University, Ekpoma, Nigeria, spent the 1994-95 year in residence at the law school.

On the teaching front, NELPI created a certificate program. Students who took a designated array of required and elective courses were awarded the REEL Certificate—Certificate in Resources, Energy and Environmental Law. The REEL Certificate joined the Native American Law Certificate as another specialty program recognized at the school in the mid 1990s.

NELPI continued its traditional activities. Students continued to edit the *Energy Law Journal*, the annual *Year-in-Review*, and the *Tulsa Law Journal Mineral Law Symposium* issue. Marla Mansfield continued to edit the *Mineral Law Newsletter*. NELPI continued to be involved in CLE activities, such as the annual Federal Energy Regulatory Commission (FERC) Conference, continued to sponsor an annual Energy Law Essay Competition, and continued to coach the Pace Environmental Moot Court team.

COMPARATIVE AND INTERNATIONAL LAW PROGRAMS

The fields of comparative law and international law took off dramatically during John Makdisi's deanship. Before this time, two faculty members, David Clark and Rex Zedalis, had been teaching and writing in these areas, but there were no "programs." Here is an example of the confluence of goals of President Donaldson and Dean Makdisi, along with those of Clark and Zedalis, shaping an academic area at the school. Donaldson, a political scientist with expertise in Russian issues, was focusing the energies of the University in the areas of globalization and interdisciplinary work. Makdisi, whose own academic interest was Islamic law, had met Josef Moravcik, dean of the law school at Comenius University in Bratislava, Slovakia, in the late 1980s and the two men had worked out a plan for academic exchange between their two schools. Makdisi started to put the plan into action upon first arriving at Tulsa. In the fall of 1991, he secured the approval of Donaldson and the law faculty for a wide-ranging teaching and scholarly exchange between Comenius University and The University of Tulsa.[10] The agreement was implemented the following year. In the fall of 1992, Professor Juraj Kolesar, on the law school faculty at Comenius University, was a visiting professor at TU. In the summer of 1993, the first Summer Institute in Law in Bratislava was held in Bratislava, Slovakia. Professsor Dennis Bires directed and taught in the Institute, along with Professor David Clark. The Institute was co-sponsored by TU and Cleveland-Marshall Law School for several years, and, later, by TU alone. That first summer 35 students attended, including 17 from TU. They took four weeks of courses, listened to guest speakers and took field trips. This was the first of a number of foreign programs that would follow.

The Summer Institute in Law in Bratislava, Slovakia was the first of a number of study-abroad programs that the College of Law sponsored. It was held each summer from 1993 through 1996. *Courtesy Dennis Bires.*

Summer Institute in Law
Bratislava, SLOVAKIA

July 4 – August 3, 1994

The University of Tulsa
College of Law
Cleveland-Marshall
College of Law
Comenius University
Law School

The Bratislava Program was originated by Dean Makdisi. In contrast, the *Journal of Comparative and International Law* was conceived and carried out by students. In December of 1992, students, led by Glenn DuPree, came to Dean Makdisi, wanting to start a journal in the areas of comparative and international law. He told them that they would have to prove the interest of students in the idea and its viability. The students took up the challenge, formed an editorial board, raised $8,000 in funds from the community, and published the first issue in the fall of 1993, all without law school funding or academic credit.[11] Only in the fall of 1994 did the law school begin to fund the *Journal* and did participating students begin to receive academic credit.

If the idea for the Bratislava Program originated with the dean, and the *Journal of Comparative and International Law* originated with students, the idea for a Comparative and International Law Center originated with the faculty. Professor David Clark, aided by Professor Rex Zedalis, saw that a critical mass of activity in the area was developing and wanted to create an organization that would develop and coordinate this activity. In the spring of 1993, the Comparative and International Law Center was created to promote and organize symposia in this field, course offerings, visiting faculty and guest speakers, the Summer Institute in Law in Bratislava and the *Journal of Comparative and International Law.*

The final component created in this area was a Certificate in Comparative and International Law. As in the other certificate programs, students who completed designated requirements were recognized as having acquired certain knowledge and were awarded the certificate at graduation. By the end of the deanships of John Makdisi and Tom Arnold, the Comparative and International Law Center served as an umbrella entity which drew together the Summer Institute in Bratislava, and the Comparative and International Law Certificate into a cohesive program.

LEGAL CLINIC

On another front, pressure had been building since the mid-1980s for the law school to have an in-house legal clinic. It had been discussed by students, faculty and attorneys.[12] Members of the 1990

The first students and staff at the Legal Clinic. Left to right: David Gregan ('93), student; Professor Winona Tanaka, director; Carrie Sue Van Nostren Genisio ('93), student; Sharon Edington, administrative secretary; and, Dan Baldwin ('93), student. *Courtesy Winona Tanaka.*

graduating class had made a $10,000 gift toward this end at the Hooding ceremony. This pressure found release in two directions. First, a strong sense of social responsibility by Dean Makdisi, Professor Jim Thomas, and attorney Maynard Ungerman, along with others, helped found the Neighbor-For-Neighbor Legal Clinic. Soon after Makdisi arrived, Jim Thomas told him about the $10,000 student gift and put him in touch with Ungerman and Dan Allen, Director of Neighbor-For-Neighbor, a charitable organization providing assistance in a number of areas for Tulsa's low-income population. Makdisi toured the facility, observed other clinics operating within the organization and immediately realized the potential of a pro bono legal clinic.[13] With $20,000 in seed money from TU and the Church of

the Resurrection, a local Catholic church, a pro bono legal clinic, staffed by volunteer attorneys, volunteer students, along with a full-time director, was started in January, 1992.[14]

Second, the hiring committee that had interviewed John Makdisi impressed upon him the growing sentiment toward starting a legal clinic at the law school, and he came with such a mandate.[15] Soon after arriving, he asked Professor Winona Tanaka, who had a background in helping set up judiciary programs while in practice, to write a grant proposal for an in-house legal clinic to the U.S. Department of Education. In May, 1992, the law school received a three-year, $300,000 grant, requiring matching funds from TU, which the University met through using in-kind funds such as salary, fringe

benefits and space and furniture rental. The clinic started in the summer of 1992, with Winona Tanaka as director, Richard (Rick) Howard as clinical instructor, and three students.[16] It was housed in a small university-owned bungalow close to the school at 825 S. Evanston Avenue, and furnished with furniture and equipment donated by local law firms. Within a year, it moved to a larger location, formerly medical offices, at the corner of Fourth Street and Harvard Avenue. At the beginning, the case load consisted of landlord-tenant, social security, consumer fraud, and other areas that would benefit its clientele, the low-income population of Tulsa.

Professor Tanaka served as director from 1992 until 1997. A number of attorneys served as clinical instructors in the early years.

A bungalow on Evanston Avenue served as the first home of the Legal Clinic during 1992 and 1993. *Courtesy Winona Tanaka.*

Rick Howard was followed by Brent Rowland, Sherry Taylor and Suzanne Levitt. The Clinic operated on Department of Education (DOE) ("soft") money for its first three years. At the end of that time, the law school assumed the funding and created necessary faculty lines. The nature of the clinic program evolved over the first half of the 1990s. In 1993, Professor Tanaka had contact with the Tulsa Area Agency on Aging and, through that contact, applied for and obtained the Older Americans Law Project grant. Thus, in 1993-94, there were two programs: 1) the Civil Clinic, continuing the work theretofore being done; and 2) the Older Americans Law Project, focusing on matters such as will drafting and elder abuse. Morris Bernstein was hired in the summer of 1993 as a clinical instructor to operate the Older Americans Law Project. As the DOE grant began to phase out,

so did the general civil caseload of the Civil Clinic. The Older Americans Law Project began to make Clinic personnel aware of the health needs of the elderly, an area of interest to both Sherry Taylor and Suzanne Levitt. During 1995 and 1996 the Legal Clinic would evolve to encompass two areas: 1) the Health Law Project, handling such issues as Social Security disability, guardianships, AIDS and black lung disease; and 2) the Older Americans Law Project, dealing with a variety of the needs of the elderly, such as will drafting, elder abuse, Veterans Administration benefits and landlord-tenant issues. This configuration would remain intact for some time.

ACADEMIC PROGRAM

At the heart of the discussion over the desirability of an in-house legal clinic at the school had been the nature of the time-honored program for teaching lawyering

A building which earlier housed medical offices served as the second home of the Legal Clinic from 1993 to 2003. *Courtesy The University of Tulsa College of Law archives.*

skills to students at TU—the legal internship program. The two programs had contrasting characteristics. The legal "internship" program had, in reality, always been an externship program, placing students outside the law school and in the offices of attorneys and various agencies. Thus, the education had been performed by those outside the law school, not by internal personnel. The setting in which students operated had been, of necessity, work driven, not education driven; therefore, education of students had to compete with needs of the employer and clientele, rather than be coordinated with it. The degree of supervision had been looser and varied, depending on the capabilities and interest of the employer.

The legal internship program was inherently less expensive for the school. Each clinical instructor in the in-house clinic typically supervised no more than seven students; whereas, the faculty supervisor in the legal internship program traditionally supervised many times that number.

A student in the in-house clinic received academic credit, but no monetary compensation; whereas, students in the legal internship program, up to that time, received both academic credit and compensation from employers. Because this double benefit violated American Bar Association accreditation rules, the law school had long relied on an ABA waiver of the ban in order to maintain the program. This swirl of differences had been debated for years by the faculty.

For a short time both programs continued as described. But the 1993 ABA inspection ultimately brought

change to the legal internship program. The program was criticized on a number of bases.[17] In response, the faculty approved a number of significant changes to the legal internship program intended to eliminate the specific deficiencies listed and strengthen the program generally. One of the changes was to no longer allow a student to receive both academic credit and compensation for participation in the program. With these changes, the legal internship program came in line with its companion, the judicial internship program. From the middle 1990s on, the in-house legal clinic, the legal internship program, the judicial internship program, along with various simulation courses within the law school, provided lawyering skills for TU students.

The groundwork was laid in the early 1990s for expansion of the American Indian law program. In the previous decade, the direction of the program had turned from scholarship to instruction. At the turn of the 1990s, Gloria Valencia-Weber had organized the American Indian Law Certificate Program. The 1991 College of Law Strategic Plan called for an active search for minority and women faculty members, particularly for the American Indian law program. When Judith Royster joined the faculty in 1992, she took over the program, the name of which was changed to the Native American Law Certificate Program. Professor Royster brought an interest in combining the fields of Native American law with natural resources and environmental law. The stage had been set for important developments in the Native American Law Program during the deanship of Martin Belsky.

The Alternative Dispute Resolution (ADR) Program was formalized during the first half of the 1990s. In the previous decade Professor Martin Frey had introduced the concept of ADR into the curriculum, although courses were taught by adjunct professors. Beginning in the 1990s, Professor Frey began to teach in the area and was joined by Professor Vicki Limas. A core curriculum was created: introduction to alternative methods of dispute resolution; interviewing, counseling, and negotiation; mediation; and arbitration. All of this activity culminated in the creation of a Center on Dispute Resolution in January, 1994, to coordinate all activities in the area.[18] By the end of 1994, an ADR Certificate had been recognized by the faculty. Students who took designated courses, wrote a scholarly article in the area, and participated in an ADR competition and an ADR practicum would be awarded the Certificate at graduation.

JOHN W. HAGER DISTINGUISHED LECTURESHIP

This period saw the passing of an era with the death of John Hager in 1991. There was an outpouring of sentiment by alumni to do something to honor the memory of Professor Hager. Dean Makdisi channeled this feeling into two specific actions. First, an oil portrait of Professor Hager was commissioned of Glenn Godsey, professor of art, which hangs in the law school student lounge ("the Pit"), along with a portrait of John Rogers. Second, the John W. Hager Distinguished Lectureship was established. Dean Makdisi realized that this was the right purpose for which to re-energize and re-organize the alumni and the Law Alumni Association. A number of alumni played an important role in this effort, including W. Thomas Coffman, who was Association president during 1992-94; Kenneth Brune, who was president during 1994-95; and, Nancy Gourley, who was president during 1995-96. The fund-raising effort to establish the Lectureship was very successful. Professor Hager's family and the law school established two criteria for the Lectureship: 1) the speaker should be a person of national prominence; and 2) lectures should emphasize the twin themes of law and justice. The first lecture was held in March, 1996, with Richard A. Posner, chief judge, United States Court of Appeals for the Seventh Circuit, as the speaker.

LIBRARY

Over the years, providing adequate resources for the law library was one of the most difficult challenges for any dean. This proved to be the case with Dean Makdisi. Among the assurances he received at the outset of his administration from Provost Gilpin was this one: "Enhancement

Judge Richard A. Posner, chief judge, United States Court of Appeals for the Seventh Circuit, was the first speaker in the John W. Hager Distinguished Lectureship series. He is seen here with Professor Hager's daughter, E. Elizabeth Hager, beside an unfinished oil portrait of Professor Hager. This portrait now hangs in John Rogers Hall. *Courtesy The University of Tulsa College of Law archives.*

of the University library is a goal of the strategic plan, and the Law Library will receive its appropriate share of new Library allocations in the University."[19] Some of the provost's assurances to the new dean were specific; this one ("appropriate share") was not. Dean Makdisi would achieve some success in obtaining an appropriate share for the library, but would also face the realization that University funds alone would never provide an adequate financial base for the library.[20] However, progress was made. The amount spent on library acquisitions increased from $330,221 in fiscal year 1991 to $513,137 in fiscal year 1995.[21] The largest increases came in fiscal years 1994 and 1995, in response to findings and conclusions made during the 1993 ABA inspection.[22] As a result, holdings, particularly in the specialized areas of energy and environmental law, comparative and international law, and Native American law, were improved.

One important change occurred in the area of control over the library's budget. The law library had historically been a part of the University Libraries system for budget purposes. Although budget recommendations would originate in the law library, final budget authority rested with the director of University libraries. Dean Makdisi engineered a change in this structure in August, 1992, whereby the law library became autonomous of the University library system and became a part of the law school. Although there would continue to be close cooperation between the law library and the University library system, control now rested in the dean of the law school.

Dean Makdisi and his wife, June Mary, personally enhanced the holdings of the library through the purchase and donation of the George Lee Haskins Collection in 1993. This collection of 829 books, many of them rare legal and historical works, were a valuable support to many users, particularly the two Chapman Distinguished Professors, Bernard Schwartz and Paul Finkelman.

PHYSICAL PLANT

Aside from collection enhancement, space was the other critical need that the law library had at the beginning of the 1990s. The East Wing had provided breathing room for a few years. The library expanded into the lower floor of that two-level structure and hoped to someday have the upper floor as well when a planned additional floor was added. The law school occupied the upper floor for other purposes and an additional floor was never added. Thus, by 1990, the library was once again squeezed for space.

Groundwork was laid in the first half of the 1990s for an addition to the library, but it would take another dean to complete the project in the last half of the decade. As has been mentioned, the President Donaldson/Dean Makdisi eras were taken up with strategic planning. The University Strategic Plan called for each college to have a plan. The updated College of Law Strategic Plan of 1992, in the law library section, added this language: ". . . and build a new addition to the law school." This goal was refined in the 1993 Plan to state: "Obtain administration and trustee approval for planning and funding to build an addition to the law building to accommodate changes in the law

library and other needs of the law program." The dean and faculty set about to have this goal included in the University's Strategic Plan, which would allow inclusion of the project in the University's upcoming "New Century Campaign", to be launched in connection with the University's centennial celebration in 1994. This effort was successful and the project was included in the University's Plan and Campaign.[23] The law school obtained preliminary plans and cost estimates from Rafael Peruyera, an architectural consultant for the University.

The remainder of the decade would be spent planning and raising funds for this project, which would culminate in the Mabee Legal Information Center. The first funds were raised by Acting Dean Arnold and Library Director Ducey. They obtained a $1 million grant from the Sarkeys Foundation.[24] As of June, 1995, the estimated cost of the expansion was $5,500,000,[25] a figure that would ultimately prove to be much too low. The first public description of the addition was given by Acting Dean Arnold to alumni at the first annual Chilifest, held February 16, 1995. Preliminary sketches were shown which indicated that, unlike the existing library, the addition would be above ground and benefit from existing light.[26]

There was little actual change in the physical plant during the first half of the 1990s. However, just as Dean Walwer had looked to the East Wing to solve space needs a decade earlier, so did Dean Makdisi during this period. He reconfigured the space to add offices for faculty, the development director, and the *Journal of Comparative and International Law*. In addition, he created two additional classrooms.

These actions were only palliative, however. The school needed more than reconfiguration of existing space; it needed additional space. The site team conducting the ABA inspection in 1993 came to this conclusion: "The faculty and administration feel strongly that the mission of the law school is hampered by its current space constraints. New office space is at a premium…, thus complicating plans to add new faculty and staff…, and the library is desperately short of space for both current needs and future growth."

Dean Makdisi and the faculty were successful in having a law school goal of an addition to John Rogers Hall placed in the University's strategic plan and fundraising campaign. And, Acting Dean Arnold and Library Director Ducey were successful in obtaining a $1 million grant from the Sarkeys Foundation to begin the fundraising effort. It would fall to the next dean, Martin Belsky, along with many others, to complete the fundraising and turn this dream into a reality.

FINANCES

John Makdisi had ambitious goals for attracting and retaining high quality students and faculty and for enriching existing programs and beginning new ones. How were these ambitious plans to be financed? Two methods were used—University money through tuition and outside money through fundraising. Law school tuition increased from $350/credit hour in 1991 to $450/credit hour in 1995, a twenty-eight percent increase. Much more income was being generated by the school during Makdisi's tenure as dean. The question was how much of this money could the law school keep

and how much must be turned over to the University in the form of "overhead"? This is a perennial question which all law schools and universities face. Law schools want to retain as many tuition dollars as possible, while universities believe it appropriate to charge a reasonable amount for all the services provided, such as building use, utilities, personnel costs, etc. But, what is "reasonable"? Debate over this issue between Dean Makdisi and the University proved to be the most controversial aspect of his deanship, as will be discussed later.

The other method of obtaining revenue—raising outside dollars from alumni and friends of the school—proved to be one of Dean Makdisi's successes. The combination of organizational structure, people and ideas that he brought to this task resulted in the most successful fundraising campaigns up to that time. He started out by securing the right of the school to have its own development director engage in fundraising efforts for the school,[27] and with the school having the right to retain all money raised.[28] The dean hired Jane Kolesnik, who proved to be very popular with alumni and an effective development director. He later hired Leslie Weeks as director of alumni relations and special projects. This was also a new position and one which would stay at the law school and be held later by Jane Kolesnik, although the development director's position would eventually return to the University's development office.

With the organizational structure and the staff in place, Makdisi utilized innovative ideas to raise money for program enhancement purposes. In his first year he channeled alumni desire to honor

the memory of John Hager into an effort to create the John W. Hager Distinguished Lectureship. The 1991-92 fund drive was dedicated to this effort. W. Thomas Coffman ('66), the Alumni Association president and Professor John F. Hicks were co-chairs of an effort that ultimately involved 86 alumni and friends of the school soliciting gifts from law firms, alumni classes and others. Forty-seven law firms participated in the effort, which went over its $100,000 goal, with the help of a $10,000 challenge donation by the Leta McFarlin Chapman Memorial Trust.[29]

The 1992-93 fund drive was focused on a law-school-course-sponsorship program. Former Dean Joe Morris served as honorary chair, and co-chairs Ben P. Abney ('68) and Stuart Price ('82), presided over a drive that once again resulted in raising over $100,000 from over 66 law firms and corporations, with many firms reporting 100% participation by firm alumni.[30]

The 1993-94 fund drive was headed by Don Marlar ('69) and Jean Coulter ('81). They and their volunteers secured participation by over 75 law firms and corporations. Dean Makdisi had energized the alumni to aid the programs of the law school in innovative and professional ways.

ALUMNI

Alumni were active during John Makdisi's deanship in ways apart from fundraising. The Law Alumni Association was reinvigorated and reconstituted under the direction of then - President Tom Coffman('66) and others.[31] The Association re-incorporated and adopted new by-laws. Standing committees were created that brought involvement

by many alumni. Alumni news
was distributed by an *Alumni
Newsletter* and, later, in the student
newspaper, the *Baculus*. In addition
to activities that had been held
before, such as the alumni lunch
at the Oklahoma Bar Association
meeting and the annual spring
dinner dance, new activities were
started. The Association sponsored
tailgate parties before football games
and became involved in the annual
Chilifests, the first one of which was
held in February, 1995, due to the
inspiration and hard work of one
alumnus, Joe Bohannon.

CONTROVERSY

Dean Makdisi's record of
accomplishments was accompanied
by a variety of controversies
throughout his deanship. During
his very first semester as dean, a
controversy arose between the law

school and the University over the
law faculty's actions concerning the
job recruiting program of the career
services office. In October, 1991,
the faculty voted to ban the military,
CIA and FBI from interviewing
students for jobs within John Rogers
Hall because of their employment
practices which discriminate
on the basis of one's "sexual
preferences."[32] The law school had
a non-discrimination policy and a
fair employment practices statement
which listed specific categories
where discrimination would not be
tolerated; one category was "sexual
orientation."[33] This action made
headlines in the *Baculus*.[34]

Most of the comments by
students were critical of the faculty's
action, some on the merits, some
on the lack of student input into
the decision, but most based on
concern over perceived diminished

employment opportunities. Dean
Makdisi was quick to point out
that the ban applied only within
the building and did not prohibit
recruiting activities elsewhere. The
faculty and students held a later
debate. The Student Bar Association
passed a resolution protesting the
action and forwarded it to President
Donaldson. Donaldson quickly
barred implementation of the
faculty action because the language
in the law school documents was
incompatible with the language in
the University's Non-Discrimination
Policy.[35] For the balance of the fall
and into the winter the law school
and the University worked to
negotiate a compromise. Agreement
was finally reached in the spring
of 1992: the law school would be
allowed, under agreed conditions,
to publish and enforce standards on
non-discrimination that included

the category of "sexual orientation," but, "by law" the military and government agencies would be exempt from some of the non-discrimination policy.[36]

The most serious controversy during this period involved Dean Makdisi's struggle with the University over the issue of the University's annual budget for the law school. Makdisi had obtained financial assurances from the University at the outset of his administration that enabled him to realize many of the goals he had set.[37] Yet, during his deanship, he became so convinced that the University was not providing appropriate resources for the school that he ultimately resigned in protest, the only dean as of this writing ever to take that action.

Two budgetary issues formed a backdrop for this controversy: 1) the appropriate share of tuition and other income generated by the law school it would be appropriate for the University to retain as "overhead," a topic mentioned earlier; and 2) the procedures to be used in determining the annual school budget. On the first issue, there was, at the time, an unwritten rule in the law school world that a 25% retention as overhead served as the boundary between what was acceptable and unacceptable.[38] By the time of John Makdisi's deanship, the overhead was exceeding 30%.[39] Dean Makdisi calculated the overhead to be even higher (41% in FY 1993 and 38% in FY 1994.)[40] He concluded that the magnitude of

An assembly of past and present deans gathered together in 1992 for a meeting of the Tulsa Title and Probate Lawyers Association, where Professor John F. Hicks gave a talk on the history of the law school. Left to right: Bruce Peterson (1962-69), Joseph W. Morris (1972-74), Frank K. Walwer (1980-91), and John Makdisi (1991-94). *Courtesy The University of Tulsa College of Law archives.*

M. Thomas Arnold served as acting dean during 1994 and 1995. *Courtesy The University of Tulsa College of Law archives.*

following recommendations by the dean. It was centralized in the hands of the provost and president and highly secretive. In 1992, Provost Gilpin changed this system and introduced "Responsibility Center Budgeting" and created a "Responsibility Center Management Council" (RCMC.)[42] The concept underlying this new system was to focus responsibility and accountability on colleges, not the central administration, in the budgeting process. Budgets would be constructed from needs expressed by each dean and worked out in a group setting, which would bring transparency to the process.[43] The process set up a type of "formula" to determine the distribution of money across the campus. Dean Makdisi placed faith in this system, believing it would result in a more appropriate monetary share coming to the law school. By his third year, however, he had concluded that the RCMC would not be given the power to implement the budgets it devised and that the underfunding he saw as the core problem at the school would continue. Therefore, he resigned on March 14, 1994 "in protest of the budgetary policies of this University."[44] Makdisi would later become dean of two other law schools — Loyola University, New Orleans, and St. Thomas University in Miami, Florida.

ACTING DEANSHIP OF M. THOMAS ARNOLD

Tom Arnold, a long-time member of the faculty, was appointed acting dean upon Makdisi's resignation and served from June, 1994, until Martin Belsky arrived in June, 1995, to assume the duties as dean of the law school. Arnold held his

the resulting underfunding exceeded $1 million.[41]

He had hoped that a new procedure by which the school budget was determined each year would make a difference. Prior to 1992, the annual budget for the law school had been determined by the central University administration, undergraduate degree from Ohio University and his law degree from the University of Michigan. Before coming to Tulsa, he had served as professor at Capital University Law School in Ohio. He had already served as associate dean twice, once under Dean Walwer and once under Dean Makdisi. He would later again serve as associate dean under Dean Belsky.

His acting deanship accrued during a tough economic year for the University. Declining enrollments and revenues caused a $2 million shortfall in the total University budget and forced budget cuts around the University.[45] There were staff cuts throughout the University[46] and the new provost, Lewis Duncan, announced that there would be no faculty or staff pay raises the following year.[47] Despite this generally gloomy fiscal picture, Acting Dean Arnold was able to

improve the budget situation in some areas at the law school. There were some enhancements to existing programs, brought about by the University's response to the concerns of the American Bar Association arising out of the 1993 inspection, and areas of improvement, such as library staff and faculty academic needs.[48] At the end of the year, through a combination of limited enhancements and tight spending controls, Arnold was able to present a balanced law school budget to incoming Dean Belsky.[49]

Despite the tight fiscal circumstances of the University and the law school, there were a number of positive developments during the acting deanship of Tom Arnold. Foremost was "The Warren Court: A 25 Year Retrospective," a conference organized by Professor Bernard Schwartz and presented by the law school October 10-13,

1994. It brought together scholars, judges, writers and others from across the country and abroad to review the accomplishments of the United States Supreme Court under Chief Justice Earl Warren and the impact that the Chief Justice and the court had on the nation. Also, as mentioned earlier, Acting Dean Arnold and Library Director Ducey secured an important $1 million gift from the Sarkeys Foundation to begin the fundraising campaign for an addition to the law library. Finally, one important personnel change occurred. Mary Birmingham ('77), assistant dean for career services, resigned and was replaced by an equally capable individual, Vicki Jordan ('92).

In June, 1995, Martin H. Belsky assumed the deanship of the law school and ushered in a period of dynamic development.

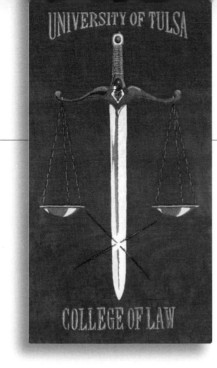

Chapter VI

BECOMING A "LEGAL EDUCATION CENTER"

(1995-2003)

INTRODUCTORY NOTE: This chapter was written in 2003 and 2004, and all information and data are presented from that time perspective.

INTRODUCTION

B
y the beginning of the twenty-first century, eighty years after its founding and eight years into the deanship of Martin Belsky, the College of Law had a profile far removed from that of its predecessor, the old Tulsa Law School. It had evolved into a mature institution of approximately 575 students, eighty percent of whom were attending full-time, forty-three percent of whom were women and seventeen percent of whom were minority. These students were being taught by thirty-six full-time faculty and more than twenty-five adjunct faculty, all backed up by six associate and assistant deans, eighteen program directors and forty-seven staff members. There were both full-time and part-time students but there was no longer a "day" division or "evening" division.

In eight decades the curriculum had expanded from a handful of required courses to over one hundred required and elective courses. In the first year, traditional required courses such as contracts, property and torts had been compacted somewhat to make room for more research, analysis and writing experiences, as well as more elective choices that would allow students to begin a "specialization" earlier and which would allow them more small-class experiences with greater individual attention. Upper class courses emphasized more lawyering skills and specialization opportunities from an institute and four centers, eight certificate programs, five study-abroad programs, and two masters programs for law graduates. An array of conferences, symposiums, lectures, colloquies, and scholars / practitioners / judges / alumni in residence created an environment which enriched the lives of students, faculty and others at the school. In addition, student life was enriched by scores of student organizations in which students could participate.

The institution had developed a "legal information center" where students, faculty and others had available for use a traditional library of over 280,000 books, other materials and traditional services, as well as electronic materials, state-of-the-art electronic equipment and services, all backed up by a number

Martin H. Belsky, eleventh dean, 1995-2004. *Courtesy The University of Tulsa College of Law archives.*

of professional librarians and staff. The institution had developed professional admissions and career counseling offices providing services for applicants, students and graduates through local, regional and nation-wide activities conducted by a number of J.D. professionals and staff using state-of-the-art computer equipment and programs. The physical plant had expanded to four units: John Rogers Hall, the East Wing, the Mabee Legal Information Center, and, in a separate building, the Boesche Legal Clinic. Tuition had increased to over $20,000 per year per full-time student, partially off-set by over $1.5 million awarded in merit-and-need-based scholarships. The end product of all this investment -- alumni -- practiced in all fifty states and abroad, and were members of an active alumni organization highly organized and functioning independently of the school, but in coordination and support of it.

In truth, the institution had evolved beyond a single "law school" of years past into a "legal education center," a complex entity providing a variety of legal services to various constituencies in both traditional and new ways. Such a "center" was beginning to be formed during the deanship of John Makdisi; it was realized during the deanship of Martin Belsky. This final chapter tells the story of how this transformation occurred.

Martin H. Belsky arrived as dean in the summer of 1995. He came from Albany Law School, having served as dean there from 1986 to 1991. Belsky had earned his bachelor's degree from Temple University and his law degree from Columbia University. His background showed a variety

of experiences in addition to legal education. He had served as an assistant district attorney in Philadelphia, as counsel to several committees in the U.S. House of Representations, and as assistant administrator of the National Oceanic and Atmospheric Administration. He was on the faculty of the University of Florida College of Law before moving to Albany Law School as dean. Belsky came with a number of firsts. He was the first dean at Tulsa with prior decanal experience. He joined the faculty along with his wife, Kathleen Waits. Although not the first husband and wife team on the faculty, Christen (Chris) and Marianne Blair having had that distinction, they were the first dean and wife combination. He was the first Jew to serve as dean, although there had been Jewish faculty members at the school ever since Phil Landa taught in the 1940s.

What Dean Belsky did have in common with his predecessors was a distinguished background. Educated at Columbia Law School, he had interest and experience in criminal law, constitutional law, international law and environmental law.[2] Most important, he came with an "agenda of change," believing that Tulsa had potential for improvement and was ready to take the steps necessary to do so.[3] He and the law school were about to continue the changes begun under John Makdisi, and, in the process, create a "legal education center."

STUDENTS

The size of the student body between 1995 and 2003 fluctuated from a high of 615 in 1999 to a low of 526 in 2000, reflecting changing demographics and other

factors. Applications decreased in the last half of the 1990s, but later rose again. Increasing or decreasing application rates necessarily affected the question of acceptance rates and presented hard choices. The dean and admissions committee were faced with the question of how to approach the admissions process. Increasing the acceptance rate when applications were down could dilute the academic profile of the entering class. Not doing so might mean a smaller entering class, which would have negative financial repercussions in a private school which was heavily tuition-dependent, as was Tulsa.[4] It was a delicate balance which the dean and admissions committee had to strike. The average GPA of entering students rose slightly between 1995 and 2003, while the average LSAT score declined somewhat during the same period.

The dean and faculty took a number of innovative steps to protect and improve this academic profile and, more fundamentally, to improve the quality and effectiveness of the academic program at the school. First, the school's investment in recruiting and admissions personnel was increased. After years of very effective service, Velda Staves, the admissions director, took semi-retirement, but remained a consultant to the admissions program for several years, totally retiring in 2003. In early 2000, George Justice became the assistant dean of admissions and financial aid. For the first time, he was joined in late 2000 by a second professional staff member, Karen Bouteller ('94), who was later replaced by April Fox ('93). Thus, as of 2003, the office had two J.D. professionals, supported by the senior staff member at the school,

Students enjoying the Student Lounge [the "Pit"] of John Rogers Hall.
Courtesy Mabee Legal Information Center.

Rosemarie Spaulding. They engaged in recruiting and admissions activity on a state, regional and national level.

Secondly, the law school increased its scholarship awards dramatically. Until the late 1990s, only merit-based scholarships were awarded. In 1997, need-based scholarships began to be awarded for the first time, opening up added possibilities for qualified students with financial needs to realistically consider private legal education at Tulsa. Considering both need-based and merit-based scholarship awards, the level of total awards grew from under $500,000 to over $1,500,000 by 2003.

Third, the school started a spring semester entering class in 1998. This was the first time since the school left the trimester system in 1973 that

students had the flexibility of fall or spring matriculation.

Fourth, the school instituted an Academic Support Program in the summer of 1998. At the outset it was reminiscent of the Summer-Admission-by-Performance Program in the late 1970s during Dean Read's administration. It started the same: students with marginal academic profiles, but with other indicators of ability to successfully complete law school, were admitted to a summer contracts course. There, the similarity ended. The new Program was more thorough. Students admitted were guaranteed admission with the entering fall class. They were taught in a small-class atmosphere with intensive instruction by a professor and student assistants. In the fall semester they received continuing academic assistance and took a lighter-than-normal course load. In the spring semester, the program was opened up to any first-year student whose GPA fell below a certain level. This program combined the selection of students with non-traditional indicators of promise with continuing help to a larger pool of students. Both students and the law school benefited. The program was headed by Winona Tanaka from its inception until 2003, when Catherine Cullem was named director, following Tanaka's appointment as vice-provost of the University.

Finally, the admissions office, along with the career counseling office, was handsomely renovated in 2001 to create a professional,

efficient and welcoming space, as will be discussed later in the chapter.

During Dean Belsky's administration through 2003, full-time student enrollment, as a percentage of total enrollment, hovered in the 75-80% range. This permanent prevalence of full-time over part-time students led the faculty in 1997 to make a historic change in the "day division/evening division" concept of education at the law school, as will be detailed later. By 2003, the number of women at the school rose to over 40% of the total enrollment. The minority population in the school rose from about 12% in the mid-1990s to close to 20% by 2003. One of the reasons cited for this increase was the availability of need-based scholarships since 1997, in addition to merit-based scholarships.[5]

In 1997, Dean Belsky shared with the faculty ideas that had been presented at a deans' meeting about the nature of the law student of that time, the so-called "Generation X Student."[6] This student, among other characteristics, (1) demanded personal attention, (2) wanted small classes, (3) liked special programs, (4) liked clinics, and (5) liked technology. Between 1997 and 2003, the law school responded to this contemporary fact of life in a number of ways:[7] (1) the Dean adopted a philosophy of considering students as "alumni in waiting"[8]; (2) Dean Belsky would meet with all entering students in a variety of small-group settings; and, (3) the academic program was changed to include some small-class sections, a year-long research and writing program, special programs, clinics and technology throughout the school. On the University level, in the fall of 2000, the University opened the newly-built University Square Apartments for occupancy by law students. This $7.3 million complex was located at Fourth Place and Delaware Avenue, within walking distance of the law school.

The number and variety of student organizations continued to increase during the Belsky administration. There continued to be "traditional" organizations such as the Student Bar Association, the *Baculus* newspaper and the legal fraternities. Added to these were organizations based on ethnic identity,[9] religious identity,[10] legal interest,[11] and other identities.[12]

Individual students continued to garner national awards. As examples, in 1998, Donna DeSimone received the Elaine Osborne Jacobson Award for Women in Health Law, sponsored by the Roscoe Pound

Mattie Bolden, left, senior records clerk who, for many years, greeted the public at the counter of the front office and Velda Staves, right, the long-time director of admissions, retired in 2003. They flank TU First Lady Marcy Lawless at their retirement recognition party. *Courtesy The University of Tulsa.*

Foundation and Elizabeth Mosley Guse received the 1998 Phi Delta Phi International Graduate of the Year Award.

The nature of the office of the associate dean of students was altered in 1996 when Dana Lamb left the office. She and a number of her predecessors had been non-faculty full-time administrators. Dean Belsky moved to another model, the faculty/administrator, and appointed

Professor Dennis Bires to occupy the position, which he held for three years before returning to full-time teaching and was replaced by Professor Vicki J. Limas, who had previously been associate dean of students.

STAFF

In the front office, Clara Flinn, the long-time school registrar, retired in December, 1997. Virginia

Personnel in the admissions and career services offices. Left to right: Terry Saunders, Jennifer Flexner, April Fox ('93), Vicki Jordan ('92), George Justice, Velda Staves, Rosemarie Spaulding.
Courtesy Ervin Photography.

Personnel providing assistance to the faculty and to various programs conducted by the College of Law. Top to bottom and left to right: Sarah Koepp, Randy Lewin, Sharon Schooley, Jane Kolesnik, Larry Curtis, Todd Gourd, Sharon Miller, Wendy Buss, Cyndee Jones, Kathryn Burgy, Tish Eaves, Sandy Plaster, Terry Kerr. Personnel not pictured: Shane Blackstock, Rita Langford, and Sue Lorenz. *Courtesy Ervin Photography.*

Personnel in the offices of the dean, the associate dean for academic affairs and the associate dean for student affairs. Front row: M. Thomas Arnold, Martin H. Belsky, and Vicki Limas. Back row: Flo Edwards, Kathy Parsons, Sherry Walkabout, Martha Cordell, Sukran Taner, Virginia Richard. Not pictured: Janet Johnson. *Courtesy Ervin Photography.*

Richard became the coordinator of registration and records. Mattie Bolden, the long-time receptionist and "friendly face" who greeted everyone at the front counter, retired in 2003 and was replaced by Kathy Parsons. As of 2003, other front office personnel included Sherry Walkabout, assistant to the dean; Sukran Taner, assistant to the dean for fiscal affairs; Martha Cordell, assistant to the dean for special projects; Janet Johnson, assistant to

the associate dean of students; and, Flo Edwards, assistant to the associate dean for academic affairs.

Vicki Jordan ('92) joined the law school as assistant dean of career services in the summer of 1995. As with admissions, personnel in career services were enhanced by the addition of Jennifer Flexner, who joined Terry Saunders, a long-time member of the career services staff. Together, these three individuals conducted a complex operation

increasingly dependent on high-tech methods of communication with students, alumni and prospective employers. For example, traditional physical job postings were gradually replaced with e-mail lists. There continued to be a lot of old-fashioned one-on-one contact in individual counseling sessions and job fairs, as well as group contact in weekly seminars sponsored by the office. The renovation of the student services suite which career services shared with admissions, mentioned earlier and discussed in more detail later, enhanced both the efficiency and ambience of the office.

Important changes occurred in the office of computing resources. This office evolved during the Belsky deanship to include a director, a micro-computer specialist and a media specialist. Ben Chapman, the first director and the person responsible for the technical direction of computer resources at the school, resigned in 2003 to take a similar position at Emory Law School and was replaced by Todd Gourd, who was assisted by Larry Curtis and Shane Blackstock.

FACULTY

The faculty were very active during the Belsky deanship. The capstone of this activity was the United States Supreme Court Conferences organized by Bernard Schwartz, Chapman Distinguished Professor of Law. Following up on the inaugural retrospective on the Warren Court, held in the fall of 1994, he organized two succeeding conferences. In the fall of 1996, the law school hosted a three-day national conference on the Burger Court. Nationally respected lawyers, judges, scholars and journalists discussed the legacy of the Burger Court before a national audience. Two years later, in the fall of 1998, the final conference organized by Professor Schwartz, a retrospective on the Rehnquist Court, was held. Tragically, Professor Schwartz, although having planned much of the conference, did not live to see its completion, having died in a traffic accident the preceding December. Once again, nationally prominent lawyers, judges, scholars

In 1999, the law school found a very able replacement to fill the Chapman Chair in Paul Finkelman, a historian, whose breadth of scholarship ranged from slavery to baseball. *Courtesy The University of Tulsa.*

and journalists discussed legal, philosophical and political questions surrounding the Rehnquist Court. At the time of the conference, the *Tulsa World*, in an editorial, gave this view on the contribution of Professor Schwartz:

> Schwartz indeed was a master at keeping the great jurisprudence conversation going. A product of that talent and that ability to attract other great legal minds to his endeavors are the three symposiums he organized to study the U.S. Supreme Court under Chief Justices

Earl Warren, Warren Burger and, most recently, William Rehnquist. Some of the planning for the Rehnquist Seminar, held this week, had to be carried out after his death. But throughout the three day symposium, Schwartz's presence was felt and acknowledged often.[13]

The life and work of Bernard Schwartz was recognized in the United States and abroad in a series of obituaries in over nine newspapers. A memorial service was held in TU's Sharp Chapel on February 23, 1998, at which deans, professors, students and judges acknowledged his many contributions to the law.

The activities of the faculty in 2003 extended not only to scholarly endeavors, but also in many other directions. As examples, Marguerite Chapman, with her interest in health law and ethics, served on numerous boards of health institutions, and Marianne Blair, with her interest in family law, served as advisor and draftsperson to the Oklahoma legislature.[14]

The scholarly work and activity of the faculty garnered awards. In 1998, Stephen (Step) Feldman was notified that he had been awarded a fellowship for university teachers from the National Endowment for the Humanities, which allowed him to complete the research and writing for a book on the history of jurisprudence. This marked the first NEH Fellowship to a TU law professor. Two other professors received Fulbright fellowships. David Clark, a nationally-recognized scholar in comparative law, received the Fulbright Trento Chair in Comparative Law, allowing him to spend the spring, 1999 semester in Trento, Italy. A visiting professor, Karen Kole, a specialist in international tax law, received a Fulbright award to teach and study at Jaiotong University in Shanghai, China in the spring of 2000.

The high quality of the teaching at the law school was recognized at the University level. Between 1980 and 2004, fifteen members of the law school faculty received the University's Outstanding Teacher award, given annually to three individuals selected from the entire University faculty.[15]

The quality of faculty scholarship, teaching and other activity of Tulsa faculty was a two-edged sword, however. It not only brought recognition to the law school, but also made faculty members very attractive to other law schools. A number of schools made offers to individuals "which they could not refuse." Former Dean Makdisi left to assume the deanship at the New Orleans School of Law of Loyola University. Suzanne Levitt accepted the position of executive director of clinical programs at Drake University Law School. David Clark accepted a chaired professorship at Willamette School of Law, as did Step Feldman at the University of Wyoming School of Law. Kimberly Krawiec went to the University of Oregon Law School; Larry Backer went to Dickinson School of Law, Pennsylvania State University; Lakshman Guruswamy went to the University of Colorado School of Law; Lundy Langston went to Nova Southeastern University Law Center; and, Nicholas Rostow took a position with the State of Massachusetts. In addition, Martin Frey retired from the faculty and took emeritus status, but, happily, returned to the school in the fall of 2002 to continue teaching on a limited basis. Finally, and, sadly, in addition to losing Bernard Schwartz to death in 1997, the school also lost Dona K. Broyles from the Legal Research, Analysis and Writing Program in 2002.

Both experienced and new faculty were hired to fill these positions and others. In 1999, Paul Finkelman took the position of Chapman Distinguished Professor of Law after the death of Bernard Schwartz. Also in 1999, Leslie Mansfield came from the University of New Mexico Clinical Program

After a distinguished career in private practice, government and the energy industry, R. Dobie Langenkamp became the third director of the National Energy - Environmental Law and Policy Institute. *Courtesy The University of Tulsa.*

Faculty of the College of Law. First row: Janet Levit, Marguerite Chapman, Catherine Cullem, Lyn Entzeroth, Linda Lacey, Marianne Blair, Valerie Phillips. Second row: Rick Ducey, Marla Mansfield, Kathleen Waits, Martin Belsky, Martin Frey, Leslie Mansfield, Tom Holland, Tamara Piety, Vicki Limas. Third Row: Melissa Tatum, Russell Christopher, Dennis Bires, Judith Royster, Ray Yasser, Charles Adams. Fourth row: Chris Blair, Richard Paschal, Tom Arnold, Bill Rice, Johnny Parker, John Hicks, Rex Zedalis. Faculty not pictured: Gary Allison, Barbara Bucholtz, Paul Finkelman, Russell Hittinger, William Hollingsworth, Marsha Huie, Dobie Langenkamp, Madeleine Plasencia, Lance Stockwell, Winona Tanaka, James Thomas. *Courtesy Ervin Photography.*

to become director of the Legal Clinic, following the departure of Suzanne Levitt. Upon the departure of Lakshman Guruswamy from NELPI, the school turned to an individual who had repeatedly served the law school and NELPI, R. Dobie Langenkamp. In 2001, he rejoined the faculty as visiting professor and acting director of NELPI. One year later he was appointed professor of law and director of NELPI.

An interdisciplinary appointment in the law school was given to Russell Hittinger, professor of religion and holder of the Warren Chair in Catholic Studies at the University. This followed earlier interdisciplinary appointments given to Stephen (Step) Feldman in the Department of Political Science and Lakshman Guruswamy in his involvement with the NELPI Fellows Program. Other individuals who joined the faculty during the Belsky administration include Russell Christopher; Montie Deer, who headed the Indian Law Clinic, which will be discussed later; Marsha Huie; Janet K. Levit, Richard Paschal; Valerie Phillips; Tamara Piety; Madeleine Plasencia; G. William (Bill) Rice; Lance Stockwell; Melissa Tatum; and, Kathleen (Kate) Waits. In addition, legal research, analysis and writing instructors included Evelyn Hutchison, Brian Johnson, Randy Lewin, Sharisse O'Carroll and Sharon Schooley.

A change was made in the faculty status of individuals in the clinical program and the legal research, analysis and writing program, which indicated the growth in importance of these programs to the academic programs of the school. In the Legal Clinic the status of the faculty was changed from "instructor:" to "(tenure track) professor."[16]

Likewise, in the legal reasoning authorities & writing program (RAW Law) , a status change was made from "instructor" to either "(tenure track) professor"[17] or "(contract) professor".[18]

A "first" occurred in the summer of 2003, when Winona Tanaka, clinical associate professor of law, was appointed vice provost by Provost Roger Blais and President Robert Lawless. This was the first University administration academic position to be held by a law school faculty member.

Finally, a number of visitors during the Belsky deanship enriched the life of the law school. Foreign visitors such as Peter Kresak and Leslye Obiera added substance to the growing international flavor of the curriculum. Likewise, summer visitors such as Julien Burger and Cynthia Price Cohen provided the same benefit. Two distinguished visitors— Justice Daniel J. Boudreau ('76) of the Oklahoma Supreme Court and William G. von Glahn—taught during the fall 2004 term. Other visitors, who replaced regular faculty on leave or sabbatical or for other reasons, included Stanley Adelman, Robert Chapman, Stephana Colbert, Lyn Entzeroth, Rashmi Goel, Brian Johnson, Karen Kole, and Charles Mansfield. Entzeroth later joined the full-time faculty.

The law school of an earlier day slipped further into history with the deaths of Ralph Thomas in 1998 and Bruce Peterson in 1999. As recounted in earlier chapters, these two men helped form the fledging downtown law school out of the old independent Tulsa Law School and continued on the faculty into the transformation of the school from a "downtown" law school to a mainstream university institution.

As of 2003, the faculty was an experienced and active group of professors whose service to the law school spanned forty years and five decades. They joined the faculty in the following decades:

1960s: James C. Thomas, John F. Hicks

1970s: Charles W. Adams, Gary D. Allison, Martin A. Frey, Tom L. Holland, William G. Hollingsworth, Ray Yasser

1980s: M. Thomas Arnold, Dennis E. Bires, Christen R. Blair, D. Marianne. Blair, Marguerite A. Chapman, Catherine M. Cullem, Richard E. Ducey, Linda J. Lacey, Vicki J. Limas, Marla E. Mansfield, Johnny C. Parker, Winona M. Tanaka, Rex J. Zedalis

1990s: Martin H. Belsky, Barbara K. Bucholtz, Paul Finkelman, Russell Hittinger, Janet K. Levit, Leslie Mansfield, Richard Paschal, Madeleine Plasencia, G. William Rice, Judith V. Royster, Lance Stockwell, Melissa L. Tatum, Kathleen Waits

2000s: Russell Christopher, Lyn Entzeroth, Marsha C. Huie, R. Dobie Langenkamp, Valerie Phillips, Tamara R. Piety.

In addition, there were two emeriti professors: Kent Frizzell and Orley R. Lilly, Jr. (in addition to Martin Frey, who continued to teach.)

ACADEMIC ACTIVITIES
Program Changes

Dean Belsky's "agenda of change" resulted in important alterations in various academic programs at the school. These alterations were made for both academic and functional reasons by the dean and faculty. The first alteration related to the "day division/evening division" concept. Having started as a law school for students who were working full-time and, thus, could attend classes only in the evening, Tulsa Law School began as an "evening division" school for "part-time" students. When the school started offering classes during the day to students who could attend "full-time," the concept that "day division" classes were for "full-time" students and "evening division" classes were for "part-time" students took hold. The bundling of the concepts that "day" classes were for "full-time" students, while "evening" classes were for "part-time" students created a "Berlin Wall" between the two divisions, breachable only by administrative variance. This meant that a complete curriculum had to be offered in each division. This responsibility became increasingly difficult and inefficient as the percentage of full-time students grew and reached a consistent super-majority at the school.

The dean and faculty finally unbundled these concepts in 1997, giving students much more flexibility in course selection and reducing the pressure on the school to offer a dual curriculum. The school changed from a "full-time division/part-time division" to a "full-time program/part-time program". This alteration allowed both full-time and part-time students to take courses being offered in the day or evening, as it met their curriculum and life needs. There were no longer two "divisions" at the school, only two categories of student: "full-time" and "part-time," depending on the number of credit hours being taken. The associate dean for academic affairs worked with each part-time student to fashion an appropriate schedule. Part-time students were allowed up to five years in which to complete their degree, which gave them added flexibility.

Dean Belsky's vision was to give first-year students an early start on pursuing one of the "specialization" certificates the school was creating; give them a small-class experience in core courses; and, give them more training in legal research, analysis and writing. This necessitated altering the traditional first year curriculum. That curriculum was changed in 1997 by (1) reducing contracts and property courses from six to four credit hours each and making each of them a one semester course, and (2) eliminating civil procedure II as a required course. These changes allowed (1) the constitutional law course to be moved into the first year; (2) students to take certain electives in the spring semester; (3) increase in the credit assigned to the legal reasoning, authorities & writing course (RAW Law); and, (4) multiple small sections to be offered in civil procedure, constitutional law and RAW Law.

Coordinated with these alterations was a revamping of the RAW Law Program. Professors Catherine Cullem and Vicki Limas, along with the legal writing full-time faculty, created a more comprehensive curriculum taught in small sections with a high degree of personal interaction and increased the number of research and writing assignments. In 2003, the full-time legal writing faculty included Barbara Bucholtz, Catherine Cullem, Richard Paschal and Lance Stockwell.

The reduction in credit of core courses such as torts, contracts and property and the removal of courses such as civil procedure II and constitutional law II from the required curriculum provoked continuing discussion among faculty, students and alumni. The discussion of inclusion and credit-size of courses in the required curriculum, going on since evidence was first eliminated from the required curriculum in 1969, heated up again due to the above changes and erratic performance by graduates on Oklahoma bar examinations.[19] In response to these concerns, in 2003, civil procedure II and evidence were once again made required courses.

In 2001, the faculty altered the grade scale for examination courses for the first time in many years and adopted a new mandatory first-year grading curve and suggested upper-class grading curve. The grade scale was more finely tuned, adding "plus" and "minus" to many grades beyond the traditional "C+." These changes came amid fears that grade inflation was eroding the academic meaning of the grading system and the faculty's desire to put more rigor and accuracy into the grading system.

The above alterations were made to the Juris Doctor program, the only program the school had ever had. Ever since NELPI had been created, consideration had occasionally been given to offering a master's degree in the energy area, but it was always concluded that resources were insufficient to begin such a program. However, within the first six years of the Belsky administration, two graduate programs were created, not within NELPI, but in conjunction with two "Centers" created during the Makdisi and Belsky administrations:

the Comparative and International Law Center (created in 1993) and the Native American Law Center (created in 2000.) These graduate programs are discussed in conjunction with the centers.

Institute, Centers and Certificate Programs

The creation and work of the Institute, Centers and Certificate Programs at the law school formed a hallmark of the new "legal education center." The oldest of these organizations, the National Energy-Environment Law and Policy Institute (NELPI), continued traditional activity, but branched out into new activity. Director R. Dobie Langenkamp and Associate Directors Gary Allison and Marla Mansfield continued their scholarship in the field; supervised NELPI publications;[20] operated the Resources, Energy and Environmental Law (REEL) Certificate Program; organized conferences and symposia; and, administered the Enrichment Program, which will be discussed later in the chapter.

In 2000, NELPI moved in a new direction, creating the Office of Tribal Environmental Management Services. This Office, under the direction of Earl Hatley, completed a multi-year research project for the Tribal Association for Solid Waste and Emergency Response (TASWER). Funded by a three-year, $250,000 per year grant from the Environmental Protection Agency, the Office engaged in a nationwide investigation of hazardous waste and environmental damage.[21] On a smaller scale, NELPI contracted with individual tribes to set up clean air and water plans for the tribes.[22]

An important personnel change in NELPI occurred in the fall of 2000, when the director, Lakshman Guruswamy, moved to the University of Colorado Law School. He was replaced by R. Dobie Langenkamp, as discussed earlier.

Four Centers operated at the school during the Belsky administration. The first one created was the Comparative and International Law Center, which was started in 1993. Its origins, along with the Comparative and International Law Certificate, created in 1994, was discussed in the previous chapter. This Center sponsored speakers and visitors, student competitions and the Certificate program. Two developments within the Center during the Belsky administration were the growth of study-abroad programs and a graduate program.

The first study-abroad program, the Summer Institute in Bratislava (Slovakia) was begun in the summer of 1993. It continued each summer through 1996, at which point it was discontinued because of deterioration in the political atmosphere in Slovakia and the preference of students for a second program the school was starting. The second program, the Summer Institute in International Law in Buenos Aires (Argentina), was first held in the summer of 1997 at the Universidad de Palermo Law School, under the direction of Professor Janet Levit. Having an interest in international human rights and contacts in the area, she was able to help the law school establish the program, which focused on private international law and international human rights, as taught by TU and Argentine faculty. It operated each summer until 2002, when it was

Faculty of the Native American Law Center. Left to right: Melissa Tatum, Valerie Phillips, Bill Rice, Vicki Limas, Judith Royster. *Courtesy The University of Tulsa College of Law archives.*

suspended because of the economic disruption in Argentina. It restarted in 2004.

The London Program (England), directed by Professor Linda Lacey, was developed by Professor David Clark. It was different from the other study-abroad programs in that it operated for a full semester. Students who attended receive credit transferred to their TU transcript. Courses on U.S. and foreign law were taught by both TU and British faculty. There was an externship component which placed the students in the offices of barristers and solicitors. The first program was held in the spring of 1997, when TU was a part of a consortium of law schools which operated it. Beginning in the fall of 1999, TU began operating a separate program, Autumn in London. It operated for the full semester with a curriculum which was an integral part of the law school's curriculum and taught by TU and British faculty.

The Summer Institute in European and International Law in Dublin (Ireland), also directed by Linda Lacey, was first held in the summer of 1999. In 1998, Professor Larry Backer was named executive director of the Comparative and International Law Center, with Professors David Clark and Rex Zedalis serving as directors. Backer began an ambitious program of development for the Center, including this Summer Institute. It was held at University College in Dublin, where students studied, under the guidance of TU and Irish faculty. The curriculum included courses on European law, international law and law governing families. A part of the program was held in Leuven, Belgium, where the students studied at the Irish Institute for European Studies.

In 2002, the Geneva Institute on Indigenous People's Law (Switzerland) was begun. When Larry Backer left the faculty in

2000, Linda Lacey was appointed executive director of the Center. She and Professor William (Bill) Rice developed this program, which was sponsored by both the Comparative and International Law Center and the Native American Law Center. It was held for the first time in the summer of 2002 with 49 students from 16 different law schools, all studying indigenous people's issues, international trade and international environmental law. Students could also elect to study applied European law in Leuven, Belgium.

The first graduate law degree program in the history of the school was created in 1999.[23] It was a master's (LL.M.) degree in American law for foreign lawyers. Operated out of the Comparative and International Law Center, it was designed for non-U.S. trained lawyers, with the purpose of giving them broad introduction to the American legal system. It included a one-year-long residency program, consisting of required and elective courses taken along with J.D. students. The program sat dormant for some time because of the international political situation, in part. The first student, Rolf Andreas Kastner, entered the program in 2002 and graduated in 2003.

The Native American Law Center was created in 2000. A number of faculty were involved with the Center—Judith Royster, Melissa Tatum, Bill Rice, Vicki Limas, and, Valerie Phillips. The Center sponsored speakers and visitors, student competitions, and a Native American Law Certificate Program. The Center's work included two programs. The first was a master's (LL.M.) in American Indian and indigenous law, directed by Bill Rice. It was begun in 2001,[24] with the first six students enrolling in the fall of 2001. It was designed to educate both U.S. and non-U.S.-trained lawyers in issues involving American Indians and other indigenous peoples around the world. It was a year-long residency program involving both course work and research and writing. When created, it was the first master's program in this field to be offered by an ABA-approved law school. The program graduated its first student, Patrick Moore, in 2002.

The second program that the Center created, this time in cooperation with the Boesche Legal Clinic, was the Muscogee (Creek) Nation Legal Services Clinic. The Creek Nation contacted the law school and inquired about the possibility of creating a clinic to meet the legal services needs of its members. Professor Leslie Mansfield, a former Boesche Legal Clinic Director from 1999 to 2003, negotiated a contract with the Nation for a three-year funding period as a joint project of the Nation and the law school. The Clinic provided: 1) rural and community legal services to enrolled Creek Nation members under a direct services contract with the Nation; and 2) legal services for the Creek Nation, the National Council Committee and the Tribal Council. The Clinic was staffed by a supervising attorney, aided by a clinical legal fellow, Lorie Guevara, who was an LL.M. graduate of the American Indian and Indigenous Law Program, and by a paralegal secretary. Students began in the Clinic in the fall of 2002. It became the third program at the Boesche Legal Clinic, joining the Older Americans Law Project and the Health Law Project.

The third Center, the Alternative Dispute Resolution Center, focused on the ADR Certificate. Students obtained the Certificate by taking designated ADR courses and participating in ADR activities in the federal district court for the northern district of Oklahoma, the Oklahoma courts and the Boesche Legal Clinic. In 2000, with the retirement of the founder of the program, Martin Frey, Vicki Limas became the director.

The Nonprofit Law Center, became the fourth Center to be created. This Center operated under the direction of its founder, Barbara Bucholtz. Professor Bucholtz taught courses on nonprofit law and worked with nonprofit organizations and lawyers who practiced in this area. Students in the program, which did not have an allied Certificate, researched legal issues and wrote papers which were utilized by nonprofit organizations and attorneys. The Center operated out of the Parc Center Building in downtown Tulsa, site of the former downtown branch of the law library, the Law Research Center, which was closed in 1997.

In addition to the four Certificates offered in conjunction with the Institute and Centers discussed above,[25] four other Certificates were offered as of 2003. The Public Policy Certificate was created by Professor Gary Allison in 1995. The Health Law Certificate was created by Professor Marguerite Chapman in 1996. The Lawyering Skills Certificate, premised on the concept that students who go into solo or small-firm practice need transactional and advocacy training, was created by Professors Chris Blair and Lance Stockwell in 1999. The Entrepreneurial Law Certificate was

created by Professor Tom Arnold in 2000.[26] All of these Certificates had similar components: 1) a schedule of required and optional courses; 2) a research and writing requirement; and 3) a practicum requirement.

This brief survey of the Institute, Centers and Certificates operated by the law school in 2003 indicated an increasingly complex institution, beginning to go beyond the model of the traditional law school. The next type of academic activity discussed, the enrichment programs of the school, further indicated this movement.

Enrichment Programs

There had always been stimulating intellectual activity outside of class at the law school. What separated the activity from the 1980s onward from previous eras was the degree and institutionalization of this type of activity. During the Walwer years, the faculty began getting together periodically to discuss a faculty member's work in progress, and, in the process, the Faculty Colloquy Program was born. This process accelerated during the Makdisi years and flowered during the Belsky years. This activity was formalized as the annual Enrichment Program at the school, supervised by the NELPI director, first Lakshman Guruswamy and, later, Dobie Langenkamp. There were at least five different components to the Enrichment Program.

First, faculty colloquies continued to be held.[27] Second, a variety of conferences and symposia, both one-of-a-kind and annual, were held each year. The major conferences on the Warren, Burger and Rehnquist Courts, organized by Bernard Schwartz, have been discussed. In addition, each year the law school sponsored a U.S. Supreme Court review, at which major cases of the previous term were discussed by the faculty and other speakers. These talks were collected and placed in an issue of the *Tulsa Law Review*.

An annual Symposium on Scholarship was begun in 2001, which was placed in the *Tulsa Law Review*. The Spring 2001 Symposium featured the scholarship of Morton J. Horwitz, Charles Warren Professor of American Legal History at Harvard Law School. Other symposia followed.[28]

NELPI continued to sponsor yearly conferences, symposia and lectures on a variety of topics in the energy, natural resources, and environmental law fields. For example, in addition to the annual Federal Energy Regulatory Commission Conference, conferences on topics as diverse as "BioBanking and BioInvestment," "The Energy Industry and Risk Management" and "Toxic Mold, Human Health and the Law" were held.[29]

In the summer of 2001, the Sovereignty Symposium, an annual conference on Native American topics, was held in Tulsa and was co-sponsored by the three law schools in the state: The University of Tulsa, the University of Oklahoma and Oklahoma City University. Other examples of seminars sponsored by the law school during this time included, "Elder Care: Critical issues for Aging Family Members," held during the 1999-2000 academic year, and "Intelligence Gathering and International Law and Diplomacy," held during the 2000-2001 academic year.

As a third component of the Enrichment Program, the law school

founded several important lecture series. The last chapter discussed the endowment of the John W. Hager Distinguished Lecture Series. The first annual lecture was held in March, 1996, with Richard A. Posner, chief judge, United States Court of Appeals for the Seventh Circuit, as the speaker.[30] In 1998, The University of Tulsa and the Tulsa Jewish Federation established the Rabin Lecture, honoring the life of the late Yitzhak Rabin, prime minister of Israel and winner of the Nobel Peace Prize. The speaker that year was Joel Singer, special advisor to Mr. Rabin during the Oslo Accords.[31] Through the efforts of Chapman Professor Paul Finkelman, the school established the Buck Colbert Franklin Memorial Civil Rights Lecture, named in honor of a pioneering African-American lawyer in Tulsa who was deeply involved in the Greenwood district before and after the 1921 race riots. The first speaker was his son, the distinguished historian, John Hope Franklin.[32] This series was also part of the TU Presidential Lecture series. Later additions to the Enrichment Program were the Bernard Schwartz Distinguished Lecture series in Constitutional Law, named in honor of TU's late scholar, and a Joint Lecture in Law and Political Science, sponsored by the College of Law and the Department of Political Science.

The fourth component of the Enrichment program was the In-Residence Program which Dean Belsky started in 1997. This Program brought scholars, practitioners, judges and alumni to the law school for several days.[33] While in residence, these individuals would speak in classes, give lectures, and meet students, faculty and alumni in informal settings.

The Buck Colbert Franklin Memorial Civil Rights Lecture series drew national leaders in the field to speak at the College of Law. The 2003 speaker was Julian Bond, chairman of the NAACP. L-R: Jim Goodwin ('65), Lecture chairman; Julian Bond; Chapman Professor Paul Finkelman; and, Dean Martin Belsky. *Courtesy The University of Tulsa.*

The law school was fortunate to have a number of United States Supreme Court justices visit during the Belsky administration. Before 1996, the only justice who had visited the school was William Rehnquist, who was present to dedicate John Rogers Hall in 1973. After 1996, four justices visited. In the summer of 1996, Sandra Day O'Conner visited during the Ninth Annual Sovereignty Symposium. Clarence Thomas visited twice, first in 1997, and, again, in 2000, when in Tulsa to receive the Oklahoma Citizenship Award from the Oklahoma Council of Public Affairs. Ruth Bader Ginsberg visited in 1997, and Stephen R. Breyer visited in 1999, while he was in Tulsa for Law Week. These visits complemented the annual U.S. Supreme Court Review program held each year at the school in which faculty members and others analyzed the decisions of the previous term of the Court.

Law Journals and Review

The law school sponsored three publications as of 2003. The *Energy Law Journal*, a joint project of NELPI and the Federal Energy Bar Association, focused on federal energy law, the global nature of energy issues and the interrelationship between environmental law and energy policy. The *Journal's* board of editors

also published the *Year-In-Review* in cooperation with the ABA Section on Natural Resources, Energy and Environmental Law. The law school's second publication, the *Tulsa Journal of Comparative & International Law*, dealt with a wide range of topics in these fields, from international commerce to human rights issues to international energy and environmental law topics. The law school's third publication, its oldest, underwent a name change in 2001. The *Tulsa Law Journal* became the *Tulsa Law Review*. The nature of the *Review* did not change; the purpose of the change was meant to clarify its nature as a publication of general interest and national scope, publishing articles on a wide variety of legal topics.

Competitions

At the turn of the twenty-first century, students at the school participated in a wide variety of intramural and intermural competitions that gave them experience in settings such as trials, negotiations and mediations, and appellate advocacy situations. In mock trial, students participated in the American Trial Lawyers Association National Student Trial Competition and the National Trial Competition. In negotiations and mediation, students participated in the ABA Client Counseling Competition, ABA Negotiations Competition, ABA Mediation Competition, and the 1L (First Year) Negotiation Competition. In appellate advocacy, students

participated in the Phillip C. Jessup Moot Court Competition, National Native American Law Student Association Moot Court Competition, National Health Law Competition, Frederick Douglass Competition, and the John W. Hager Memorial Torts Competition.

This large array of competitions was organized and managed by the Board of Advocates, a student group. The Board, in turn, relied on sitting judges, practitioners, alumni and professors to serve as coaches and judges.

Reflective of the quality of the performance of TU students in these competitions, two students—Pansy Moore-Shrier and Mia Johnson— won the 2003 National Health Law Competition. They were coached by Bruce A. McKenna ('80) and aided by the Board of Advocates and the Law and Medicine Society.

Boesche Legal Clinic

The previous chapter discussed the creation of the Legal Clinic in 1992 and its early personnel and evolution to encompass two programs, the Older Americans Law Project and the Health Law Project. The Older Americans Law Project, under the supervision of Professor Morris Bernstein, until his resignation from the University in 2003, continued to provide its designated clientele with such services as estate-planning documents, advice on landlord/tenant issues, and advice on mortgage foreclosure problems. The Health Law Project, under the supervision of Professor Suzanne Levitt from 1996-1999, and Professor Leslie Mansfield from 1999 through the time of this writing, represented clients in several settings. The "Guardian ad litem" Project, started in 1996 in cooperation with Judge Edward Hicks of the probate division of the Tulsa County district court, allowed students appointed as guardian ad litem in cases to be the "eyes and ears" of the court in guardianship and conservatorship matters. The Health Law project also represented coal miners and uranium miners who had federal disability rights due to lung disease. In 2003, both the Older Americans Law Project and the Health Law Project were aided by a clinical legal fellow, Jason Fields.

A third program, the Muscogee (Creek) Nation Legal Services Clinic,

RIGHT: Personnel in the Boesche Legal Clinic. Left to right: Lori Guevara, Devra McManus, Catherine Zilahy Welsh, Dyan Bramwell, Jason Fields, Leslie Mansfield and Candice Kuykendall. *Courtesy Ervin Photography.*

ABOVE: United States Supreme Court Justice Ruth Bader Ginsburg and her husband, Professor Martin Ginsburg, visited the College of Law in 1997. Left to Right: Professor Ginsberg, Justice Ginsberg, Dean Martin H. Belsky, and, his wife, Professor Kathleen Waits. *Courtesy The University of Tulsa.*

under the supervision of Professor Montie Deer until his resignation in 2004 to become attorney general of the Muscogee (Creek) Nation, was opened in 2002. Kathy Supernaw became supervising attourney in 2005. As discussed earlier in this chapter, this Clinic provided legal services to enrolled members of the Creek Nation, and also to the National Council Committees and Tribal Council.

Another project the Legal Clinic undertook stemmed from a tragic incident in Tulsa's history—the 1921 Tulsa race riot. After being dormant for decades, renewed interest and concern over appropriate contemporary response to this loss of life and property arose. The Clinic became involved in this process through the filing of a riot survivors' lawsuit. In 2004, the federal district court dismissed the action, which was pending on appeal at the Tenth Circuit when this book was published.

Professor Winona Tanaka served as Legal Clinic director from the time of its founding until 1997. When she returned to full-time teaching, Dean Belsky served as acting director until Professor Suzanne Levitt, who had been on the staff as a clinician since 1996, was appointed director in 1998. When Levitt left to become executive director of the Drake Law School Clinics in 1999, Professor Leslie Mansfield, who had been at the Legal Clinic at the University of New Mexico Law School, was hired as director. Professor Montie Deer became Legal Clinic director in 2003 when Mansfield returned to full-time teaching and research. That same year he was also appointed to the Sac & Fox Supreme Court. He resigned in 2004 to serve as attorney

general of the Muscogee (Creek) Nation. At the time of this writing, Richard Paschal, a professor of research and writing, was the director.

In 1996, the faculty status of the staff clinicians was changed from "instructor" to that of "professor" on tenure track. This change applied to the two clinicians, Morris Bernstein and Leslie Mansfield, as discussed earlier in this chapter. In addition, the University made a commitment to provide funding for the Legal Clinic in the regular law school budget. Before this change occurred, the Clinic had relied on "soft" money from outside funding sources.

Each of the three Legal Clinic programs accommodated up to 20 students per year, meaning that a total of 60 students could participate in this lawyering skills activity. The Legal Clinic was staffed by two full-time clinical professors, an office administrator, a secretary, former clinic students who served as "law clerks," and a "fellow" (a practicing lawyer).

The Legal Clinic began operation in 1992 in a small university-owned bungalow close to the school at 825 S. Evanston Avenue. In 1993, it moved to a larger location, a former health clinic building, at the corner of Fourth Street and Harvard Avenue. In February, 2002, the Legal Clinic moved into its new $600,000 home, the Boesche Legal Clinic Building, directly across Fourth Place from the law school. The history of this move is discussed later in this chapter.

FINANCES

Finances were an area of dramatic change during the Belsky administration. It will be

remembered that this issue was a most critical one in the Makdisi administration, leading to his resignation.[34] Dean Makdisi had protested University overhead charges exceeding 30%.[35] In negotiating an agreement on this issue with the University prior to coming, Dean Belsky made significant headway toward solving the problem. He and President Robert Donaldson agreed to a reduction of the overhead down to twenty percent over a three year period.[36] The agreement also provided that the law school could keep all money raised through fundraising.[37] Belsky then took a second step toward controlling the school's overhead charges. After Robert W. Lawless became president of the University in May, 1996, Dean Belsky concluded a new agreement with him concerning overhead charges owed the University. Under the new agreement, the school would pay a set amount for overhead (initially calculated to be $1.5 million) and then be responsible for ensuring that the revenue the school collected covered its expenses.[38]

Importantly, the school could retain all revenue above the agreed amount. The impact on the percentage of law school revenue flowing to the University was dramatic: by FY 2000, overhead had been reduced to 17.9%.[39] Equally important, in the words of Dean Belsky, "as long as I come up with the right numbers, the law school decides how to spend its money."[40]

Being heavily dependent on tuition, the school increased tuition in order to pay for an increasingly complex educational operation. In 1995-96, tuition was $470/credit hour; by 2003-04, it had risen to the equivalent of $770/credit hour for entering students. However, in a second break with the financial past, in 1997, Dean Belsky altered the method by which tuition would be charged. Beginning in the fall of that year, tuition charges moved from a credit hour basis to a flat sum for a range of credit hours during the academic year.[41]

TU faced the same battle all private higher education faced: justifying to students and others tuition which was substantially higher than that of public higher education. Justification had, at a minimum, two basic facets. First, was whether the nature of the experience of the student was sufficiently superior to justify the difference. This concept was basic to the law school's multiple actions which were moving it from a traditional "law school" to a complex "legal education center" offering variety and flexibility to each student. Second, was whether the price of the individual school was a "good buy" in private higher education. TU had always attempted to, and generally had been successful at, demonstrating its relatively lower tuition compared to other law schools in the region.[42]

Besides tuition, the other main source of school revenue was gift giving through fundraising. This source had not been historically significant except for landmark activities. The funding of John Rogers Hall was an example. It was built with a $1 million dollar gift from Leta M. Chapman, coupled with a $500,000 campaign among alumni, friends and area businesses, as described in chapter two. Although law school personnel were involved, the campaign was directed by the University. As described in

chapter three, raising the nearly $1 million to build the East Wing was different. It was a "two-man" show involving Tom Read and Bill Bell. Throughout these times, fundraising for the law school was not an ongoing year-in, year-out activity. In the 1980s, Frank Walwer started an annual Law Alumni Fund Drive, having only modest success because, at least in part, of constraints placed on the process by the University, as discussed in chapter four. More sustained fundraising activity commenced during John Makdisi's deanship. In the early 1990s, Makdisi acquired control over law school fundraising activities and hired Jane Kolesnik as the law school development director. Together, they launched successful campaigns for designated projects such as the John W. Hager Distinguished Lecture Series and course sponsorships, as discussed in chapter five. The school's fundraising position was lost in the University's financial belt-tightening in the mid-1990s (although Jane Kolesnik came back to the law school as director of alumni affairs and special projects.)

Fundraising reached a new level under Dean Belsky. Having the right to retain all funds raised, as discussed earlier, and, working in conjunction with the administration of President Lawless and the Vice President for Institutional Advancement, Jan Cavin Zink, Belsky teamed up with fundraisers assigned to the law school full-time from the office of development (Luke Doyle, Vicky Stone, and, later, Terry Kerr) to raise unprecedented amounts of money for special projects, on-going needs and endowment.[43] Both the physical plant and the program of the school reflected these successful fundraising efforts.

PHYSICAL PLANT

During Marty Belsky's deanship, the law school embarked on the fourth major set of building projects in its history and its first set of multiple projects. The first project, the building of the downtown facility at 512 S. Cincinnati in 1948-49, gave the school a home of its own for the first time in its history and helped achieve ABA accreditation. The building of John Rogers Hall in 1971-73, changed the direction of the law school by giving it a modern facility on campus, helping it enter into the mainstream of legal education. The need for additional library space drove Dean Read to obtain funding for the East Wing, which was built in 1979-80. By the early 1990s, the library had again run out of room. The 1993 ABA Site Evaluation Report was critical of the situation: "The Library ...'has a critical need for more space and renovation of some existing space.'"[44]

Mabee Legal Information Center.

The ABA Report had stated the obvious. In 1992, the "College of Law Strategic Plan" included "building a new addition to law school." In 1993, the Plan was updated and expanded to include "planning/funding for library and other needs." In 1994, Dean Makdisi was successful in having a John Rogers Hall-building-addition goal included in the University's "New Century Campaign."

During the acting deanship of Tom Arnold in 1994-95, planning turned to action. Arnold and Library Director Rick Ducey obtained a $1 million grant from the Sarkeys Foundation. Preliminary sketches of a new addition to John Rogers Hall were exhibited by Arnold at the first Chilifest in February, 1995.

Dean Belsky told the story that when he arrived in the summer of 1995, he was given "good news/ really good news" information: the good news was that, "you are going to have a new library building;" the really good news was that, "you are going to have to pay for it."[45] He would spend the next five years doing that. The name to be given to the new facility evolved quickly. In an August, 1995 interview in the *Baculus* student newspaper, Belsky indicated that $3 million of the $7 million needed for the "library addition" had been raised.[46] Both the name and the cost of the project would change.[47] Three months later, in the *Shrimper*, a short-lived newspaper published by Jewish law students, Belsky called the addition an "information resource center."[48] By February, 1996, once again in a *Baculus* article, he referred to the addition as the "legal information center."[49] This became the permanent name for the facility. Dean Belsky explained the name this way:

> I am often asked why we decided to call this renovation and new construction project a "legal information center." . . . there are elements of a traditional library—bookshelves, offices for our library staff, and space for reference material and assistance—alongside the newest technology necessary for a state-of-the-art law library—carrels and tables with electrical and modern connections, an online cataloguing system, compact shelving, and group discussion rooms with video viewing sites. . . .

Our College provides students and users from the law community "With every possible form of legal information. But there is even more. Space is available for our alumni and other visitors to have an office-away-from-home. Our three journals and Board of Advocates have new offices close to the resources they need. Four center sites hold special collections and facilitate work by researchers. Two new classrooms—the Technology Training Center and a dispute resolution facility—provide innovative ways for students and others to learn and use new information sources.[50]

The facility was truly a legal information center.

LEFT: Sharon Bell ('85), individual trustee of the Chapman-McFarlin Interests, and her husband, Greg Gray ('85) served as co-chairs of the Legal Information Center Campaign Committee. *Courtesy The University of Tulsa.*

BELOW: A "Hard Hat" party was held during construction of the Mabee Legal Information Center, attended by many donors, law school and University personnel, alumni and the general public. Left to right: Charles Kothe, Doug Dodd, Robert Rizley, Charles Norman, Greg Gray, Donne Pitman, Sharon Bell, Mark Skaggs, Pamela Jones, Martin Belsky, Kathleen Waits, Drew Edmondson, Jim Secrest, Robert Lawless, Marcy Lawless, C.S. Lewis, Floyd Walker, Virginia Walker, John Conway, Jan Cavin Zink, Melissa Henke Sartin, Richard Small, Norma Rowell, Jim Wallis, Norma Small, Frank Henke, Ron Rickets. *Courtesy The University of Tulsa.*

THE UNIVERSITY of TULSA

COLLEGE OF LAW
"A Law School for the 21st Century"
MARCH 31, 1999

The staff of the law library, along with the books, were dispersed across campus during the construction of the Mabee Legal Information Center. Here, left to right, Susan Johnston, administrative assistant; Rick Ducey, director; and Lou Lindsey, associate director, are seen in their temporary office in the Allen Chapman Activity Center's administrative conference room. *Courtesy Mabee Legal Information Center archives.*

In January, 1996, the Legal Information Center Campaign Committee,[51] appointed to assist the dean in raising the funds for the facility, met to review architectural drawings and create a plan of action. Judge Joseph W. Morris, the former dean, was honorary chair, while Sharon J. Bell ('85) and Greg Gray ('85) served as co-chairs. Four subcommittees were formed to contact 1) foundations, 2) law firms, corporations and solo practitioners, 3) government entities, and 4) individuals about gifts in wills and estates.[52]

By 1998, firmer information on the nature of the facility was emerging. It would be a three-story structure connected to the southwest corner of John Rogers Hall and cost between $10-11 million. It was designed by the Hillier Group of Princeton, New Jersey.[53]

Work on the structure began in late 1998. Preliminary work began in September, with construction starting in October. By November, there was a breakthrough of the walls of John Rogers Hall. Not only was the building to be high-tech, but, so to was the recording of its construction. The computer and media office, under the direction of Ben Chapman and his staff, regularly placed updated photos of the construction process on the web pages of the law school and the library. Well into construction, on March 31, 1999, a "Hard Hat" Party was held for donors, law school personnel, University personnel, alumni and the general public.[54] By that point, $8.5 million of the projected $10.4 million cost had been raised, including a $3 million challenge grant from the J.E. and

L.E. Mabee Foundation. In all, there were fifteen major donors to the project,[55] in addition to the myriad other contributors. Supporters buried a time capsule, scheduled to be opened in 2024, in the building.

Because the Taliaferro-Savage Library in John Rogers Hall, which was an integral part of the Mabee Legal Information Center, was scheduled to be renovated as a part of the construction process, it was necessary to move the contents and offices into temporary quarters for the year it would take to renovate. The scope of this move dwarfed the relocation of the library from downtown to campus in 1973. Following the end of final exams

for the 1998 fall term, the library closed on December 19, 1998, and was dispersed among three locations in Allen Chapman Activity Center, McFarlin Library and off-campus by the start of the spring term on January 11, 1999.[56] Close to 60% of print material and all microform material were retrievable under an intricate plan devised by the library staff. The library served its patrons well under these conditions until the new facility was opened one year later, on January 17, 2000. Construction had been completed in December, 1999, and the library staff supervised the move of the collection from the disparate locations into its new and renovated home.

The facility was dedicated on March 2, 2000, as the Mabee Legal Information Center. The keynote speaker, William Paul, president of the American Bar Association, was joined by President Lawless, Dean Belsky, the faculty and staff of the school, alumni, donors and friends, all celebrating this milestone in the life of the school.

Why a milestone? In the words of the Fall 2000 College of Law ABA Self-Study, the Mabee Legal Information Center (MLIC) had "start[ed] a new era of the library's influence and integration into the life of the College of Law."[57] A few brief facts will show why. The MLIC could seat over 100% of

Mabee Legal Information Center. *Courtesy The University of Tulsa College of Law archives.*

the student body at any one time. The new three-story expansion and the renovated Taliaferro-Savage Library, together, total 70,500 gross square feet. The permanent and compact shelving allowed the print collection to grow from its then-size of 142,718 volumes to 220,000 volumes. The original plan was to have even greater volume capacity through the installation of additional compact shelving. However, the decision was made to put more resources into the legal research and writing program in 2002 and a writing suite, housing legal writing faculty, was built in the space originally intended for additional compact shelving. A large percentage of the tables and carrels in the new and renovated portions were wired to the College of Law computer network and to the world wide web. There were three computer labs; a technology training center; specialty rooms for law school centers; and, offices for student organizations, the alumni, the Law Alumni Association, and the career services office.

There was beautiful artwork located throughout the facility. The centerpiece, located in the lower rotunda, was an alabaster sculpture of the Oglala Sioux chief, Crazy Horse, donated by Professor Vicki Limas in memory of her mother, Doris Jean Jones.

In addition to the "bricks and mortar," there was the all-important human dimension to the MLIC.[58] As of 2003, the MLIC was under the direction of Director Rick Ducey and Associate Director Lou Lindsay, who joined the staff in 1995. There were eight full-time librarians and eight support staff. The director and associate director had both J.D and M.L.S. degrees. Five of the staff had

Personnel in the Mabee Legal Information Center. Front row, left to right: Lou Lindsey, Susan Johnston, Ruth Whitson, Carol Arnold, Mira Greene, Faye Hadley. Back row, left to right: Kathy Kane, Susan Julian, Karen Bouteller, Marta Swanson, Mark Mayer, Melanie Nelson, Rick Ducey, Dan Bell, Courtney Selby, David Gay, Margaret Nunnery. Personnel not pictured: Threresa Eubanks, Margaret Enright, Mike Weibel. *Courtesy The University of Tulsa College of Law archives..*

law degrees, while six of the full-time librarians had masters' degrees. This increase in the number and qualifications of personnel over the years was merely one facet of Ducey's fundamental objective during his tenure to provide ever-improving service to faculty and students.

The law school's computer and media support program originated in the library. Ben Chapman, the director of computing resources during the construction of the MLIC was a J.D. holder who was first hired from private legal practice as media/electronic services and copyright law librarian. The program evolved into the present office of computing resources, with a director, a micro-computer specialist and a media specialist. Chapman resigned his position in the summer of 2003 and was replaced by Todd Gourd. As of 2005, computer resources were handled by Shane Blackstock, Larry Curtis and Chris Farwell.

It would be a mistake to believe that all was "wine and roses" in the MLIC, however. Difficulties involving financial support continued. The Fall 2000 College of Law ABA Self-Study pointed out that, "The acquisitions budget over the past seven years has been relatively stable and increasing most years…, but it has not adequately kept up with the cumulative effects of inflation."[59] The 2001 ABA Site Evaluation Report pointed out the strengths and weaknesses of the MLIC: "While many financial concerns remain, the new Library physical plant has alleviated all of the former space problems and has made the Library the focal point of the Law School."[60] The Report, however, went on to list three areas of concern.[61] In response, Dean

Belsky committed to increasing the MLIC acquisitions budget.[62] As the traditional law library transformed into a legal information center, a new difficulty arose, at least for accreditation purposes: how should the institution account for resources going into traditional library resources and those going into modern technology? In 2002, Dean Belsky commented on the question:

> We are in the top 25% of library funding—but there is a dispute now as to distribution—more and more of our information resources will be from technology based information sources—and where do we count these[?] If we put together those bases—library and computer resources—and add in annual maintenance of MLIC—and also add in increased staff and increased salaries for library and computer resources—this has been our single biggest investment in the last seven years—nearly a doubling of financial support. This conflict between a library and a legal information center is what we will have to adjust to.[63]

Boesche Legal Clinic

Just as the Mabee Legal Information Center was a milestone in the dissemination of legal information at the law school, so was the Boesche Legal Clinic in the imparting of lawyering skills at the school.[64] In 1992, the Legal Clinic opened under the direction of Professor Winona Tanaka in a small University-owned bungalow close to the law school at 825 S. Evanston Avenue. After operating there for one year, it moved into larger quarters

in a former medical building at the corner of Fourth Street and Harvard Avenue. Between 1993 and 1998, as the program grew from a single civil law focus into two programs, the Older Americans Law Project and the Health Law Project, the size and functionality of the building became increasingly inadequate. After the Boesche Legal Clinic building was built and occupied, a third program, the Muscogee [Creek] Nation Legal Services Clinic, was opened in the fall of 2002.

In the winter of 1998, Dean Belsky obtained funds from the Mervin Bovaird Foundation and the Estate of Jay C. Byers ('61) for a new Legal Clinic building. The trustees of the Bovaird Foundation made their gift in the name of Fenelon Boesche, who was involved with the Foundation since its inception in 1955 and served as its president until his death in 1993. Jay C. Byers had arranged in his will to leave a legacy to the law school.

The years 1998 through 2000 were planning years for the new project. After Professor Tanaka left the directorship in 1997, Dean Belsky served as acting director of the Clinic for a year before appointing Professor Suzanne Levitt, the head of the Health Law Project, to the position in 1998. Professor Leslie Mansfield became the director one year later, in 1999, when Levitt took a position at another school. Mansfield served in that capacity until 2003, when Professor Montie Deer was appointed director. He resigned in February, 2004, to serve as attorney general of the Muscogee (Creek) Nation, whereupon, Dean Belsky once again assumed the position of acting director. All of these individuals, with the exception of Deer, were involved in the

Boesche Legal Clinic. *Courtesy The University of Tulsa College of Law archives.*

planning process. A new location for the Legal Clinic proved troublesome and delayed the process. Originally, the plan was to place the Clinic on the corner of Fourth Place and Gary Avenue, but land acquisition proved difficult and the location was abandoned. Ultimately, the corner of Fourth place and Florence Avenue was chosen as the location for the new building. Although it took away some parking from the school, it had the advantage of being immediately across the street from John Rogers Hall.

Construction began in spring of 2001. In February 2002, the Boesche Legal Clinic building was dedicated. It was a $600,000 facility of 3,850 square feet. It contained a reception area, six offices, a student work room with sixteen work stations equipped with network-connected PCs and telephones, two interview rooms, a room for law clerks, a library, secretarial pool space, and a lounge/ kitchenette area. It was designed by Lotti Krishan and Short, with interior design by Woody Design Associates, the same firm which designed the interior of the Mabee Legal Information Center.

East Wing

Dean Belsky was the third dean to make renovations to the East Wing. In baseball terms, it had served as a "utility infielder," meeting differing needs over the years. Dean Walwer took the empty ground floor and made offices so that the admissions and career counseling offices could move into the law school building. As space became increasingly tight in John Rogers Hall, Dean Makdisi found space for additional offices in the Wing. As space once again became tight in John Rogers Hall, Dean Belsky turned once more to the East Wing for additional offices for faculty, staff and students. In addition, he built an "electronic" classroom which gave the professor and students the ability to access tapes, CD ROMs and the world wide web for classroom use. Finally, work on the East Wing culminated in 2001 with the dedication of the Jay C. Byers Student Services Center, financed by a gift from the Estate of Jay C. Byers ('61.) The Center contained the admissions and financial aid office and career counseling office. There was a warm and inviting reception area for prospective students, current students, employers and guests of the law school. Existing offices and the career counseling library were refurbished and new offices created,

along with a kitchen for providing refreshments to visitors.

John Rogers Hall

Important renovations to the main building of the law school were made by Dean Belsky in order to

insure that the physical plant met the needs of students in the twenty-first century. All the classrooms were converted to "electronic" classrooms, having the same capabilities as the "electronic" classroom in the East Wing, described above. In the summer of 2003, the law school became "wireless" throughout John Rogers Hall, the Mabee Legal Information Center, the lawn between John Rogers Hall and the Allen Chapman Activity Center,

A Lifetime of Achievement

ABOVE: John L. (Jack) Boyd ('50) received the College of Law's Lifetime Achievement Award from Alumni Board President Michael Zacharias ('71) at the 2003 Alumni Gala. *Courtesy The University of Tulsa.*

RIGHT: The renovated Model Courtroom in John Rogers Hall was re-named the Wm. Stuart Price and Michael C. Turpen Courtroom in honor of the two principal donors. L-R: Linda Price ('80), Stuart Price ('82), Michael Turpen ('74), and Susan Turpen. *Courtesy The University of Tulsa.*

and extending into that Center. Students no longer needed to be tethered to outlets to have computer access to the internet.

The Model Courtroom was renovated in 2002-2003. On April 15, 2003, it was dedicated as the Wm. Stuart Price and Michael C. Turpen Courtroom. It was remodeled to serve three functions. It would serve as an academic courtroom for simulation courses. It was fitted with electronic capabilities for taping, presentations and other uses, as well as having its acoustical qualities improved. It would also serve as a sitting courtroom in which state and federal courts would hear oral arguments. Finally, it would be used as an "electronic" classroom which could be separated from

the courtroom by state-of-the-art-partitioning.

Present at the dedication were the donors—Wm. Stuart Price (JD '82) and Linda Mitchell Price (JD '80); Michael C. Turpen (BA '72, JD '74); the Leta McFarlin Chapman Memorial Trust, represented by Trustee Sharon J. Bell; and, the Richard P. and Norma T. Small Foundation, represented by Richard and Norma Small. Keynote remarks were made by Robert H. Henry, judge, U.S. Court of Appeals for the Tenth Circuit and taped remarks were made by Governor Brad Henry and former U.S. Senator George J. Mitchell. Ben Chapman, director of computing resources, discussed the electronic capabilities of the courtroom.

Along with all of the programs at the law school which have been described earlier, these physical improvements and electronic enhancements transformed the law school into a legal education center of the twenty first century.

ALUMNI

Eighty years after students first started studying at the Tulsa Law School, alumni and the Law Alumni

Association worked along side the law school as partners, benefiting both the alumni and students and organizations at the school. The Law Alumni Association was involved with a number of regularly-held activities throughout the year, such as tailgate parties before football games and get-togethers before basketball games, the OBA annual meeting alumni lunch, regional receptions as the dean and administration traveled around the country, the annual Chilifest, and the annual Law Alumni Gala Dinner Dance. The Association recognized both alumni and non-alumni with the Outstanding Faculty Member Award, the Outstanding Alumnus/ Alumnae Award, and the Honorary Alumni Award.

Alumni and the Association were very involved with law school programs. In 1997, the Association began an Alumni Mentoring Program. The concept was that a second or third year student would be paired with an attorney who would give the student insight into the everyday practice of law. It emphasized one-on-one interaction between the student and the mentor, supplementing knowledge and understanding the student was gaining in law school work. Alumni worked with the "Dean and Team," as Marty Belsky, George Justice, Vicki Jordan, Jane Kolesnik and others traveled around the country recruiting students and developing relationships with alumni. The dean and faculty presented CLE programs to alumni in various locations, with the aid of a gift by Ken Brune ('74), who created the Annette Watkins Brune Lecture Series, in memory of his wife.

These activities and others were facilitated by an effective alumni

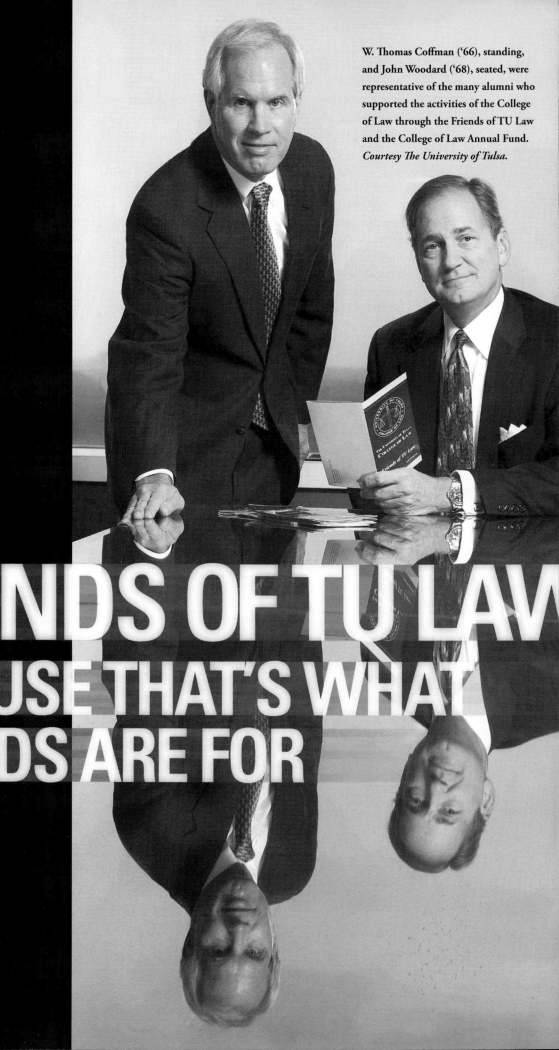

W. Thomas Coffman ('66), standing, and John Woodard ('68), seated, were representative of the many alumni who supported the activities of the College of Law through the Friends of TU Law and the College of Law Annual Fund. *Courtesy The University of Tulsa.*

FRIENDS OF TU LAW
BECAUSE THAT'S WHAT FRIENDS ARE FOR

organization. In 1993 the Law Alumni Association re-incorporated and adopted new by-laws and a standing committee system.[65] The organization was composed of a group of officers,[66] a board of directors, and nine standing committees.[67]

Communication between the law school and the alumni and among alumni was facilitated by an alumni magazine started by Dean Belsky in 1996, the *Tulsa Law Magazine*. It published articles about the law school and about alumni. In 2001, a "class correspondent" (a member of each year's graduating class) concept was initiated so that alumni could direct information about themselves to a classmate who would forward it to the school for inclusion in the magazine.

In chapter two the story of the integration of the law school was discussed. One of the early African-American graduates was Charles L. Owens ('60.) In recognition of his pioneering activity as the first African-American assistant state attorney general in 1963 and the first African-American to be appointed an Oklahoma district court judge in 1968, and in recognition of his service to the people and State of Oklahoma, alumni and friends established the Charles L. Owens Endowed Scholarship to aid law students on either a merit or need basis.

Over the years other alumni distinguished themselves in many realms. For example, Daniel J. Boudreau ('76) was appointed a justice on the Supreme Court of Oklahoma in November, 1999.

Three young graduates, Tim Graham ('03) Diane Hall ('03) and Vivi Maddox ('03) were representatives of the generation of alumni who were beginning to make their mark in the legal profession as of 2003. Upon graduation, each earned a Presidential Management Internship with the federal government. Courtesy The University of Tulsa.

He was appointed by Governor Keating to fill a vacancy left by the retirement of Robert D. Simms, himself a 1950 graduate of the law school. The third graduate to serve on the Court was Robert Lavendar ('53). Charles S. Chapel ('69) served on the Oklahoma Court of Criminal Appeals before and during the Belsky years.

AN ENDING AND A NEW BEGINNING

As the ninth decade in the life of the College of Law unfolded, Martin Belsky's tenure as dean ended in August, 2004. The school had enjoyed great progress during his administration.

Catherine Cullem, a long-time member of the faculty, was appointed acting dean. She had earlier served as an associate dean and as director of the legal writing program. Her appointment marked the first time that a woman had held the position of dean in the school's history. She served during the 2004-2005 academic year.

In June, 2005, Robert Butkin, the Treasurer of the State of Oklahoma, assumed the deanship. He came with a background in both the practice of law and government service. Holding an undergraduate degree from Yale College and a law degree from the University of Pennsylvania, he was awarded a Henry Luce Scholarship immediately after law school and served as Visiting Fellow at the University of the Philippines Law Center. He then practiced law in Washington, D.C. for several years before serving as an assistant attorney general for the State of Oklahoma between 1987 and 1993.

In 1994, Butkin ran for the position of Treasurer of the State of Oklahoma. He enjoyed widespread support and was endorsed by both the *Tulsa World* and *Daily Oklahoman* in each of his campaigns. He was elected to the position three times by the voters of Oklahoma.

During his terms of office Butkin was involved in a number of important initiatives. He drafted legislation creating the Oklahoma College Savings Plan—the "'529' Savings Program," which provided an effective way for Oklahomans to save for the college education of a child or grandchild. He wrote and secured passage of legislation creating a low interest loan program to stimulate the building of affordable housing in rural and underserved urban areas in Oklahoma. He also co-chaired the successful effort to obtain passage of important State Questions. State Questions 680 and 681 were constitutional amendments that permitted Oklahoma's state supported colleges and universities to engage in technology transfer and commercial development of ideas developed on college campuses. State Question 692 created a permanent constitutional trust fund for Oklahoma's tobacco settlement moneys.

Robert Butkin came into the deanship with a number of important qualifications for success. He had significant experience in the legal profession, both private and public. He had become a state leader in areas of public service and public policy. His background had shown administrative, team building and strategic skills that could prove useful in his new position. Finally, having raised campaign funds, he was a knowledgeable fundraiser, an ability critical to any modern-day dean. He brought abilities to the College of Law that would be important as the school moved toward its first century of service.

Eight decades brought amazing changes to the College of Law. The school began in 1923 with a handful of students studying at night in rental space and being taught by practicing lawyers only. By 2003, the school had evolved into an institution of over 500 students, being taught both during the day and at night by over 30 full-time professors and scores of practitioners. This complex operation was supported by almost 40 professional and staff personnel and housed in multiple buildings totaling over 100,000 square feet.[1]

One can make only an informed prediction as to what the College of Law of the future will look like. Whatever its nature, it is very likely that its objective will be the same: to help men and women become both lawyers capable of handling the legal needs of a wide variety of clients and individuals capable of being productive citizens in local, state, regional, national and international arenas.

Based on its past and on the present situation, The University of Tulsa College of Law should be successfully involved in these pursuits into the indefinite future. The purpose of this work is to help the generations of the future better understand the origins and evolution of the College of Law during its first eight decades.

Preface: Although this history refers to events on the local, state and national level on occasion, it does not attempt to comprehensively weave the history of the law school into those histories. Readers who may be interested in comprehensive histories in these other areas can find them in the following works:

- **History of American Legal Education**

    Stevens, Robert. *Law School: Legal Education in America from the 1850s to the 1980s.* Chapel Hill: University of North Carolina Press, 1983.

    Friedman, Lawrence M. *American Law in the Twentieth Century.* New Haven: Yale University Press, 2002.

- **History of the State of Oklahoma**

    Baird, W. David, and Danney Goble. *The Story of Oklahoma.* Norman: University of Oklahoma Press, 1994.

    Gibson, Arrell M. *The History of Oklahoma.* Norman: University of Oklahoma Press, 1984.

    Morgan, H. Wayne, and Anne Hodges Morgan. *Oklahoma: A History.* New York: W. W. Norton & Co., 1977.

- **History of the City of Tulsa**

    Blakey, Ellen Sue, Robbie Boman, Jim Downing, Ina Hall, John Hamill, and Peggi Ridgway. *The Tulsa Spirit.* Tulsa: Continental Heritage Press, 1979.

    Butler, William. *Tulsa 75: A History of Tulsa, Oklahoma.* Tulsa: Metropolitan Tulsa Chamber of Commerce, 1974.

    Goble, Danney. *Tulsa!: Biography of the American City.* Tulsa: Council Oaks Books, 1997.

- **History of The University of Tulsa**

    Logsdon, Guy Willliam. *The University of Tulsa.* Norman: University of Oklahoma Press, 1977.

    Olsen, Claire, ed. *The University of Tulsa: 1935-1958.* Tulsa: The University of Tulsa Press, 1958.

CHAPTER ONE

1. *Tulsa Times—A Pictorial History: The Boom Years,* (World Publishing Co. 1987).
2. Logsdon, *The University of Tulsa,* 78 (Univ. of Okla. Press 1977).
3. This is an estimate of William C. Kellough, a Tulsa attorney involved in writing the history of the Tulsa County Bar Association (TCBA) for the TCBA Centennial. TCBA records do not exist prior to 1930. Interview with William C. Kellough, attorney (Sept. 21, 2003).
4. McKown, *The Dean—The Life of Julien C. Monnet,* 149 (Univ. of Okla. Press 1973).
5. Logsdon, Supra n. 2 at 114.
6. Ibid.
7. The *Tulsa Tribune,* Oct. 21, 1960.
8. Ibid.
9. Ibid.
10. The *Tulsa World,* Jan. 22, 1995.
11. Martindale-Hubbell Law Directory (1940).
12. By 1944, toward the end of his long association with the law school, a law school document listing officers of the University and law school faculty shows him as having not only an LL.B from Illinois Wesleyan University, but also an LL.D from Atlanta Law School.
13. Supra n. 10.
14. The 1941-42 Law School bulletin indicates that Hanson was the founder. It states: "The Tulsa Law School was founded in 1922 by E.E. Hanson, a member of the Oklahoma Bar, as an educational institution and not for profit. The Honorable Wash E. Hudson was elected Dean, and has served in that capacity ever since."
15. Interview with Preston Kors, class of 1941 (Oct. 7, 1993). (University of Tulsa College of Law Archives)
16. Supra n. 10.
17. The *Tulsa World,* Jan. 24, 1995.
18. Interview with Charles W. Adams, Prof. of Law (Feb. 25, 2003). (University of Tulsa College of Law Archives)

19. Univ. of Tulsa *Kendallabrum*, 1925-1926.

20. Minutes, Tulsa County Bd. of Educ. Sept. 10, 1923; Feb. 4, 1924; Aug. 18, 1924; Feb. 4, 1924; Aug. 18, 1924; Aug. 4, 1925; Sept. 7, 1926; Aug. 26, 1927; and Sept. 6, 1927.

21. Univ. of Tulsa *Collegian*, Oct. 1, 1926.

22. *Tulsa Tribune*, Sept. (unknown date), 1925.

23. W.E. Green (insurance, legal biography), Harry Halley (damages), E.E. Hanson (bailments and carriers, personal property, domestic relations, pleading), Robert D. Hudson (moot court), Wash E. Hudson (dean), Bryon Kirkpatrick (conflict of laws), John Ladner (code pleading, federal jurisdiction), F.D. Leonard (wills, partnership), William H. McClarin (equity), A.E. Montgomery (suretyship), Lewis W. Pratt (torts), Thomas F. Serviss (international law, legal ethics), I.J. Underwood (contracts, corporations), Thomas Wallace (criminal law).
Just two years later, the faculty included: Henry Gray (real property), Horace Hagen (bills and notes, oil and gas), Harry Holley (damages), James L. Hull (contracts), M.M. Mahaney (legal bibliography, taxation), William Melton (bankruptcy), Lawrence Mills (indian land titles), Charles Skalnik (Blackstone), H.L. Smith (bailments and carriers), J.B. Underwood (agency, sales), H.R. Williams (constitutional law). Univ. of Tulsa *Kendallabrum*, 1927.

24. Section 10652, compiled Oklahoma Statutes, 1921, as amended by Chapter 9, Session Laws, 1925: "Authority is hereby granted to the respective boards of control of the . . .
The Tulsa Law School of Tulsa [one of twelve institutions listed] upon recommendations of their respective faculties to grant the academic and profession degrees, usually and customarily granted to graduates of institutions of collegiate rank."

25. However, it is certainly possible that the critical privileges were granted one year before students first graduated in 1926, which would be the case if classes were first held in 1923.

26. How suspect is this article? Its source has not been identified. It contains two factual errors relating to the month of incorporation and the identity of the institution as being a part of the University. One can only speculate on whether this casts doubt on the date classes are said to have started. However, the central idea of the article that the school opened in the fall of 1923, is corroborated in more contemporary articles. A general article in the *Collegian* about the law school, refers to it having been organized in 1923 with eighteen students. Univ. of Tulsa *Collegian*, Oct. 1, 1926.

27. Univ. of Tulsa *Alumni Magazine*, July 1973. By 1926, tuition had been "increased" to $75 per semester. Univ. of Tulsa *Kendallabrum*,1926-27.

28. Minutes, Board of Trustees Univ. of Tulsa, (Mar. 12, 1925, and June 2, 1925).

29. Supra. n. 24.

30. Unidentified newspaper article, Oct. 1, 1926.

31. Unidentified newspaper article, Summer, 1925; unidentified newspaper article, Sept.1925.

32. 1926 - 9 graduates; 1927 - 10 graduates.

33. 1928 - 9 graduates; 1929 - 22 graduates; 1930 - 18 graduates.

34. Univ. of Tulsa *Kendallabrum*,1927-28.

35. Interview with Mrs. Ben F. Murdock, secretary to Mr. Hanson during the 1920s and 1930s, (Mar. 8, 1993). (University of Tulsa College of Law Archives)

36. Univ. of Tulsa *Collegian*, Feb. 4, 1927.

37. Ibid.

38. Univ. of Tulsa *Collegian*, Feb. 18, 1927.

39. Interview with Ben F. Murdock, ('29) (Sept. 10, 1992). (University of Tulsa College of Law Archives)

40. The Univ. of Tulsa *Bulletin*, vol. 31, no. 1, Apr. 1925.

41. Ibid.

42. Ibid.

43. Ibid.

44. Ibid.

45. Ibid.

46. Univ. of Tulsa *Collegian*, Oct.1, 1926.

47. Ibid.

48. Minutes, Univ. of Tulsa Bd. of Trustees (Feb. 9, 1927).

49. Minutes, Univ. of Tulsa Bd. of Trustees (Feb. 23, 1927).

50. Supra. n. 39.

51. Interview with A. Allen King, ('41) (May 7, 1988). (University of Tulsa College of Law Archives)

52. Minutes, Univ. of Tulsa Bd. of Trustees (undated, but between Feb. 23, 1927 and July 1, 1928).

53. Ibid.

54. Supra n. 22.

55. Supra n. 51.

56. Ibid.

57. Interview with Ben Henneke (Oct. 29, 1992). (University of Tulsa College of Law Archives)

58. Logsdon, Supra. n. 2 at 203.

59. Ibid.

60. See Supra n. 51.

61. Interview with Charles Kothe (July 19, 1998). Mr. Kothe was an attorney who taught at the school during this period. (University of Tulsa College of Law Archives)

62. Supra n. 51.

63. Between 1925 and 1935, Charles Skalnik was a practicing attorney who taught a number of courses, including legal bibliography, and managed the library, weeding out duplications and acquiring working sets of books. Between 1936 and 1943, Polk's Tulsa City Directory lists five other individuals as "librarian": Emmett V. Rosser, Jr. (1936); J. Norman Barker (1937); Marvin Kennworthy (1938-39); Ruth Bachelder (1941); and Marie Smith (1942).

64. Following is a list of all individuals known to have taught between 1929-42 and the courses they taught:

Name	Courses
John Cantrell	Oil and Gas
Phil W. Davis, Jr.	unknown
George Downey	unknown
T. Austin Gavin	Contracts
Grace Elmore Gibson	Domestic Relations, Ethics Practice and Procedure
Henry W. Gray	Real Property
W. E. Green	Insurance
Horace Hagan	Bills and Notes, Constitutional Law, Oil and Gas
Harry Halley	Municipal Corporations
Barney A. Hamilton	Criminal Law
Emory E. Hanson	Bailments and Carriers, Criminal Law, Domestic Relations, Legal Bibliography, Personal Property, Pleading
Russell R. Hayes	Agency, Municipal Corporations
Paxton Howard	unknown
Robert D. Hudson	Moot Court
Wash E. Hudson	unknown (probably taught no courses)
Roy M. Huff	Probate, Wills and Trusts
James A. Hull	Contracts
Hawley C. Kerr	Oil and Gas, Partnerships, Wills
Bryan Kirkpatrick	unknown
Charles A. Kothe	Bills and Notes, Corporations Labor Law
John Ladner	Evidence

Name	Courses (continued)
Phillip N. Landa	Federal Courts, Practice and Procedure
Gentry Lee	Torts
Fred D. Leonard	Conflict of Laws, Partnerships, Wills
Stewart Lynch	unknown
M. M. Mahaney	Taxation
William H. McClarin	Equity, Partnerships
William Melton	unknown
Lawrence Mills	Indian Land Titles
A.E. Montgomery	Suretyship, Trial Practice
Dwight A. Olds	Property
Louis W. Pratt	Torts
Hal Rambo	unknown
Rogers S. Randolph	Conflict of Laws, Taxation
McKeriel C. Rodolf	unknown
John Rogers	Constitutional Law, Contracts
Remington Rogers	Agency and Partnership, Code Pleading, Constitutional Law, Insurance, Trial Techniques
Charles Skalnik	Blackstone, Code Pleading, Common Law Pleading, Legal Bibliography
Thomas F. Serviss	unknown
H.L. Smith	Bailment and Carriers, Trial Practice
I.J. Underwood	Corporations
J.B. Underwood	Agency, Evidence
Elsie Waddle	unknown
Thomas L. Wallace	Criminal Law
H.R. Williams	Constitutional Law
W.I. Williams	unknown

65. Supra n. 58 at 216.

66. Supra n. 61.

67. Interview with George Downey, law school instructor 1933-36 (May 6, 1988). (University of Tulsa College of Law Archives)

68. Charles Kothe, who taught from 1938-58, stated that faculty pay was $25.00 per night. Supra n. 61.

69. Supra n. 67. (Faculty pay was $100.00 month).

70. Ibid.; interview with Hawley C. Kerr, law school instructor 1929-42, (Apr. 27, 1992). (University of Tulsa College of Law Archives)

71. Interview with Ben L. Murdock, ('29), (October, 1987). (University of Tulsa College of Law Archives)

72. Supra n. 51; Interview with Peggy Wilson, secretary at the law school 1946-1962 (Apr. 2, 1992). (University of Tulsa College of Law Archives)

73. Ibid.

74. Supra n. 61.

75. Supra n. 67.

76. Interview with George Sandel, attorney/instructor (Apr. 22, 1992). (University of Tulsa College of Law Archives)

77. Supra n. 67 & 76.

78. Supra n. 61.

79. Interview with Alma Sheilds Nelson, ('44), (Mar. 5, 1993). (University of Tulsa College of Law Archives)

80. Supra n. 67, 68 & 76.

81. Interview with F.A. Petrik, ('35) (Sept. 9, 1993). (University of Tulsa College of Law Archives)

82. TU's President, C.I. Pontius, as part of his message welcoming students at the start of the 1942-43 school year, stated: "We are engaged in total war. This means that every physically fit boy and man is a candidate for the Armed Forces of the United States." Univ. of Tulsa *Collegian,* Sept.18, 1942.

83. During early 1943, the TU newspaper discussed a survey of the nation's colleges and universities, showing a 9.5% decline from the previous year in the number of full-time students. Univ. of Tulsa *Collegian*, Jan. 22, 1943.

84. The following number of students graduated between 1929 and 1935:

    1929: 22
    1930: 18
    1931: 3
    1932: 13
    1933: 6
    1934: 12
    1935: 4

85. The following number of students graduated between 1936 and 1945:

    1936: 13
    1937: 11
    1938: 17
    1939: 19
    1940: 21
    1941: 16
    1942: 13
    1943: 5
    1944: 6
    1945: 5

CHAPTER TWO

1. TU *Alumni Magazine*, Vol. 12, No. 1, July, 1973.

2. C. Morris, *The Cutting Edge: The Life of John Rogers*, (Univ. of Okla. Press 1976).

3. Minutes, Univ. of Tulsa Bd. of Trustees, (Aug. 23, 1943).

4. Ibid.

5. Minutes, Univ. of Tulsa Bd. of Trustees, (Aug. 25, 1943).

6. Minutes, Univ. of Tulsa Bd. of Trustees, (Sept. 16, 1943). In fact, Judge Hardy was never paid a salary during his tenure as Dean.

7. Minutes Univ. of Tulsa Bd. of Trustees, (Sept. 28, 1943).

8. In September, 1943, Emory Hanson, in looking back over the previous twenty years, released the following statement about the accomplishments of the soon-to-be dissolved Tulsa Law School:

    The Tulsa Law School has had a colorful record. Its founders, with its faculty members, look with justifiable pride upon the illustrious years of the school's achievements. Its scholastic record is evident by the fact that there have only been six failures in the State Bar Examinations in the past 22 years. It is a member of the National Association of Law Schools and is approved by the State Board of Bar Examiners, and the Supreme Court. It has chapters in three National Legal Fraternities: The Phi Beta Gamma, Phi Delta Delta, and the Delta Theta Phi. The local chapter of the Delta Theta Phi was named in honor of a faculty member, Major T. Austin Gavin.

    The Tulsa Law School was a pioneer in this educational enterprise. The founders usually selected for their faculty members leading jurists and lawyers. The school was always without endowment, other than the courage and faith of its founders and faculty. It has continued, self-supporting throughout its career. Today the Tulsa Law School alumni is scattered throughout the United States and on all the world battle-fronts. A recent survey shows that 75 percent of its graduates are engaged in the practice of Law.

    * * *

    Press release of E.E. Hanson, (Sept. 23, 1943).

9. Interview with Gatra Marvin Bradshaw, ('67) (June, 9, 1992). (Granddaughter of Judge Hardy) (University of Tulsa College of Law Archives)

10. Univ. of Tulsa press release, released at the time

of Judge Hardy's appointment as dean (undated) (University of Tulsa College of Law archives).

11. Judge Hardy's son, Milton, later became an adjunct professor at the law school, thus creating the second father-and-son team, following in the footsteps of Wash Hudson and his son, Robert.

12. Supra. n. 7.

13. Minutes, Univ. of Tulsa Bd. of Trustees (Sept. 28, 1943). According to the TU Bd. of Trustees Minutes of October 1, 1943, the assets of the Tulsa Law School were:

Bank Balance	$ 288.49
Balance due on accounts receivable (unpaid student tuition)	504.50
	$ 792.99

Although the comparison is inexact, to appreciate the transformation in the nature of the enterprise of legal education at the University between 1943 and 2002, consider the fact that the total expenditures for the Univ. of Tulsa College of Law for 2001-02 were $12,526,457.00.

14. Supra Chap. 1, n. 48.

15. Supra Chap. 1, n. 58.

16. TU *Alumni Magazine*, July, 1973.

17. Ibid.

18. In a letter from Dwight Olds, a lawyer who taught property courses at the school, to John Rogers, Olds remarks: "I believe that he [Hanson] must have had something on the ball to do as well as he did with his old Law School. But that very loyalty made him drag his feet in connection with the new Law School - or at least that is the impression I received." Letter from Dwight Olds, property instructor, to John Rogers (June 30, 1946) (TU McFarlin Lib. Spec. Collections).

19. Upon Hanson's death, W.C. Franklin became the Assistant Dean, directing the day-to-day operation of the school. He served in that capacity until 1949, when he was replaced by A. Allen King, who became "administrative" dean under John Rogers.

20. "The sudden death of Mr. Hanson had projected the Law School into a new phase of its growth. . . . Now that he is dead I believe a new perspective should be sought. . . . Our immediate aim is to qualify for ABA approval." Supra n. 18.

21. Ibid. Olds outlined two major areas of recommended change to Rogers:

1. He first recommended an overhaul of the curriculum, concentrating on his own field, property. He suggested that the law school study the curriculum of major law schools, mentioning Harvard, Columbia and Michigan, as well as the University of Oklahoma. He suggested a move away from emphasis on bar exam courses, suggesting that the school focus on the "tougher fields on law, together with a heavy sense of his [the student's] social responsibility."

2. He recommended a move away from reliance on textbook instruction in favor of the casebook method of instruction.

22. File memo from W.C. Franklin, Assistant Dean, (Dec. 8, 1947). This memo refers to a visit by a "Mr. Sullivan" who inspected the law school for the ABA, examining the records and indicating what requirements would need to be met for the school to receive accreditation.

23. *Tulsa World*, June 19, 1994.

24. It is estimated that the government spent over 14 billion dollars educating World War II veterans. Ibid.

25. *Tulsa World*, Aug. 17, 1947.

26. Ibid.

27. Supra n. 22.

28. Interview with A. Allen King, ('41) (May 7, 1988). The school started a true full-time program ten years later, in 1957.

29. Following is the four-year curriculum for 1948-49, showing the courses and instructors:

Course	Hours	Instructor
FIRST YEAR		
First Semester		
Contracts I	2	W. E. Green
Torts I	2	R. Rogers
Property I	2	D. Olds
Civil Procedure I	2	M. V. Hardy
Legal Method I	2	W. P. Woodruff
Second Semester		
Contracts II	4	W. E. Green
Torts II	3	R. Rogers
Property II	2	D. Olds
Legal Method II	1	W. P. Woodruff
SECOND YEAR		
First Semester		
Civil Procedure II	2	M. V. Hardy
Property III	2	D. Olds
Equity I	2	R. Rogers

SECOND YEAR

First Semester *(continued)*

Course	Hours	Instructor
Criminal Law Agency &	2	W. Mausey
Partnership	2	P. N. Landa

Second Semester

Course	Hours	Instructor
Property IV	2	D. Olds
Equity II	2	R. Rogers
Trusts	2	R. Huff
Bills and Notes	2	G. Lee
Agency & Partnership II	2	P. N. Landa

THIRD YEAR

First Semester

Course	Hours	Instructor
Constitutional Law I	2	J. Rogers
Private Corporations	2	W. P. Woodruff
Evidence I	2	T. Milsten
Electives	4	

Second Semester

Course	Hours	Instructor
Constitutional Law II	2	J. Rogers
Private Corporations I	2	W. P. Woodruff
Evidence II	2	T. Milsten
Electives	4	

FOURTH YEAR

First Semester

Course	Hours	Instructor
Oklahoma Practice I	2	R. Rogers
Administrative Law	2	W. P. Woodruff
Electives	6	

Second Semester

Course	Hours	Instructor
Oklahoma Practice II	2	R. Rogers
Judicial Administration	2	G. Klein
Electives	6	

Courses sufficient to complete the elective requirements could be selected from the following courses:

Course	Hours	Instructor
Damages	2	P. N. Landa
Insurance	2	P. N. Landa
Creditor's Rights	2	J. Rogers
Restitution	2	unknown
Security	2	W. C. Franklin
Domestic Relations	2	unknown
Sales	2	M. V. Hardy
Property V (Wills)	2	R. Huff
Property VI (Future Int.)	2	D. Olds
Conflict of Laws	2	unknown
Criminal Procedure	2	unknown
Indian Land Titles	1	unknown
Taxation I and II	4	unknown
Oil and Gas Law	2	unknown

Course	Hours	Instructor
Municipal Corporations	2	unknown
Public Service Companies	2	unknown
Labor Law	2	unknown
Federal Jurisdiction and Procedure	2	unknown

30. Supra. Chap. 1, n.2 at 216.

31. Interview with Bruce Peterson (Feb. 26, 1992).

32. *Tulsa Tribune*, Aug. 26, 1949. By this time, although the administrative office and some classes were located in the Ault-Kirkpatrick Building on Third Street, other classes were still being held at Central High School. The library remained at the county courthouse.

33. Interview with George Sandel (Apr. 22, 1992) (The University of Tulsa College of Law archives).

34. *Tulsa Tribune, Jan. 5, 1950.*

35. Ibid. Compare the fact that, in 1969, when the law school was in the throes of deciding whether to move out of the 512 South Cincinnati building for lack of space to adequately conduct law school operations, the enrollment of the law school, which alone occupied the building since the departure of the Downtown Division in 1963, was only 312 students.

36. Interview with John W. Hager (Mar. 25, 1989) (The University of Tulsa College of Law archives).

37. Delta Theta Phi, Phi Alpha Delta, Phi Beta Gamma and Phi Delta Delta.

38. Univ. of Tulsa *Collegian*, May, 1953.

39. *Tulsa World*, Oct. 26, 1951.

40. *Tulsa Tribune*, Mar. 5, 1954.

41. Univ. of Tulsa School of Law Bull., 1957-58; unknown newspaper article, (March 16, 1956) (The Univ. of Tulsa McFarlin Library Spec. Collections).

42. Below are selected enrollments between 1957 and 1973 in each division:

Year	Full-time Division	Part-time Division
1957	15	201
1960	55	166
1968	108	204
1973	361	110

43. Interview with A. Allen King, ('41) (May 7, 1988) (The University of Tulsa College of Law archives).

44. Ibid.

45. See Sipuel v. Board of Regents of University of Okla., 68 S. Ct. 299 (1948); Fisher v. Hurst, 68 S. Ct. 389 (1948) After graduation from law school, Ms. Fisher practiced law, taught at Langston University for many years and, ultimately, was appointed to the University of Oklahoma Board of Regents in 1992. *Tulsa World*, Oct. 20, 1995.

46. Interview with Mrs. Edward L. Goodwin, Sr. (Mar.11, 1992) (The University of Tulsa College of Law archives).

47. Dones' wife asserted the former, while the school registrar, Peggy Wilson, asserted the latter. One factor giving credence to Dones' wife's view is the fact that the admission criteria for entrants at this time was loose and students without undergraduate degrees were often admitted as regular students. Why was Dones treated differently?

48. Supra n. 46; interview with Peggy Wilson (Apr. 2, 1992) (The University of Tulsa College of Law archives).

49. Supra n. 46. Mrs. Goodwin recounted that her husband had been inducted into one of the men's fraternities and that she was welcomed into the Law Wives Association.

50. Over the next seven years, only three African-Americans would graduate: Robert Copeland ('59), Charles Owens ('60) and James O. Goodwin ('65).

51. For his long-time service to the University, he was awarded an honorary LL.D. degree.

52. The three previous deans—Wash Hudson, Summers Hardy and John Rogers—had been practicing lawyers who had been titular heads who delegated day-to-day responsibilities to others.

53. Interview with Peggy Wilson (Apr. 2, 1992) (The University of Tulsa College of Law archives).

54. *Tulsa World*, Aug. 23, 1959.

55. *Tulsa World*, Nov. 14, 1959.

56. TU *Alumni Magazine*, July 1973.

57. TU *Alumni Magazine*, July 1973.

58. Supra n. 43.

59. Interview with Ben G. Henneke (April 28, 2003) (The University of Tulsa College of Law archives).

60. Ibid.

61. *Tulsa Quarterly*, Winter 1963 (published by Univ. of Tulsa Law School).

62. TU *Alumni Magazine*, Fall, 1966.

63. *Tulsa Tribune*, Oct. 16, 1962.

64. *Tulsa Tribune*, June 26, 1964.

65. The Univ. of Tulsa College of Law *Bull.*, 1965-1966.

66. Minutes, Univ. of Tulsa Bd. of Trustees, May 26, 1965.

67. Interview with Bruce Peterson (Feb. 26, 1992) (The University of Tulsa College of Law archives).

68. This division, composed of undergraduate students, is not to be confused with the law school's evening division of law students.

69. *Tulsa Tribune*, Sept. 13, 1962.

70. *Tulsa World*, Oct. 20, 1963.

71. Following are total school enrollments for most of the remaining decade, based on University data:
Fall, 1963:   241 students
Fall, 1964:   282 students
Fall, 1965:   324 students
Fall, 1966:   321 students
Fall, 1967:   325 students
Fall, 1968:   312 students

72. *Tulsa World*, Oct. 20, 1963.

73. By the fall semester, 1968, enrollment had grown to 350. Tulsa World, Nov. 13, 1968 (Discrepancy between this figure and that found at supra note 71. This could be explained both by different methods of counting and by Dean Peterson's penchant for "puffing." He believed that more was always better when it came to enrollment.)

74. *Tulsa Tribune*, Feb. 25, 1953.

75. *Tulsa Tribune*, Mar. 1, 1963.

76. The petition requested the following improvements:
   • a variety of physical improvements in the building
   • an improved student-faculty ratio
   • increased budget allowances for student activities
   • expansion of available parking
   • establishment of a fund-raising foundation

   The following improvements were announced :
   • renovation to several classrooms
   • renovations necessary to add additional faculty offices
   • increased work area for clerical staff
   • enlargement of the student lounge
   • space provided for the *Tulsa Law Journal* and the Student Bar Association
   • Library renovations: additional study areas and additional shelving necessary to increase capacity from 42,000 to 60,000 volumes.
   Tulsa Tribune, Dec. 20, 1968.

77. Interview with J. Paschal Twyman (June 22, 1987).

78. Three years earlier, the University and the law school had investigated, but abandoned, the possibility of expanding the law school into a building at 310 W. Sixth Street. *Tulsa Tribune*, Apr. 30, 1965.

79. Letter from Carol Wilson, widow of the then-deceased former dean, (May 13, 1992) The University of Tulsa College of Law archives.)

80. Memo from Edgar H, Wilson, Dean, College of Law, to J. Paschal Twyman, President, Univ. of Tulsa (Jan. 26, 1970) (The University of Tulsa College of Law archives).

81. The eight reasons cited for a downtown location are these:

    1) Clinical offerings such as legal aid, public defender, legal clerkships and other programs which provide practical experience can best be developed and maintained from a downtown location.

    2) The proximity of the Law School to the courts gives students an opportunity to observe "law in action."

    3) The availability of the Law School Library to members of the Bar renders a service to the Bar and brings students and faculty in closer contact with practicing lawyers.

    4) A location in the heart of the city brings about a closer association between the faculty and practicing attorneys.

    5) Being off campus help keeps the Law School independent from the rest of the University.

    6) Association with undergraduate students would be detrimental to the professional atmosphere which should be maintained in the Law School.

    7) The downtown location provides travel convenience for evening students.

    8) Students in a downtown Law School have greater job opportunities.

The nine reasons cited for a campus location are these:

1) A campus location makes possible interdisciplinary studies.

2) Availability of the resources of the main campus is essential to a good law school.

3) The availability of the Law Library to other disciplines is an asset to the University.

4) Administration of the Law School is more convenient and efficient when the building is located on the main campus.

5) Law professors and students have a greater allegiance to the University when the law building is located on campus.

6) A campus location gives law students and faculty the use of facilities such as the student union, cafeteria and bookstore.

7) Students spend more time at the Law School when it is located on the main campus.

8) A campus location discourages students from seeking outside employment.

9) A law school located on the main campus of a University attracts better qualified students from a broader geographical area. Ibid.

82. Ibid.

83. Interview with John Dowgray (May 10, 1989) (The University of Tulsa College of Law archives).

84. Interview with Gordon McCune, of McCune, McCune & Associates, architects for John Rogers Hall and other campus buildings (Oct. 1, 1992) (The University of Tulsa College of Law archives).

85. This view is confirmed by his daughter, Sharon Bell, who was, as of 2003, the Chapman Trusts trustee. Interview with Sharon Bell (July 31, 2002) (The University of Tulsa College of Law archives).

86. *Tulsa World* Nov. 21, 1970. Although this gift was officially "anonymous" for many years, it was widely known that it had come from Leta M. Chapman, widow of James A. Chapman, and was publicly acknowledged as such after her death (The University of Tulsa College of Law archives).

87. Interview with Edwin M. Schmidt (May 15, 1992) (The University of Tulsa College of Law archives).

88. The Cabinet, including Taliaferro and Savage, was comprised of:

William H. Bell	Raymond Kravis
Byron V. Boone	Bert McElroy
Robert Bresnahan	Joseph W. Morris
Lambert Fielder	Claude Rosenstein
Russell Hunt	Eugene Swearingen
Max Knotts	Don Turner

89. Interview with Royce Savage (Apr. 10, 1992) (The University of Tulsa College of Law archives).

90. The drive began in December, 1970 and was completed by October, 1971. Minutes of the Univ. of Tulsa Bd. of Trustees for October 5, 1971 (Oct. 5, 1971). President Twyman announced that "…the fund drive for John Rogers Hall, in the amount of $500,000, which was co-chaired by Mr. Paul Taliaferro and Judge Royce Savage, has been completed and actually oversubscribed." Ibid.

91. *Tulsa World*, Nov. 21, 1970.

92. Minutes, Univ. of Tulsa Bd. of Trustees (May 5, 1971).

93. Univ. of Tulsa *Collegian*, May 13, 1971.

94. Supra n. 87.

95. Interview with Professor James C. Thomas (Feb. 26, 1993) (The University of Tulsa College of Law Archives).

96. *Tulsa World*, June 19, 1971.

97. Ibid.

98. The letter, dated June 14, 1971, was on University stationary and signed by Twyman in his capacity as president of The University of Tulsa.

99. *Tulsa Tribune*, June 20, 1971; *Tulsa Tribune*, June 23, 1971; *Tulsa World*, June 24, 1971; *Tulsa World*, June 25, 1971; *Tulsa World*, June 30, 1971.

100. The report of the ad hoc committee, which is undated, is entitled, "REPORT OF THE AD HOC COMMITTEE TO INVESTIGATE THE CHARGE BY PROF. JAMES THOMAS THAT THE UNIVERSITY HAS VIOLATED ITS ACADEMIC FREEDOM AND TENURE POLICIES.." The local AAUP report (Aug. 19, 1971) is entitled "AAUP THOMAS COMMITTEE REPORT." Both reports are located in the College of Law archives. *Tulsa World*, July 14, 1971; *Tulsa Tribune*, July 14, 1971.

101. Interview with Allen R. Soltow (Oct. 1, 2003) (The University of Tulsa College of Law archives).

102. Twyman continued to maintain that he had the right to criticize a faculty member's actions as long as he did not threaten the faculty member. Thomas continued to maintain that he had the right to express what he believed. He felt vindicated because of Twyman's position of "criticism without threats." See Endnote 95, supra.

103. See the statement, entitled "Allen Soltow, President, Local Chapter American Association of University Professors, Univ. of Tulsa, (Aug. 24, 1971)," The University of Tulsa College of Law archives.

104. A summary of the incident and a student appraisal of its meaning can be found in the University of Tulsa *Collegian*, (Sept. 2, 1971).

105. Interview with J. Paschal Twyman, see endnote 77, supra.

106. Memo from Imogene Harris to Dean Morris and Library Committee (Jan. 11, 1973).

107. Interview with Imogene Harris (July 29, 1992) (The University of Tulsa College of Law archives).

CHAPTER THREE

1. Statement drafted by William H. Bell (The University of Tulsa College of Law archives).

2. Interview with Joseph W. Morris (Apr. 17, 1992) (The University of Tulsa College of Law archives).

3. For example, John Hager had produced, along with others, a definitive eight-volume work on Oklahoma forms and practice. He also produced a casebook on the law of torts, which he used in his course. W. Paul Gormley had written extensively on admiralty.

4. Interview with J. Paschal Twyman (June 22, 1987). Monies from the James A. Chapman Trust were beginning to flow into the University. President

Twyman viewed this as providing the capability of reducing teaching loads and freeing up time for faculty to seek research grants and engage in more scholarship. When John Dowgray, the new provost, arrived at the University in 1969, he told the College of Arts and Sciences, with deliberate exaggeration, that he found TU to be a "fine four-year community college," but not a "research institution." With the help of the Chapman monies, he and President Twyman set out to change this. Interview with John Dowgray (May 10, 1989).

5. Grace Elmore Gibson had taught at the Tulsa Law School in the 1930s; however, she was a practitioner who taught part-time.

6. Interview with Georgina Landman (Oct. 10, 1992). (The University of Tulsa College of Law archives) See, also, an article about women in the law school and the founding of the Women's Law Caucus. *Tulsa World*, May 19, 1974.

7. In 1975, there were 76 women in a total population of 544 students, equaling 14% of the enrollment. *Tulsa Tribune*, Oct. 8, 1975.

8. Univ. of Tulsa *Alumni Magazine*, Mar. 1973.

9. *Tulsa Tribune*, Sept. 5, 1973.

10. Ibid.

11. Interview with Rennard Strickland (May 21, 1992). (The University of Tulsa College of Law archives)

12. In 1975, enrollment passed the 500 mark for the first time. Supra n. 7.

13. These new faculty members were: John Choate, William G. Hollingsworth, Patrick H. Martin, Carol Ann Potter, David M. Treiman, Raymond Yasser, and, as librarian, Joel Burstein.

14. Interview with Mrs. Edward L. Goodwin, Sr. (March 11, 1992). (The University of Tulsa College of Law archives)

15. *Tulsa Tribune*, Apr. 20, 1972.

16. The courses involved were administrative law, business associations, commercial law I, conflict of laws, decedents' estates and trusts, evidence and tax I.

17. The courses involved were comparative law, international law, jurisprudence and legal history.

18. This concept was the cornerstone of the Read Deanship. It permeated faculty discussions and decisions and appears in the law school documents of the day. See e.g. Univ. of Tulsa College of Law *Bulletin*, 24 (1975-76).

19. See Report of the Special Board ad hoc Committee for Long Range Planning and Faculty Steering

Committee for Long Range Planning to the Board of Trustees (Dec. 1, 1975).

20. See Implementation Suggestions: The College of Law's Preliminary Response to the 1975 Cresap, McCormick and Paget Report (1976).

21. Renard Strickland,15 Tulsa Law J., 720 (1980).

22. Supra n. 13.

23. The six new faculty members were: Gary Allison (visiting), Edna Ball, Martin Frey, Gunther Handl, Eric Jensen and Rennard Strickland.

24. Supra n. 5.

25. The *Tulsa Tribune* printed an article on female students and professors in the law school. *Tulsa Tribune*, Sept. 23, 1976.

26. In 1974, the percentages of students in the full-time division and part-time division were 84% / 16%. By 1979, the percentages were 67% / 33%.

27. Supra n. 14.

28. *Tulsa World*, July 24, 1974.

29. *Tulsa World*, Apr. 15, 1977. See *Tulsa Tribune*, Apr. 14, 1977 (a more complete story about the SBA resolution and its aftermath).

30. *Tulsa World*, May 8, 1978.

31. Univ. of Tulsa *Collegian*, Sept. 7, 1978.

32. Interview with Velda Staves, (Apr. 23, 1992).

33. Univ. of Tulsa College of Law *Bulletin*, Map, (1979-80).

34. *Tulsa World*, July 13, 1975.

35. Interview with Anthony Bastone, II (Sept. 30, 1988). (The University of Tulsa College of Law archives)

36. Supra n. 33.

37. *Tulsa World*, Oct. 22, 1951.

38. Memo from Tom Holland, professor, to Reynard Strickland, dean (July 18, 1974) (Univ. of Tulsa McFarlin Library Special Collections. (detailed . . . what had been done during the recent fund-raising campaign and what needed to be done in the future).

39. *Tulsa World*, Nov. 9, 1975.

40. Tuition increased during this time as follows:
    1973-75 $52/credit
    1975-76   62/credit (19% increase)
    1976-77   70/credit (12% increase)
    1977-78   75/credit (7% increase)
    1978-79   85/credit (13% increase)
    1979-80   90/credit (6% increase)

41. Memo from Tom Holland, assistant dean to Tom Read, dean, "Building Addition." (Oct. 2, 1978).

42. Memo from Frank T. Read, dean to John Dowgray, vice president for academic affairs and John Evans, director of development, "Law School Ten Year Plan." (Nov. (year unknown)).

43. *Tulsa Tribune*, Oct. 6, 1978.

44. Interview with Frank T. Read (Jan. 29, 1988).

45. *Tulsa Tribune*, June 5, 1979.

46. Memo from McCune & Associates to Tom Read (Oct. 10, 1978).

47. Memo from Sharon J. Bell to John F. Hicks (Aug. 15, 2002) (listing contributions to the Univ. of Tulsa College of Law from the J.A. Chapman and Leta M. Chapman Charitable Trust (1966) and the Leta McFarlin Chapman Memorial Trust).

48. Interview with Tom L. Holland (Aug. 29, 2002). (The University of Tulsa College of Law archives)

CHAPTER FOUR

1. The Univ. of Tulsa *Annual*, 11 (1984-85).

2. The Univ. of Tulsa *Annual*, 19 (1981-82) ("As the pool of high school graduates continues to shrink annually, competition among colleges and universities for able students intensifies. Each year it is necessary to recruit from larger numbers of prospective students in order to achieve our objectives for the freshman class.").

3. Univ. of Tulsa *Annual* 13 (1982-83) (indicates the focus the University was about to take under his direction: "Staley is most concerned with the University's undergraduates. . . . Since these undergraduates are the University's future, their academic programs - indeed, their entire undergraduate experience - are Dr. Thomas Staley's main concern.")

4. "From 1981-88, TU experienced seven years of declining enrollment. Three factors appeared to influence the decline: a shrinking freshman applicant pool; an excessive attrition rate; and a sharp decline in the number of non-traditional and part-time students." Exit Report from Dr. E. Joe Middlebrooks, acting president Sept. 1989 to June, 1990, to Univ. of Tulsa Faculty (June 11, 1990).

5. *Baculus*, 5, April / May, 1991 (a publication of Univ. of Tulsa College of Law).

6. Applications reached a high of 1,390 in 1977; by 1987, they had fallen to 615.

7. In 1976, the school was the most selective, offering admission to 46% of all applicants; by 1980, the number of applications accepted had risen to 65%; the percentage continued to rise until it hit a high of 74% in 1987, before falling back to 64% by 1990.

8. In 1980, the average GPA of the entering class was 3.02; by 1987, it had declined to 2.95. It continued

to fall, reaching a low point of 2.87 in 1990, before
beginning to rise again. The Law School Admission
Test (LSAT) score average in 1983 was 32; by 1987, it
had fallen to 29, before rising again to 32 by 1990.

9. In 1970, total enrollment stood at 251; by 1978,
    it had risen to an all-time high of 728. In contrast
    to this trend, in 1980, enrollment stood at 650; by
    1986, it had fallen to 553, before increasing to 635 by
    1990.

10. In 1990-91, the school awarded scholarships to 141
    students, including 22 full-tuition scholarships and
    47 John Rogers Scholarships. See Dean's Annual
    Report 1990-91, 8 (1990-91).

11. *Briefly* (Univ. of Tulsa College of Law, Oct. 2, 1987).

12. Classified in law school statistics as African American,
    Asian, Hispanic and Native American.

13. Marianne Blair, Marguerite Chapman, Catherine
    Cullem, Linda Lacey, Vicki Limas, Marla Mansfield,
    and Winona Tanaka.

14. Christen Blair, M. Thomas Arnold, Dennis Bires,
    Richard Ducey (library director), Johnny Parker, and
    Rex Zedalis.

15. Swygert and Gozansky, "Senior Law Faculty
    Publication Study: Comparisons of Law School
    Productivity," 35 J. Legal Ed. 373, Table 5 (1985).

16. See the discussion in the previous chapter on how
    Dean Read secured the funds for the East Wing
    outside of the "Dimensions for a New Decade
    Campaign."

17. ABA Self-Study Report, The Univ. of Tulsa College of
    Law, 71 (Spring, 1987).

18. Advanced advocacy, advanced legal writing,
    alternative methods of dispute resolution, evidence
    workshop, and pre-trial practice.

19. Introduction to alternative methods of dispute
    resolution; mediation; arbitration; and interviewing,
    counseling, and negotiation.

20. An enhanced classroom component was added to the
    Program, enhanced faculty supervision of attorney/
    supervisors was added, and an orientation program
    for attorney/supervisors was started.

21. Professors Gary Allison and Chris Blair debated the
    subject. *Baculus*, Apr./May 1989.

22. Editor-in-chief of the *Baculus* asked the question,
    "Why Doesn't TU Have a Legal Clinic?" and asked
    for reader response. Todd Singer, *Baculus*, Mar. 1990.
    A local attorney, Maynard Ungerman, discussed a
    model clinical program.

23. These new courses included banking law, consumer
    transactions, corporate finance, environmental

policy, financing energy development, hazardous
substance control, health law, international business
transactions, international energy law, legal rights of
children, oil and gas transactions, real estate finance
and sports law.

24. ABA Self-Study Report, The Univ. of Tulsa College of
    Law, 86 (Spring 1987).

25. "Legal Aspects of Enhanced Oil
    Recovery," prepared for the U.S. Congress, Office
    of Technology Assessment (1976-77) [$9,000].
    "Legal Aspects of Transporting Coal by Slurry
    Pipeline," prepared for the U.S. Congress, Office
    of Technology Assessment (1976-77) [$30,986].
    "Legal Analysis of PURPA (Public Utility Regulatory
    Policies Act of 1978)," prepared for the Oklahoma
    Corporation Commission (1978-79) [$10,000].
    "Public Utility Regulatory Policies Act," State
    Implementation Grant awarded by the U.S.
    Department of Energy (1979-80) [$200,000].
    "Conference on Nuclear Power Generation", grant
    awarded by the National Science Foundation
    (1980-81) [$38,964].
    "Economic Development Alternatives for Oklahoma's
    Third Congressional District," grant awarded by
    the Kiamichi Economic District of Oklahoma
    (1981-82) [$10,000].
    "Energy Sectionalism and the American Legal System:
    Approaches to Reconciliation," prepared jointly
    with the ABA Special Commission on Energy Law
    (1982-83) [$15,000].

26. ABA Self-Study Report, Univ. of Tulsa College of
    Law, 80 (Spring 1987).

27. Ibid. at 84.

28. Report of the Oversight and Planning Committee to
    the Faculty, 11 (Nov. 5, 1987).

29. Ibid. at 9.

30. Mary N. Birmingham (1986-95), Vicki D. Jordan
    (1995 - to the time of this writing).

31. E.g. Dean's Annual Report (1987-88) (indicates that
    45% of 1987 graduates were practicing in twenty-two
    states outside of Oklahoma); but see Dean's Annual
    Report (1990-91) (indicates that 32% of 1990
    graduates were located in sixteen states outside of
    Oklahoma).

32. See a discussion of these events earlier in this chapter.

33. "TU's Presidential Search High Stakes," *Tulsa World*,
    Feb. 14, 1990.

34. "A Dean's Eye View, 1980-1991, and Beyond,"
    Baculus, 6 Apr./May, 1991).

CHAPTER FIVE

1. "The College of Law Strategic Plan for 1992-97," adopted in the fall of 1991, had, as its first goal: Achieve the indicators of success that establish The University of Tulsa College of Law as an institution on the level of SMU, George Washington, Ohio State, Washington University and Illinois.

2. Memo from George Gilpin, Provost, to John Makdisi, Dean Designate, "Understanding in Regard to Resources Needed for the College of Law." (May 24, 1991). This Memo gives financial assurances in regard to the goals listed in the text as follows:

   1. Development Officer:
      As discussed with President Donaldson and Vice President Gibson, a development officer for the College of Law will be appointed in Fiscal Year 1991-92.

   2. Computers:
      Up to $50,000 will be made available for academic computing in the College of Law in Fiscal Year 1991-92.

   3. Additional Faculty Positions:
      Three new faculty lines will be allocated to the College of Law, and at least one of these lines may be fitted for Fiscal Year 1992-93. Lines for all three positions will be available no later than Fiscal Year 1994-95. (President Donaldson has committed to find support as soon as possible for at least one chaired professorship).

   4. Faculty Salaries and Summer Research Grants:
      I recognize that salaries in the College of Law need to be raised to the national average, and I commit to increasing them to that level during a three-year period beginning Fiscal Year 1992-93. In addition, during the same period of time a program of summer research grants will be funded.

   5. Admissions/Recruitment Publications:
      You will review the existing resources for these publications and advise me if additional funds outside the budget for the College of Law are needed.

   6. Library Enhancement:
      Enhancement of the University Libraries is a goal of the strategic plan, and the Law Library will receive its appropriate share of new library allocations in the University. You will review the current needs and advise me about what is required.

3. Total University enrollment dropped from 4,922 in 1992 to 4,579 in 1994. These decreases in enrollment required the University to adjust its budgets to reflect the resulting diminution in tuition and associated revenues. See "Findings" in a letter, dated June 26, 1995, to President Donaldson and Acting Dean Arnold from James P. White, Consultant of Legal Education to the American Bar Association.

4. 1) Globalization Program
   2) Environmental Studies Program
   3) Math and Science Education Programs
   4) High Quality "bridge" Programs to help "at risk" students
   5) Multicultural emphasis throughout the curriculum.

5. "The University of Tulsa Strategic Plan 1991-96", p. 99.

6. Ibid.

7. "Area Lawyers Hit Hard by Economy," *Tulsa World*, Jan. 5, 1992.

8. In 1991, 56% of all students taking the LSAT during the relevant period scored at or below the TU average (and, conversely, 44% of all students scored above the TU average). In 1992, this figure had improved to 67% of all students scoring at or below the TU average. The numbers stayed close to this point for the remainder of Makdisi's deanship.

9. He once remarked that he thought that his years at Tulsa were proving to be his most productive, which was remarkable in light of the quantity of scholarship he produced in over forty years on the faculty of New York University. For a brief assessment of his scholarship while at NYU, see the *NYU Alumni Magazine*, 20 (Autumn 1992).

10. Academic Exchange Agreement Between The University of Tulsa and Komenius University, appended to a faculty Memo (Nov. 13, 1991).

11. *Baculus*, Mar. 1994 (a publication of Univ. of Tulsa College of Law).

12. See Supra chap. 4, n. 21.

13. Interview with John Makdisi (Apr. 29, 1996).

14. See *Baculus*, Nov. / Dec. 1991; Tulsa County Bar Association *Lawyer* (Feb., 1992).

15. Interview with Winona Tanaka (Oct. 30, 2002). (The University of Tulsa College of Law archives)

16. See *Baculus* (Oct. / Nov., 1992).; Univ. of Tulsa College of Law *Alumni Newsletter* (Summer, 1993).

17. A letter, dated June 26, 1995, from James P. White, Consultant on Legal Education to the ABA, to President Donaldson and Acting Dean Arnold, listed these criticisms: (1) participating students, rather than the College, select their field supervisors; (2) training

is not provided for the field supervisors; (3) field supervisors are evaluated by the School primarily on the basis of information maintained by the students; (4) placement sites are rarely, if ever, visited by the faculty member who directs the program; and (5) the program's classroom component, at least in the view of some faculty members, is weak and lacking in rigor.

18. See *Baculus*, Mar., 1994.

19. Supra n. 2.

20. Dean's Report to the Alumni (Spring, 1992). Makdisi summarized the progress made during his first year in the areas covered by the Provost's assurances. In discussing the law library, he said this: "The one area in which the law school has serious needs that have not yet, nor probably can be, completely met by the University alone is the support of the Law Library. Our acquisitions budget and our space needs are critical, but my hope is that the University and the alumni will join in supporting this most critical need of the law school." Ibid.

21. Memo from Rick Ducey, Lib. Dir., to John F. Hicks (Oct. 31, 2002) (supplying figures).

22. Supra n. 3.

23. Memo from Makdisi, Dean. to Univ. of Tulsa Faculty and Staff, "John Rogers Hall Expansion Building Project" (Feb. 1, 1994).

24. Interview with Tom Arnold (Oct. 30, 2002). (The University of Tulsa College of Law archives)

25. Supra n. 21.

26. *Baculus,* Mar. 1995 (a publication of Univ. of Tulsa College of Law).

27. Supra n. 2.

28. Supra n. 13.

29. *Baculus*, Aug. / Sept. 1992, (a publication of Univ. of Tulsa College of Law).

30. *Lawyer* (Tulsa County Bar Association May, 1993), *Alumni Newsletter* (Univ. of Tulsa College of Law Fall 1993).

31. *Baculus*, Oct. 1994 (Univ. of Tulsa College of Law).

32. Minutes of the Regular Faculty Meeting, (Oct. 1, 1991).

33. A "Fair Employment Practices" statement had been adopted November 15, 1988; Minutes, Regular Faculty Meeting. (Sept. 3, 1991). (Non Discrimination Policy)

34. *Baculus*, Oct., 1991 (a publication of Univ. of Tulsa College of Law), *Baculus*, Nov./Dec., 1991 (a publication of Univ. of Tulsa College of Law).

35. *Tulsa World*, Oct. 11, 1991; Memo from Robert Donaldson, President, to John Makdisi, Dean (Dec. 2, 1991).

36. Memo from Makdisi, Dean to Univ. of Tulsa Faculty (Apr. 17, 1992).

37. Supra n. 2.

38. Interview with Tom Holland (Aug. 29, 2002). (The University of Tulsa College of Law archives)

39. See Supra n. 3.

40. Memo from John Makdisi, Dean, to ABA Inspection Team," Financial Situation of The University of Tulsa College of Law" (Sept. 2, 1993).

41. Ibid.

42. Memo from Gilpin, Provost, to University Faculty (Aug. 11, 1992).

43. Supra n. 13.

44. Memo from John Makdisi, Dean, to Law Faculty and Staff, "Resignation" (Mar.14, 1994).

45. Memo from Thomas Arnold, Acting Dean, to Faculty (Nov. 9, 1994).

46. Address by Robert Donaldson, President (Feb. 6, 1995) (discussing the reductions and the larger fiscal picture at the University).

47. Memo from Lewis Duncan, Provost, to Univ. Community, "The University's 1995-96 Budget" (Mar. 1, 1995).

48. Supra n. 24.

49. Ibid.

CHAPTER SIX

1. See "Dean's Message" Univ. of Tulsa College of Law Catalog (2002-2003) (Dean Belsky discusses the concept of a "legal education center"); Martin Belsky, "Law Schools as Legal Education Centers," 34 U. Toledo L. Rev. 1 (Fall 2002).

2. After graduating from law school, he returned to his home town, Philadelphia and worked in the District Attorney's office for five years, becoming chief prosecutor. Moving to Washington, D.C., he worked in government for the Judiciary Committee of the U.S. House of Representatives, the Special Committee on Offshore Oil and Gas and the National Oceanic and Atmospheric Administration, while teaching as an adjunct at Georgetown Law School. He moved into full-time teaching and administration at the University of Florida College of Law as a professor and director of the Public Policy Center, before moving to Albany Law School as dean.

3. Interview with Martin H. Belsky, (Mar. 3, 2000). (The University of Tulsa College of Law archives)

4. 2001 ABA Site Evaluation Report, 53 (May 4, 2001). Dean Belsky worked to reduce this dependence by

increasing endowment income, as discussed later in this chapter.

5. See Univ. of Tulsa College of Law Self-Study, 69 (Fall 2000).

6. Memo from Martin Belsky, Dean, to Faculty and Senior Staff "Report - ABA Deans' Meeting - January 29 - January 31st." (Feb. 3, 1997).

7. Supra n. 1.

8. This concept is consistent the approach taken on a University-wide level by President Robert Lawless of treating students as valued consumers of the University's products.

9. Black Law Student Association, Hispanic Law Students Association, Jewish Law Students Association, Native American Law Student Association.

10. Christian Legal Society, Jewish Law Students Association, Latter-Day Saint Student Association.

11. Entertainment and Sports Law Society, Environment and Natural Resources Society, International Law Society, Law and Medicine Society, Lesbian, Gay, Bisexual, Transsexual Law Caucus, Women's' Law Caucus.

12. The Part-Time Student Association, Significant Others Society (the successor to the Law Wives Club of years past).

13. *Tulsa World*, Sept.19, 1998.

14. See *Tulsa Law Magazine*, 19 (Spring 1997).

15. 1980 - John W. Hager
    1981 - Martin A. Frey
    1982 - John Forrester Hicks
    1983 - M. Thomas Arnold
    1988 - Marguerite A. Chapman
    1989 - Orley R. Lilly, Jr.
    1992 - Marianne Blair
    1993 - Ray Yasser
    1994 - Bernard Schwartz
    1995 - Larry C. Backer
    1998 - Winona Tanaka
    2000 - Richard Ducey
    2001 - Johnny Parker
    2002 - Catherine Cullem
    2004 – Rex Zedalis

16. This change affected the status of Morris Bernstein and Leslie Mansfield.

17. This change applied to Barbara K. Bucholtz.

18. This change applied to Richard Paschal and Lance Stockwell.

19. Supra n. 4 at 30.

20. *Energy Law Journal, Year- in- Review, Tulsa Law Review, Mineral Law Symposium* and the OBA Mineral Law *Newsletter*.

21. See NELPI 2000-2001 Year-End Report.

22. See NELPI 2001-2002 Year-End Report.

23. ABA action letter from John A. Sebert, Consultant on Legal Education to the American Bar Association, to President Lawless and Dean Belsky, (Aug. 6, 2001).

24. Ibid.

25. Resources, Energy and Environmental Law Certificate; Comparative and International Law Certificate; Native American Law Certificate; and, Alternative Dispute Resolution Certificate.

26. This program, and similar ones at other law schools, is discussed in the magazine *Prelaw*, vol. 7, no. 3 (Winter 2004).

27. See e.g. 2001-2002 Annual Report of the Enrichment Committee (lists thirteen colloquies held during that academic year).

28. To 2003, the Series focused on the scholarship of these individuals: Morton J. Horwitz, Charles Warren Professor of American Legal History at Harvard Law School (2001); Sanford Levinson, W. St. John Garwood & W. St. John Garwood, Jr. Professor of Law at the University of Texas Law School (2002); Frank I. Michelman, Robert Walmsley University Professor of Law at Harvard Law School (2003).

29. See the annual NELPI End-Of-Year Reports (pub. annually).

30. To 2003, the Series featured these speakers: Richard A. Posner, chief judge, U.S. Court of Appeals for the Seventh Circuit (1996); Isaac C. Hunt, Jr., commissioner, Securities and Exchange Commission (1997); Stewart G. Pollock, associate justice, Supreme Court of New Jersey (1998); Guido Calabresi, circuit judge, United States Court of Appeals for the Second Circuit (1999); James P. White, consultant on legal education to the American Bar Association (2000); Fred R. Harris, professor of political science at the University of New Mexico and former United States Senator from Oklahoma (2001); Deanell Reece Tacha, chief judge, U.S. Court of Appeals for the Tenth Circuit (2003); Derrick Bell, visiting professor of Law, New York University (2004).

31. To 2003, the Series featured these speakers: Joel Singer (1998); Martin Edelman, professor of political science and Judaic studies at the University of Albany; (2000); Aharon Barak, president, Supreme Court of Israel (2002).

32. To 2005, the Series featured these speakers: John Hope Franklin (2000); Morris Dees, chief trial

counsel for the Southern Poverty Law Center (2002); Charles Ogletree, professor of law at the Harvard Law School (2002); Julian Bond, chairman of the NAACP (2003), Rennard Strickland, professor of law at the University of Oregon and a former professor and acting dean at the Collge of Law (2005).

33. **Scholars-In-Residence** to 2003 included:

Steven J. Burton, Wm. G. Hammond professor of law of the University of Iowa; James Anaya, professor of law at the University of Iowa (1999); John Hope Franklin, professor emeritus of history at Duke University (2000); Mark V. Tushnet, Carmack Waterhouse professor of Constitutional law at Georgetown University Law Center (2000); Douglas O. Linder, professor of law at the University of Missouri, Kansas City (2001); Michael McConnell, then professor of law at the University of Utah and, currently, circuit judge, United States Court of Appeals for the Tenth Circuit (2001); Howard Gillman, professor of political science and law at the University of Texas (2002).

Practitioners-in-Residence to 2003 included: William G. von Glahn, senior vice president and general counsel, The Williams Companies, Inc. (1997); Jerome Shestack, Wolf, Black, Schorr and Solis Cohen, LLP (1999); Gerald Stern, attorney and author (2001); James J. Hoecker, former chairman of the U.S. Federal Regulatory Commission, 1997-2001 (2001); Robert J. Woolsey, former CIA director (2001).

Judges-In-Residence to 2003 included: Robert Henry, judge, U.S. Court of Appeals for the Tenth Circuit (1997); Susan Weber Wright, chief judge, U.S. District Court for the Eastern District of Arkansas (2000); Ronald M. George, chief justice, Supreme Court of California (and, also, speaker at the Darcy O'Brien Lecture) (2002); Deanell Reece Tacha, chief judge, U.S. Court of Appeals for the Tenth Circuit; Stephanie Seymour, circuit judge, United States Court of Appeals for the Tenth Circuit (2004).

Alumni-In-Residence in 2003 included: Joe Cannon ('66), Judicial Arbiter Group, Inc, Denver and Colorado Springs, Colorado (2000); Elizabeth Crewson Paris ('87), attorney and tax counsel for the U.S. Senate Finance Committee (2001); Kevin L. Patrick ('78) attorney, Aspen, Co.; Sharon L. Corbitt ('82), attorney and former chair of the ABA Family Law Section (2003).

34. See Chapter 5
35. Ibid.

36. "Q & A with Dean Belsky." *Baculus*, Feb.1996.
37. Ibid. In the interview, Belsky gave credit to Dean Makdisi and Acting Dean Arnold for paving the way for such an agreement.
38. See supra n. 4 at 52; Interview with Martin H. Belsky, (Dec. 7, 2002); Interview with Robert W. Lawless, (Oct. 15, 2002). (The University of Tulsa College of Law archives)
39. Supra n. 4 at 52.
40. Interview with Martin H. Belsky, (Dec. 7, 2002). (The University of Tulsa College of Law archives)
41. For 1997-98, tuition for a full-time program for the academic year was $15,250; for a part-time program for the academic year, it was $10,200; other than full-time or part-time, it was $510/credit hour. For 2002-2003, tuition for a full-time program for the academic year was $19,425; for a part-time program of 8-11 hours per semester (four year program), for the academic year it was $13,175; for a part-time program of 4-7 hours per semester (five year program), for the academic year it was $9,975; other than full-time or part-time, it was $725/credit hour.
42. E.g. Supra n. 5 at 77, ("Tuition at the University of Tulsa College of Law has traditionally been about $3,000 below the national average for private schools. This is roughly 15-20% below the national average.") Dean Belsky comments that current and planned future tuition at the school" . . . would still make us the lowest price private school in the four state area (Texas; Oklahoma (OCU); Arkansas; Missouri) and in the bottom 10 in tuition for private schools nationwide." Supra n. 36.
43. Between 1995 and 2002 Belsky organized efforts to successfully raise $21.85 million in cash and endowments and $11 million in future endowment:

$11,700,000	Mabee Legal Information Center
600,000	Boesche Legal Clinic
150,000	East Wing and the Jay C. Byers Student Services Center
600,000	Classrooms and Model Courtroom
2,000,000	Annual Giving (1995-2002)
1,800,000	Special Projects (conferences, speakers, etc.) (1995-2002)
2,000,000	Chapman Trusts [beyond MLIC and Chapman Chair monies] (repairs, computers and technology, general support) (1995-2002)
3,000,000	Endowment Gifts
$21,850,000	TOTAL

$11,000,000 Estate Gifts (future endowment) Supra n. 40.

44. Letter from James P. White, Consultant on Legal Education to the American Bar Association, to President Donaldson and Acting Dean Arnold, 4 (June 29, 1994) (stating the Findings of the ABA Accreditation Committee).

45. See "Dean's Message" *Tulsa Law Magazine* (Summer 2000).

46. See *Baculus*, Aug. 1995 (a publication of Univ. of Tulsa College of Law). .

47. The estimated cost of the project rose from an original estimate of under $6 million, during the initial planning stages under Acting Dean Arnold, to an over $10 million actual cost According to Dean Belsky, the cause was twofold: 1) incomplete and inaccurate architectural work at the beginning, which omitted many cost factors; and, 2) added features to the original plans. Supra n. 40.

48. See *Shrimper*, Nov. 16, 1995.

49. See *Baculus*, Feb. 1996.

50. *Tulsa Law Magazine*, 1 (Summer 2000).

51. Campaign Committee members were Doug Dodd, Tom Coffman, Katherine Coyle, Robert Farris, Martin Frey, Nancy Gourley, John Hicks, Tom Holland, David James, M.M. McDougal, Joe McGraw, Charles Norman, Millie Otey, Margaret Swimmer, John Turner, Mike Turpen and David Winslow.

52. See *Tulsa Law Magazine* (Spring 1997).

53. *Tulsa Law Magazine* (Fall 1998).

54. See *Tulsa World*, Apr. 12, 1999.

55. J.E. and L.E. Mabee Foundation; J. A. and Leta Chapman Charitable Trust; Sarkeys Foundation; H.A. and Mary K. Chapman Charitable Trust; Mervin Bovaird Foundation; Oklahoma Family Law and Mediation Services, LLC; Frank M. Rowell, Jr.; Riggs, Abney, Neal, Turpen, Orbenson and Lewis; Peggy and Lloyd Stephens; Gable and Gotwols; Bonnie and Frank Henke III; W. Mitchel Hill and Jim Secrest; Richard P. and Norma T. Small Foundation; James Wallis; Virginia and Floyd Walker.

56. The library put information in print and on the world wide web concerning the timetable of construction and information on services of the library during construction.

57. Supra n. 5 at 95.

58. ABA Site Evaluation Report 9-10 (Aug. 6, 2001).

59. Supra n. 5 at 101.

60. Supra n. 4 at 42.

61. The areas of concern listed were 1) a small base budget that has never recovered from University-imposed freezes and cutbacks in the mid-1990s; 2) the fact that restricted funds which make up a sizable portion of the resource budget must be devoted to basic purchases and not collection enrichment; and 3) uneven restricted fund allocations, which create uncertainty every year as to whether there will be support for the basic collection or the need to cancel subscriptions.

62. See Letter from Martin Belsky, dean, and Robert Lawless, president, to John Sebert, consultant on legal education to the American Bar Association (May 31, 2001 & May 1, 2002).

63. Interview with Dean Martin Belsky, (Dec. 7, 2002) (conducted by e-mail). (University of Tulsa College of Law archives).

64. See Leslie Mansfield, "Inside the New Boesche Legal Clinic," *Tulsa Law Magazine* (Fall 2002). The article contains a description of the history and status of the Clinic programs as of 2002.

65. See Chapter 5.

66. The following individuals have served as Association President since the re-incorporation: W. Thomas Coffman ('63) [1992-94], Kenneth Brune ('74) [1994-95], Nancy Gourley ('83) [1995-96], David Winslow ('64) 1996-97], Jim Lang ('64) 1997-98], George Otey ('90) 1998-99], Julie Evans ('89) [1999-2000], Richard Studenny ('67) [2000-01], Rachel Blue ('88) [2001-02], Molly McKay ('90) [2002-03], C. Michael Zacharias ('71) [2003-04].

67. Alumni Relations, Judicial Intern, Library and Information Services, Long Range Planning, Membership Services, Mentoring, National Alumni Coordinating, Nominations and Awards, and Student Recruiting.

EPILOGUE

1. The law school's 2003 American Bar Association Questionnaire information breaks the square footage down this way in Question 22:

Classroom/Seminar
    Rooms .... 11,106 sq. ft.
Library facilities ..... 52,745 sq. ft.
Faculty offices .... 9,076 sq. ft.
Administrative offices 5,670 sq. ft.
Student organizational
    & common areas 17,645 sq. ft.
Clinical .... <u>4,700 sq. ft.</u>
             100,948 sq. ft.

Deans of The University of Tulsa College of Law

Washington E. Hudson	May, 1923 – September, 1943
Summers Hardy	September, 1943 – June, 1949
John Rogers	June, 1949 – November, 1949 (acting dean)
	December, 1949 – December, 1957 (dean)
A. Allen King	June, 1949 – December, 1957 (administrative dean)
	January, 1958 – May, 1962 (dean)
Bruce Peterson	May, 1962 – February, 1963 (acting dean)
	February, 1963 – August, 1969 (dean)
Edgar H. Wilson	September, 1969 – July, 1972
Joseph W. Morris	August, 1972 – April, 1974
Rennard Strickland	April, 1974 – December, 1974 (acting dean)
Frank T. Read	December, 1974 – July, 1979
Tom L. Holland	August, 1979 – July,1980 (acting dean)
Frank K. Walwer	August, 1980 – June,1991
John Makdisi	July,1991 – May, 1994
M. Thomas Arnold	June, 1994 – May, 1995 (acting dean)
Martin H. Belsky	June, 1995 – August, 2004
Catherine Cullem	August, 2004-May, 2005 (acting dean)
Robert Butkin	June, 2005 – date of publication

1920s

John Cantrell	Bryan Kirkpatrick	Hal F. Rambo
Henry W. Gray	John Ladner	McKeriel C. Rodolf
W. E. Green	Fred D. Leonard	Thomas F. Serviss
Horace Hagan	Stewart Lynch	Charles Skalnik
Harry Halley	M.M. Mahaney	H. L. Smith
Emory E. Hanson	William H. McClarin	I. J. Underwood
Russell R. Hays	William Melton	J.B. Underwood
Robert D. Hudson	Lawrence Mills	Thomas L. Wallace
Wash E. Hudson (dean)	A.E. Montgomery	H.R. Williams
James L. Hull	Louis W. Pratt	W.I. Williams

1930s

Phil W. Davis, Jr.	Wash E. Hudson (dean)	A. E. Montgomery
George Downey	Russell R. Hays	Remington Rogers
T. Austin Gavin	Paxton Howard	Charles Skalnik
Grace Elmore Gibson	Hawley C. Kerr	H.L. Smith
Henry Gray	Charles A. Kothe	J. B. Underwood
Barney A. Hamilton	Phillip N. Landa	Elsie Waddle
Emory E. Hanson	Gentry Lee	W.I. Williams
	Fred D. Leonard	

1940s

James B. Diggs	Harold Hughes	A.E. Montgomery
W.C. Franklin	Hawley C. Kerr	Dwight A. Olds
T. Austin Gavin	A. Allen King	Rogers S. Randolph
Grace Elmore Gibson	Gerald B. Klein	John Rogers (dean)
Henry Gray	Charles A. Kothe	R. Ryan
W.E. Green	Phillip N. Landa	Remington Rogers
Emory E. Hanson	Gentry Lee	Charles Skalnik
Summers Hardy (dean)	Fred D. Leonard	H. L. Smith
Milton W. Hardy	Whit Y. Mauzy	J.B. Underwood
Roy M. Huff	James P. Melone	W. Preston Woodruff
Wash E. Hudson (dean)	Travis Milsten	

*Explanatory Note

Until the 1940s, all faculty were practicing attorneys who taught only part-time. Even after the first full-time faculty were hired in the late 1940s, and continuing through the 1950s, the size of the full-time faculty was small and the school continued to rely heavily on part-time teachers. This roster reflects this fact by listing both part-time and full-time faculty through the decade of the 1950s.

Only in the 1960s did the size of the full-time faculty reach a "critical mass" that allowed the bulk of the curriculum to be taught by them, with practicing lawyers filling out the curriculum with more specialized and practice-oriented courses. Therefore, beginning with the decade of the 1960s and thereafter, this roster lists only full-time members of the faculty.

1950s

J. B. Bailey
P. L. Baker
James E. Bush
Joye Clark (librarian)
James B. Diggs
Gerald K. Donovan
John W. Hager
Carl D. Hall
Milton W. Hardy
Roy M. Huff

Edwin S. Hurst
Lewis C. Johnson
A. Allen King (dean)
Graham Kirkpatrick
Gerald B. Klein
Phillip N. Landa
Whit Y. Mauzy
Banks McDowell, Jr.
Richard K. McGee
Travis Milsten

Joseph W. Morris
Bruce Peterson
John Rogers (dean)
Remington Rogers
Arthur E. Rubin
David M. Thornton
Ralph C. Thomas
J.S. Woodruff
W. Preston Woodruff

1960s

Robert D. Cox
W. Paul Gormley
John W. Hager
Bueford G. Herbert
James E. Herget
John F. Hicks
Charlotte Highland (librarian)

Frank G. Homan
A. Allen King (dean)
Graham Kirkpatrick
Phillip N. Landa
Orley R. Lilly, Jr.
Charles W Linder, Jr.
John F. Marvin

Bruce Peterson (dean)
Hugh V. Schaefer
E. Dale Searcy
John TeSelle
James C. Thomas
Ralph C. Thomas
Edgar H. Wilson (dean)

1970s

Charles W. Adams
Gary D. Allison
Edna Ball
Walter J. Blakey (visiting)
Anthony J. Bocchino (visiting)
Robert T. Brousseau (visiting)
Joel Burstein (librarian)
Douglas K. Chapman
John Choate
David S. Clark
Charles E. Consalus (visiting)
E. McGruder Farris (visiting)
Anthony R. Fasano
Bradley Forst (visiting)
Martin A. Frey
Kent Frizzell (NELPI director)
Donald H. Gjerdingen
Thomas W. Goldman, Jr.
Nathaniel E. Gozansky (visiting)
William A. Gregory
John W. Hager

Gunther F. Handl
Marilyn K. Harlan (visiting)
Imogene Harris (librarian)
Buford G. Herbert
James E. Herget
John F. Hicks
Tom L. Holland
William G. Hollingsworth
Eric B. Jensen
Georgina B. Landman
Orley R. Lilly, Jr.
John S. Lowe
Patrick H. Martin
Charles C. McCarter
Leah Brock McCartney (visiting)
James W. McElhaney (visiting)
Joseph W. Morris (dean)
Jerry F. Muskrat (visiting)
Thomas C. Newhouse (visiting)
Alan Ogden (librarian)
Bruce Peterson

Alan N. Polasky (visiting)
Carol Ann Potter
Margaret H. Potts
Edward H. Rabin (visiting)
Frank T. Read (dean)
Sue Titus Reid
Edwin M. Schmidt
High V. Schaefer
Harry N. Stein (visiting)
Rennard J. Strickland
John TeSelle
James C. Thomas
Ralph C. Thomas
David M. Treiman
Dale Whitman (visiting)
Edgar H. Wilson (dean)
Mary Ann Wood (visiting)
Stephen G. Wood (visiting)
Robert R. Wright (visiting)
Raymond L. Yasser

1980s

Charles W. Adams
Gary D. Allison
M. Thomas Arnold
Taunya Lovell Banks
Dennis E. Bires
D. Marianne Blair
Christen R. Blair
Reid P. Chalmers
    (Chapman vis. professor)
Douglas K. Chapman
Marguerite A. Chapman
David S. Clark
Catherine M. Cullem
Richard Delgado
    (Chapman vis. professor).
Richard E. Ducey (library director)
James W. Ely, Jr.
    (Chapman vis. professor)
Stephen M. Feldman
Judith A. Finn
Martin A. Frey
Kent Frizzell (NELPI director)

Stephen Fuller (visiting)
Gilbert Gaynor (visiting)
Donald H. Gjerdingen
John W. Hager
John F. Hicks
Tom L Holland
William G. Hollingsworth
Douglas L. Inhofe (visiting)
Henry F. Johnson (visiting)
Stephen F. Knippenberg (visiting)
Linda J. Lacey
R. Dobie Langenkamp
    (Chapman vis. professor)
Orley R. Lilly, Jr.
Vicki J. Limas
John S. Lowe
Marla E. Mansfield
Kathleen W. Marcell
Patrick H. Martin (visiting)
Peter Maxfield
    (Chapman vis. professor)
Daniel J. Morrissey

Ljubomir Nacev
Alan Ogden (library director)
Marian F. Parker (library director)
Walter Ray Phillips
    (Chapman vis.professor)
David E. Pierce (visiting)
Carol Ann Potter
Margaret H. Potts
Sue Titus Reid
Frank F. Skillern (visiting)
Rennard J. Strickland (John
    Shleppey research professor)
Winona M. Tanaka
James C. Thomas
Ralph C. Thomas
David M. Treiman
Gloria Valencia-Weber
Frank K. Walwer (dean)
Raymond L. Yasser
Rex J. Zedalis

1990s

Jason B. Aamodt
    (reasearch / writing instructor)
Charles W. Adams
Stanley E. Adelman (visiting)
Gary D. Allison
M. Thomas Arnold
Larry C. Backer
Martin H. Belsky (dean)
Morris D. Bernstein (legal clinic)
Dennis E. Bires
D. Marianne Blair
Christen R. Blair
Dona K. Broyles
    (research/writing instructor)
Barbara K. Bucholtz
Marguerite A. Chapman
David S. Clark
Stephana Colbert (visiting)
Nancy J. Conison
    (research/writing instructor)
Catherine M. Cullem
Richard E. Ducey (library director)
Stephen M. Feldman
Paul Finkelman (Chapman professor)
Judith A. Finn
Martin A. Frey
Kent Frizzell (NELPI director)

Gilbert Gaynor (visiting)
Lakshman Guruswamy (NELPI director)
John W. Hager
Kermit L. Hall
John F. Hicks
Russell Hittinger (Warren professor)
Tom L. Holland
William G. Hollingsworth
Douglas L. Inhofe (visiting)
Chris Kelsey
    (research/writing instructor)
Karen V. Kole (visiting)
Kimberly D. Krawiec
Peter Kresak (visiting)
Linda J. Lacey
R. Dobie Langenkamp
    (Chapman visiting professor)
Lundy R. Langston
Janet K. Levit
Suzanne Levitt (Clinic)
Randy Lewin
    (research / writing Instructor)
Orley R. Lilly, Jr.
Vicki J. Limas
John Makdisi (dean)
Charles F. Mansfield (visiting)
Leslie Mansfield (clinic)

Marla E. Mansfield
Daniel J. Morrissey
Johnny C. Parker
Richard A. Paschal
    (research / writing instructor)
Mark Pennington (visiting)
Madeleine M. Plasencia
G. William Rice
Nicholas Rostow
Judith V. Royster
Shelley Ryan (visiting)
Emily E. Sanderson
Donna Thompson Schneider
    (research / writing instructor)
Bernard Schwartz
    (Chapman professor).
Lance Stockwell
    (research / writing instructor)
Winona M. Tanaka
Melissa L. Koehn Tatum
Sherry N. Taylor (legal clinic)
James C. Thomas
Gloria Valencia-Weber
Kathleen Waits
Frank K. Walwer (dean)
Raymond L. Yasser
Rex J. Zedalis

2000s

Charles W. Adams
Stanley E. Adelman (visiting)
Gary D. Allison
M. Thomas Arnold
Larry C. Backer
Martin H. Belsky (dean)
Morris D. Bernstein (clinic)
Dennis E. Bires
D. Marianne Blair
Christen R. Blair
Dona K. Broyles
   (research / writing instructor)
Barbara K Bucholtz
Nicholas Capaldi
Marguerite A. Chapman
Russell Christopher
David S. Clark
Diana Clark (research/writing instructor)
Stephana Colbert (visiting)
Catherine M. Cullom
Montie R. Deer (legal clinic)
Richard E. Ducey (library director)

Lyn Entzeroth
Stephen M. Feldman
Paul Finkelman (Chapman professor)
Martin A. Frey
Lakshman Guruswamy (NELPI director)
John F. Hicks
Russell Hittinger (Warren professor)
Tom L Holland
William G. Hollingsworth
Marsh Cope Huie
Evelyn Hutchison
   (research/writing instructor)
Brian Johnson
   (research/writing instructor)
Karen V. Kole (visiting)
Linda J. Lacey
R. Dobie Langenkamp (NELPI director)
Randy Lewin
   (research / writing instructor)
Janet K. Levit
Vicki J. Limas
Leslie Mansfield (clinic)
Marla E. Mansfield

Sharisse O'Carroll
   (research/writing instructor)
Johnny C. Parker
Richard A. Paschal
   (research/writing instructor)
Valerie J. Phillips
Tamara R. Piety
Madeleine M. Plasencia
G. William Rice
Matthew Rollins
   (research/writing instructor)
Judith V. Royster
Sharon Schooley
   (research / writing instructor)
Lance Stockwell
   (research/writing instructor)
Winona M. Tanaka
Melissa L. Tatum
James C. Thomas
Kathleen Waits
Raymond L. Yasser
Rex J. Zedalis